"Read That Back, Please!"

Memoirs of a Court Reporter

John R. Reily, CSR

FITHIAN PRESS

SANTA BARBARA · 1999

Published by Fithian Press
A division of Daniel and Daniel, Publishers, Inc.
Post Office Box 1525
Santa Barbara, CA 93102

LIBRARY OF CONGRESS CATALOGING-IN-PUBLICATION DATA
Reily, John R. (date)
    Read that back, please : memoirs of a court reporter / John R. Reily.
        p.   cm.
    ISBN 1-56474-284-9 (alk. paper)
    1. Law reporters—California—Anecdotes. 2. Justice, Administra-
tion of—California—Anecdotes. I. Title.
KFC985.C6R45   1999
347.794—dc21   98-33821
                                                         CIP

This book is dedicated to Bonnie K. Estes and God *(not necessarily in that order)* for blessing me with their constant friendship and patience.

"If happy little bluebirds fly beyond the rainbow, why oh why can't I?"

"Over the Rainbow"
Lyrics by E.Y. Harburg
Music by Harold Arlen

Acknowledgements

I wish to express my deepest gratitude to all of the friends, court reporters, court clerks, attorneys, judges, bailiffs and police officers, as well as my family members, for their invaluable assistance, contributions, and encouragement in the preparation of this book. It was my original intent to thank everyone by name, but upon reflection I realized there could be some who, by a long stretch of the imagination, might consider parts of this book controversial. Because many of the people who helped me so much are still employed and part of the court system, I did not want them to suffer any embarrassment. You know who you are, however, and thanks a bunch!

I am indebted as well to the research staff of the San Jose Public Library and owe many thanks to the research department of the *San Jose Mercury News*. Both of those institutions have been of great help to me. Hopefully, I can help you all someday when you need to write your book—or at least wash your car.

Gracias!

The characters and events depicted in the following narrative are true, with the exception of those events used for purposes of illustration. Any similarity to fiction, living or dead, is purely coincidental. The names have been changed to protect the innocent—namely, me.

Contents

Prologue

IT IS MY intent in this book to acquaint the reader with the very real world of the courtroom. For that purpose, I think it is necessary to explain the job description and duties of court reporters and the unique opportunities they have for observing the human panorama that unfolds before them on a daily basis. This book is somewhat autobiographical, but it also includes many incidents experienced by others. A court reporter is the modern version of the old court stenographer who makes a verbatim record of court proceedings. Originally, the recording of court proceedings was attempted by rapid handwriting. The scribes mentioned in the Bible must have had a very fast chisel. With the invention of written shorthand, such as the Gregg and Pitman systems, the court stenographer's job became a lot easier.

There were still problems, however, because it was necessary to watch the paper as the notes were being written and the stenographer might miss a nod of the head or a gesture by the witness. So-called writer's cramp was a very real concern after scratching out notes for two hours or more. Many years later a shorthand machine was invented which used a system called Stenotype and most court stenographers chose that method for making the court record. This innovation was known to have been utilized in the late 1920s and is still in use today. Currently, most court reporters (*the term preferred today*) use computer-aided transcribing to more efficiently speed up the court process.

Court reporters are called upon to make verbatim records

of court proceedings, both prior to and during a trial. Prior to trial, each party in the litigation is permitted to engage in what is known as discovery. During that process, witnesses for the opposing parties may be ordered to give depositions. Depositions are statements given under oath which may later be used in court, if the matter eventually goes to trial. The procedure by which the deposition record is made involves the reporter writing down in shorthand everything that is said by the witness and the attorneys, then transcribing the shorthand notes into longhand typewriting and certifying the document as correct.

When court stenographers became known as court reporters, it led to some confusion on the part of the public and that confusion still exists today. A common error—even by many attorneys—is to refer to them as *court recorders*. This is somewhat understandable because they do make the *record*. But, of course, the real court recorder or county recorder is the official with whom you must file deeds to your property, record death certificates, etc. Another common misconception encountered by court reporters is that people assume they work for a newspaper, since the word *reporter* means only one thing to them.

It is my hope that this prologue will help you to better understand the perspective from which the reporter views the proceedings in court. The courtroom staff usually comprises the judge, the court clerk, the court reporter and the bailiff or deputy sheriff. The bailiff is charged with maintaining order in the courtroom as well as court security. The clerk is charged with marking and identifying exhibits when they are admitted into evidence, swearing in witnesses, maintaining a minute book containing a rough outline of the trial proceedings and a number of other important duties.

The reporter's job, as indicated, is to make a record as nearly perfect as possible. The judge, of course, makes decisions and rulings on the law and, most importantly, decides when the next recess will be taken. Hopefully, the foregoing will be of some use to you in trying to make some sense out of the following pages. If not, with proper folding, it will make an excellent beginning for a fleet of paper airplanes. Thanks for listening and please don't litter.

"READ THAT BACK, PLEASE!"

Chapter One

Genesis

WHO, INDEED, was the slayer of King Arthur? It was a dark and stormy knight! Oh well, nobody's perfect. Anyway, Snoopy already started his book that way. This is a chronicle of thirty-one years of employment as an official court reporter in the Municipal and Superior Courts of California and the District Court of Montana. Hopefully, this chronicle will serve a nobler purpose than lining the bottom of a bird cage. Ideally, I should have myself Mirandized before making any voluntary statements, but then I never gained fame for doing what was good for me. In fact, I never gained fame at all.

The average person's perception of what goes on inside a court of law consists of the cumulative knowledge gained through many hours of watching Perry Mason or Judge Wapner on television. Serving a short sentence of jury duty often brings one a little closer to the way things really happen, but to really get down to the nitty gritty, you have to breach a contract or steal a car.

Because of the potential consequences to one's liberty and/ or finances, the courts are often thought of as places of dread—places to be avoided. There are, however, many occasions when things happen that are quite humorous, even in the most serious circumstances. The general public, for the most part, is unaware that the foreboding and sometimes frightening environment of the courts can often lend itself to situations bordering on hilarity. It is my intention through this book to share some of these incidents experienced not only by me, but many other court reporters of my acquaintance—

17

although if they have any pride at all, they will deny knowing me.

In the beginning (*well, it was the Genesis of my career*) my employer was Flathead County, Montana, in the county seat of Kalispell. In December of 1959, the population of Kalispell was approximately 10,000—not counting an untold number of deer, elk, sheep and five or six cantankerous Democrats. Along with the town, I found the people to be warm and picturesque. They were still picturesque, but not quite so warm, when the mercury hit fourteen below zero. Kalispell is located just north of Flathead Lake (named for the Flathead Indian tribe) which is twenty-eight miles long and up to fifteen miles wide, making it the largest fresh water lake west of the Mississippi.

During my first winter in Kalispell, Flathead Lake froze over to the extent that when an air force plane tragically crashed through the ice, the pilot and his plane could not be retrieved until the spring thaw. Initially, I rented a large two-story house for my family, approximately eight blocks from the courthouse. On the night before the fourteen-below weather, I had neglected to put my car in the garage. But, not to worry! Had I not filled the radiator with anti-freeze and did I not have tire chains? My California logic was shattered when I attempted to start the car and found the engine would not turn over because of course the frigid weather would not allow the battery to function properly.

Where is the problem? Here I am only eight blocks from the courthouse—I'll just walk! As evidence of the fact that I had not just fallen off the turnip truck, I was garbed in a pair of long johns, shirt, tie, trousers, gloves, overcoat, muffler (borrowed from the car), socks, shoes, snow boots, fur hat and a great deal of northern naivete. When I started out, I was so forceful that I even walked on the sidewalk hidden two feet below the surface, deigning the relative ease of the street which had been recently plowed.

After about a block, I discovered that my lungs were on fire. My nose was running and froze immediately. My eyes were watering and I actually had little icicles appended to the bottoms of my eyes. Eventually I made it to the courthouse, not having encountered a single St. Bernard (or a married one, for that matter) along the way. When the court clerk asked me how I liked their Montana weather, I cannot at this time recall my exact response, but she always looked at me very strangely after that.

At the time I rented the aforementioned house in Kalispell, natural gas was not available in the area for use as a fuel. Therefore, homes were equipped with either wood burning furnaces or heating oil furnaces. This charming and spacious house had an oil furnace. Since I had never lived around snow before, it never occurred to me to inquire as to whether or not the house was insulated. I soon learned that it was not. I also learned that it came with a 2,000 gallon oil tank buried in the front yard. By comparison, the house we rented a few months later, which was fully insulated and had double paned windows, was adequately heated by a 300 gallon tank.

This house was selected originally, not only because of its proximity to the courthouse, but because it had a lovely yard our children could enjoy in the summer and it had a massive fireplace with a large supply of firewood stacked in the garage. In addition, the rent was very reasonable. I soon discovered it was so reasonable because the monthly heating oil bill was twice the amount of the rent. The kitchen had a walk-in pantry adjacent to it and one night we forgot to leave the door open to the pantry and the next morning everything in the pantry was frozen, including a ten pound bag of potatoes and all of our canned goods.

A couple of weeks after we got settled in the house, the oil pump on the furnace gave out and we were seriously considering the construction of an igloo in our living room until the repairman could come and thaw us out. But, alas! Did we not have an ample supply of firewood in the garage? I quickly made several trips to the garage and stacked a considerable number of logs in the fireplace. Shrewdly checking first to make certain the damper in the fireplace was open, I lighted the fire. I must confess I am not always successful in my efforts to start fires, but this one was a roaring inferno in no time at all.

Unfortunately, I had not anticipated the fact that the fireplace had not been used or the chimney cleaned in a number of years and a great deal of debris had evidently fallen down behind the damper, preventing it from opening adequately. Needless to say, the whole house soon filled with smoke and I was forced to extinguish the fire with several buckets of water. The most fun part of it all was that we got to open all the doors and windows in the house to get rid of the smoke, in exchange for the frigid air and wind from outside. If not for the fact that we had an electric range in the kitchen (another victory for G.E.), we would have all been potential selections for the Jolly Green Giant by the time the furnace repairman arrived.

I don't mean to suggest this house was another Amityville Horror, but to a family from sunny California, this was quite a culture shock. Fortunately, the local people were very friendly and understanding, although probably hard-pressed to suppress a giggle over some of the predicaments we got ourselves into.

In 1959, the eleventh judicial district of the state of Montana comprised two counties, Flathead and Lincoln. The county seat of Lincoln County was the town of Libby, population then about 6,000, and located ninety-two miles northwest of Kalispell. It might also be described as about midway between Kalispell and Spokane, Washington. Since the greater amount of litigation occurred in Flathead County, the procedure was to hold court four days a week in Kalispell and each Friday in Libby—with the exception of some extended trials held in Libby.

Because of the uncertainty of the weather, the judge I worked for would usually leave for Libby on Thursday evenings to ensure court starting promptly on Friday mornings. We would ride together, of course, and the journey rarely failed to be an adventure. I can recall a number of occasions trying to stay warm while a jack-knifed lumber truck was being cleared from the ice-covered highway. Quite often, deer would bolt across the road in front of the car, requiring a great deal of skill on the part of the driver to avoid a collision.

The first deposition I ever reported was taken in Libby,

Montana, and was quite memorable in many aspects. The deponent or witness was inebriated and had probably seen some court show on television at one time because he kept admonishing me to "strike that" each time he misspoke. The session lasted much longer than planned, in the hope that the witness would eventually sober up. Consequently, it was quite late when we began our return trip to Kalispell, ninety-two miles away. I had ridden with the attorney who was taking the deposition and he had chosen an older car because it had better traction on the snow and ice.

By the time we reached the outskirts of Kalispell, it was about 2:00 A.M. At that point, there was a very long grade to ascend with quite a steep drop off on our side. We made several attempts to climb the icy surface and each time the car would start sliding backwards down to the bottom of the grade. Fortunately, there was no other traffic on the road at that time, but my dry-land driving in California had ill prepared me for an experience like this, even as a passenger. The car was equipped with snow tires, but it was obvious that the greater traction of chains would be required.

Undaunted, my attorney/driver decided to park the car on the wrong side of the road, next to the embankment, so he could attach the tire chains to the car. My duty was to sit behind the steering wheel, applying the brakes as hard as possible. After the chains were attached, the attorney continued driving on the wrong side of the road, using the snow on the embankment side for additional traction, until we reached the top of the hill. If a large truck, or any other vehicle for that matter, had chosen that moment to come down the hill on that ice, there was absolutely no way a head-on collision could have been avoided.

The fact that I am now writing this would indicate that the driver's strategy was correct, but I would not recommend it as a means of escaping the early use of Grecian Hair Formula. I was finally delivered to my home about 3:30 in the morning, only to find that the fire department had been summoned there the day before because the clothes dryer had caught on fire. I never could find out what the local folks did for entertainment before we arrived in town.

⚖

As I indicated before, this was my first job as a court reporter. There was not a very heavy calendar most of the time, but I found it all interesting whether it was a murder trial, a divorce, or a juvenile proceeding. There were only two judges in this District Court and each judge had his own reporter. The reporter in the other department of the court was a veteran of almost fifty years, who used Gregg shorthand to report the court proceedings. I had nothing but admiration for this man, who did an excellent job using a system I had been taught in reporting school was completely antiquated. Later, I learned that part of his success was a result of properly training counsel to cooperate in making a good record.

Prior to the time a second department was created in the court, he had been for many years the only court reporter in the entire county. As such, he commanded a great amount of respect from the local attorneys. Often, when the inevitable chaos would occur which results when two or three attorneys try to talk at once during a trial, he would throw his pen and writing pad up in the air in exasperation and storm out of the courtroom. In order to proceed with the trial, the attorneys would go to his office and promise to conduct themselves in a proper manner. Only then, after calming him down, would the trial proceed.

This reporter was quite a remarkable man. When I first met him, he was seventy-two years of age and twice as sharp as I was. (*Big deal!*) He had never learned to drive an automobile, but had the stamina to walk for many miles. Anyone familiar with Montana knows that things are really spread out in the Big Sky Country. He had a wood burning furnace in his home and still chopped all the wood that was required for fuel. He was very patient and considerate with me and was a tremendous help in making my first reporting job successful, even though I was an *outsider* from California.

He retired about a year after I started my job and his replacement was a young man in his late twenties from Michigan, who used a Stenograph machine. The older reporter stayed around for a while to help train his replacement. It was the younger reporter's first reporting job, just as it had been mine. Evidently, the new man was told by someone of his predecessor's successful method for obtaining the cooperation of counsel in court. About a month after he was hired, he was having some difficulty with a couple of attorneys in court, so he shouted at them to slow down, stood up over his machine and threatened to leave the courtroom. They looked at him as if he was a lunatic, the judge told him to sit down and the trial resumed. The young reporter continued on with a successful career in that court, having learned a valuable lesson about the privileges of seniority.

Once, during a juvenile proceeding in Libby, the juvenile, who was in custody, escaped and ran down three flights of stairs to the outside, where he was subsequently apprehended. Several weeks later, when he was being tried on the escape charge, I was called as a witness to the escape.

At that time, I was literally the only reporter in the county so I had to report my own testimony. On cross-examination, I was asked if I was a qualified and competent court reporter and, being under oath, I had to modestly admit that I was the best reporter in the county at that time. I might also comment that that was one of the rare occasions when the witness did not speak too rapidly.

Near the beginning of the first murder trial I reported, I was requested to read back a previous question and I froze. This had nothing to do with the weather, for a change. I simply panicked and could not read my notes. Later at the recess, I looked back at my notes and I had the question down perfectly. That evening I was asked by the prosecutor to read back part of the record in his office, which I did. Obviously, he wanted to assure himself that a correct record was being made. Fortunately, I never had such an experience again in any court. As a matter of fact, I have always had very vivid dreams at night and one night I dreamed I walked out onto a stage in white tie and tails, bowed to a huge audience, and sat down at my Stenograph machine and started "playing." Eat your heart out, Liberace.

Although never awarded, special mention should be made here

of the Medal of Valor earned by my wife for maintaining her sanity and control while caring for two infants, aged one and two, in my absence. At the time, she had not learned to drive and occasionally would be snowbound for a week at a time while I was out of town in trial. I had never taken seriously the term cabin fever, but after having peeled her off the ceiling once or twice on my return, I began to understand its true meaning.

It had always been our intention to return to California after a couple of years because we were buying a home there. Additionally, we missed family and friends and wished to be part of our old community. The cabin fever simply strengthened that resolution. To that end, I flew to California in late October of 1960 for the purpose of taking the examination to become a Certified Shorthand Reporter (C.S.R.), the fancy term for a licensed court reporter in California.

⚖

That trip was quite a tale in itself. I was very fortunate in having friends who met me at the airport, provided me lodging in their home as well as transportation to San Francisco, where the examination was held. Court reporters are always expected to provide their own equipment, but I did not bring along an electric typewriter from Montana and I needed one to transcribe my notes for the examination. One of my friends who was employed in an office building in San Francisco offered to lend me an I.B.M. Selectric, with the proviso that I return it Saturday afternoon after the examination. The building was one of the few in the city that still required an operator for its elevator. When we got the typewriter, the elevator operator assured me he would be working late Saturday afternoon.

As you might guess, when I returned the typewriter after the examination, he was gone and the elevator was locked up tight. I had to carry the typewriter up seven flights of stairs to the correct office. It probably weighed around forty pounds, but it felt like 400 by the time I returned it to its proper place. After a brief period of resuscitation during which my life flashed before my eyes, I made my way back to the street where I purchased a shopping bag full of sourdough French bread, which was not available in Montana. I expected to be home the following morning and thought it would still be fresh. I returned to the home of my friends in Santa Clara, about forty miles south of San Francisco, and later that evening they drove me to the airport in San Francisco.

Upon reaching the airport, I was informed that my plane had just taken off and there would not be another until 9:00 the next morning. My friends from Santa Clara gamely brushed aside my stupidity for not checking my schedule more accurately and agreed to drive me to the home of some other friends in Pacifica, a community much closer to the airport. I spent what was left of the night (as well as one loaf of French bread) with these friends and they drove me to the airport Sunday morning.

After leaving San Francisco, the plane arrived in Portland just in time for me to miss my connection to Spokane and Kalispell. Once again, I was informed the next flight would not be available until the following morning. Fortunately, I knew a couple of transplanted Californians who lived in Portland and they came and picked me up. They agreed to let me spend the night with them in exchange for another of my loaves of French bread and drove me to the airport the next morning.

The connecting flight to Spokane was on a nonscheduled airline and the temperature inside the plane seemed very low. Upon reaching Spokane, the ice was chipped away from the loudspeaker long enough to inform the passengers there was a problem with the heating system and the plane would not be able to continue to fly over the Rockies. The airline agreed to pay for our transportation by train, which would hopefully get us the rest of the way there, and threw in a couple of meal tickets because the train was not scheduled to leave until ten o'clock that night.

Try as I might, I could not think of anyone I knew in Spokane, so I stashed my luggage and my dwindling supply of French bread in a locker and set out to explore what I could of Spokane. I soon learned that Spokane was a very nice place to visit and that one can get very tired just walking around. I saw two different movies, used my two meal tickets, and finally left on the train for Kalispell that night. At six the next morning, the train arrived at Whitefish, Montana, located about fifteen miles north of Kalispell. I was informed the train did not go directly into Kalispell and I would have to find my own transportation from that point on. Fortunately, my mother-in-law was visiting us *(now, there's a phrase you don't hear that often)* so I called her and she came and picked me up for the last leg of the trip.

I had stayed in telephone contact with my wife along the way so she knew I would be home about six or seven in the morning. She therefore set her alarm clock for 6:00 A.M., put the kids to bed and then retired at about ten-thirty. She awoke from a sound sleep, glanced at the clock and saw that it was already six o'clock and assumed the alarm had not gone off. She immediately arose, got dressed, woke up the kids and was giving them breakfast when the radio announcer informed her the correct time was 1:15 A.M. She had obviously misread 12:30 A.M. as 6:00 A.M. and the kids must have thought that was the shortest night of the year. This was one of those situations you laugh at years later *(please try and control yourself)*, but she was less than ecstatic at the time.

By the time I finally made it home, the bag of French bread, which I had guarded like the Holy Grail, had become a container of deadly weapons. I could easily have subdued a grizzly bear by using any one of the loaves as a club, using the second as a spade to dig its grave and the third as a tombstone. Luckily, we were spared any encounter with an *Ursus horribilis*. Instead, the loaves were sprinkled liberally with water and slowly warmed in the oven. Although they were a bit crunchier than usual, I doubt any French bread was ever enjoyed more than those three loaves.

Some weeks later, I was informed that I had successfully passed the test for California C.S.R. In September of 1961 I learned of a job opening in Palo Alto, California, about the same time that the tenants who had rented our house in Santa Clara were moving out. I applied for the job, I was hired, and in early October we bade farewell to all the nice folks we had met in Montana and recklessly abandoned ourselves to whatever new adventures awaited us in the Golden State.

Chapter Two

Return of the Prodigal Son

MY NEW JOB was as an Official Court Reporter in the Municipal Court of the Palo Alto–Mountain View Judicial District, as it was then known. The title *Official Court Reporter* may sound somewhat pretentious, but it merely distinguishes the regular reporter who works each day in court for the same judge from the deposition reporter or hearing reporter who may work in a different place every day.

When I left Montana, there was no Municipal Court system in that part of the state. Primary jurisdiction was established before a Justice of the Peace (who was not even required to be a lawyer) and the next step up was the District Court, comparable to the Superior Court in California. Very basically, the differences between the Municipal Court and the Superior Court are that the Municipal Court has jurisdiction over crimes known as misdemeanors and civil litigation that does not exceed a limited, specified amount. The Superior Court has jurisdiction over felony matters, unlimited civil litigation and also the authority to grant divorces, conservatorships, approve land sales, etc.

The matters that were dealt with in the Municipal Court were about twenty times as numerous as those I had experienced in Montana. Prior to this new job, I had never heard of a preliminary hearing or preliminary examination. I soon learned that when a person is accused of committing a felony, there is a right to have a hearing held before the magistrate to determine first that a crime was committed and secondly that there is sufficient evidence to suggest that the accused is guilty

27

of committing said felony. If the judge determines that sufficient evidence has been presented, the defendant is then held to answer for trial in the Superior Court at a later date.

If insufficient evidence is presented at the preliminary hearing, the charge against the defendant is dismissed. If the defendant is held to answer for trial, the court reporter must prepare a transcript of the hearing within ten days of the hearing. In addition to their salary, court reporters are paid for preparing transcripts, since it represents extra work that must be done on the reporter's own time—during lunch breaks, after court or on weekends. While the added income is very nice, the pressure to get the transcript filed on time can be tremendous. Assignment to a criminal calendar for a lengthy period usually causes the reporter to be constantly behind because new cases are being brought before the court every day. I can almost hear the attorneys now making remarks about "crying all the way to the bank," but the stress can become very difficult to manage.

One of the things a reporter must learn early is the necessity for circumspection. Court reporters enjoy a very unique position of trust and are privy to many off-the-record matters that are not meant for public consumption. Great care should also be taken in discussing even matters of public record because undue embarrassment might be caused to the parties in the litigation if the conversation is overheard by a relative or friend of the parties. My Irish heritage made this a difficult lesson for me to learn, but the following example finally taught me to keep my big mouth shut.

One of the felony cases before the court involved a gentleman charged with murder, who was alleged to have followed his wife to a motel where she had a clandestine meeting with her lover. The husband stabbed his wife's lover and was subsequently arrested for his murder. On the day scheduled for his prelim, there were a number of interested spectators, as well as many people who were scheduled to testify, milling about in the corridor.

My office at the time was the first door off the corridor and my door was usually open (*not to mention my mouth*) when I was in the office. Just prior to the hearing, a friend of mine stuck his head in the door and asked what type of case we were scheduled to hear. The case had gotten quite a write-up in the local papers so I informed him, in my most genteel and gallant fashion, that *"this is the case where the husband found his wife shacked up in a motel with her boyfriend so he stabbed him."* Only then did I look up and discover the wife of the defendant standing about a foot from my door, having a cigarette. She surely heard what I said. I could have bitten off my tongue. Unfortunately, I decided not to.

My decision not to helped immensely in removing any doubt about my idiocy a short while later when I contributed even more to this little scenario. The normal procedure, when a defendant was in custody, was that the deputy sheriff would bring the defendant up to an anteroom outside the courtroom and wait there until just before the judge took the bench. I would often wait there also because of its proximity to the courtroom. At this particular time I had been troubled for days with a severe backache. When the deputy politely asked me how my back was feeling, I responded that *"it feels like somebody just stuck a knife into it."*

As soon as I said it, I realized how this must have sounded to someone charged with stabbing a man to death. In a space of about five minutes, I had managed to make humiliating remarks in front of the defendant and his wife. To their credit, they each showed the grace I had lacked by not making an issue of it in any respect. It taught me the value of a plaque that a judge I knew had up on his bench which reminded him to *"put brain in gear before engaging mouth!"*

The crime of drunk driving or driving under the influence certainly does not jump out as a subject for humor in the minds of most people. There are, however, many instances during the trials of these cases where it is very difficult to keep a straight face. One that comes to mind involved a gentleman who testified that he had two beers—the almost universal dosage admitted by defendants to possibly explain the arresting officer's allegation that they smelled like a brewery—and that he was certainly not incapacitated as far as driving was concerned.

He further testified that the arresting officer was very dis-

courteous and rude, but that when he was placed in the rear
seat of the patrol car, the officer who sat with him back there
on the way to the station was very pleasant and he vividly recalled his friendly smile and very white teeth. When the defendant's testimony was ended, the deputy district attorney requested permission to recall the arresting officer to the witness
stand for rebuttal and the following examination took place:

> Q: Officer, did you have a partner with you the night
> of this arrest?
> A: No, sir. I was alone.
> Q: So there was no other officer in the back seat of
> your patrol car?
> A: No, sir. Just my police dog, Max.

The jury deliberated just long enough to elect a foreperson
and returned with a verdict of guilty in record time.

To me, the goal of making a verbatim record was to deliver a
transcript which would make the reader feel, as much as possible, that he or she had been in the courtroom at the time the
proceedings took place. One of the tools I used to accomplish
this was an explanatory parenthetical. In other words, if there
was an outburst in the courtroom, the transcript would read
something like this:

> The Court: Madam, if you don't restrain yourself, I'll
> have you removed from the courtroom! (speaking
> to woman in spectator section)

Now, if I were to get carried away and insert "speaking to
woman in spectator section, blond, about fifty years of age,
weighing 225 pounds, wearing a red miniskirt, torn panty-
hose, with a tattoo on her right thigh proclaiming Save the
Motel Six," I could reasonably be accused of padding the
transcript plus including my own unwarranted conclusions.
With this in mind, the attempt to get things down verbatim
must often be tempered with common sense and reporters
should use their discretion when confronted with an unusual

"GD' EVENING, OSSIFER. YOU LOOK JUSH LIKE MY MOTHER-IN-LAW."

situation, such as a witness who has a severe stammering or stuttering problem. If someone began an answer with, "ah, ah, ah, ah, ah," I would usually put down the first three ah's, to indicate to the reader of the transcript that the witness had a stammer. I always felt that to do otherwise would seem to be mocking someone's infirmity.

I did report one drunk driving case, however, where the defendant had an extreme stuttering problem and, try as I might, I could not understand his testimony without including every single stutter he uttered. As fate would have it, about ten minutes after the jury retired to the jury room for deliberation, they requested that the defendant's testimony be read back to them. This took about an hour to accomplish and I believe that was one of the most embarrassing hours of my life (and possibly the defendant's) because I imagined the jurors and everyone in the courtroom felt I was deliberately ridiculing the defendant.

That was certainly not the case and I hope, in retrospect, everyone understood that. On the other hand, attorneys often make statements on the record that are not exactly brilliant or correct grammatically and reading that back verbatim doesn't bother me in the slightest. After all, they are well paid to know the law and make a polished presentation to the public. Besides, most of the time they assume the reporter made a mistake because they know their speech is more beautiful than that.

In one jury trial I reported, the prosecutor was becoming very exasperated with the judge. It seemed that almost every effort he made to present evidence was being thwarted by defense objections that were sustained by the court. Finally, the prosecutor made a motion to the court which was denied and the prosecutor responded with a very audible, "wheoew!" which I dutifully recorded, since it was loud enough for all the jurors to hear. Later, I was requested to read back that portion of the trial to the jury and when I read back the D.A.'s "wheoew!" the jury completely cracked up. The prosecutor was not amused, but it helped to defuse the rather tense atmosphere in the courtroom at the time.

⚖

One of the preliminary hearings I had occasion to report involved a defendant accused of molesting twin sisters who were only four years old. Great care should always be taken in dealing with witnesses of tender age, not only to avoid further traumatizing them, but to guard against leading them or putting words in their mouths. Too many good intentions, however, can sometimes lead to a miscarriage of justice. In this instance, the defendant was charged with exposing himself to the children and urging them to fondle him. The testimony of these children was difficult, not only because of their age, but because they both had a slight speech defect. Their speech was slightly accented by their Filipino heritage as well.

During the crucial part of their testimony, when the prosecutor asked them what the defendant had shown them, they answered, "his peter." I have no doubt that that is what they said—and what I put down—although the way they pronounced it phonetically was "his *beedo*." The deputy D.A. asked, incredulously, "his beetle?" The girls replied firmly, "No! His peter!" Again, pronounced *"beedo."*

The question was then asked where the defendant asked them to place their hands and their response was, "on his peter (*beedo*)." Once again, the question of whether they were saying beetle was put to them and once again they vociferously answered, "No! On his peter (*beedo*)." Now, I don't know whether the prosecutor and the court were incredibly naive or had some sort of entomological fixation, but there was a finding of insufficient evidence and the charges against the defendant were dismissed.

As I previously mentioned, if a defendant is not held to answer for trial, no transcript is made of the preliminary examination. The notes are simply stored by the reporter. Several months after this incident, I was contacted by a deputy district attorney from another county who requested a transcript of the aforementioned hearing because the same defendant was charged with a similar offense in that county. I prepared the transcript, including the word peter in the appropriate portions of the children's testimony. To this day, the prosecutor in the neighboring county must be wondering why the defendant was cut loose in the previous case.

⚖️

I found it quite fascinating whenever we heard a case involving the use of police dogs. The Mountain View Police Department at that time had a K-9 unit comprised of highly trained dogs and officers, even though it got by on a bare bones budget. The dogs were German shepherds which had been trained in Germany and responded only to commands in German. The officers to whom the dogs were assigned had to learn some basic German phrases in order to control the dogs.

In addition to their obvious value in apprehending violent criminals, they played a psychological role as well. In one incident involving a drunken man who had gone berserk in a local bar, the man had broken a beer bottle and was threatening everyone in the bar with the jagged glass. The police were called and the K-9 unit responded along with several other officers. At first the officers tried to talk the man into putting down the broken bottle, but he refused, vowing to cut anyone who came near him. The officers could have used their weapons, of course, but they didn't want to have to do that under the circumstances. They signaled for the K-9 unit to enter the bar and as soon as the distraught drunk spotted the menacing dog, he immediately dropped the broken bottle and was taken into custody.

In another instance, an officer was walking a beat with his dog late at night, checking the doors of business establishments to make sure they were locked. At one dry cleaning store everything seemed to be in order, but the dog kept wanting to return there. The officer used his flashlight to inspect the insides of the premises and could see nothing amiss. The dog was so persistent, however, the officer then went to the back of the cleaning establishment and from that vantage point could see a smouldering pile of rags just inside the back door. He immediately summoned the fire department which extinguished the small fire. If not for the highly developed senses of the dog, the building would have gone up in flames.

In one of the assault cases tried before a jury, the defendant alleged police brutality, claiming that the arresting officer had ordered his dog to attack him by constantly using the command, "kill!" The prosecutor then asked the officer to bring the dog into the courtroom for a demonstration. The dog appeared quite docile. The officer was then asked to give several commands to the dog. The officer ordered the dog to "attack," "bring him down" and finally, "kill!" The dog remained seated on the floor of the courtroom and couldn't have been less concerned if the officer had read him the Gettysburg Address. Finally, tightly grasping the leash of the dog, the officer whispered the German word for danger. The dog jumped to his feet, hackles rising and bared his teeth with a snarl. The defendant growled his objections, but they were quickly muzzled by the court. Despite the jury being hounded by the defendant's claim of police brutality, the demonstration caused him to shed his credibility and he was found guilty of the assault charge. After sentencing, he left the courtroom in such a huff that he accidently barked his shins on one of the chairs. As he drove away from the courthouse, his car was observed to be adorned with a bumper sticker which read, *"Life's a bitch and then you die."*

Chapter Three

Judges

JUDICIAL NOTICE is a legal term which basically may be defined as a stipulation by the court that something is true, without the necessity of proving it. For example, a judge in Florida might take judicial notice of the fact that the streets were wet during a hurricane, without requiring testimony by meteorologists or traffic engineers. Once judicial notice is taken of something, the jury or court may consider that as a fact. Sometimes judicial notice may be expressed in a more subtle fashion which often proves amusing.

Occasionally judges say things from the bench which leave a much more profound impression on the people in the courtroom than at other times. A judge in the Municipal Court in San Jose once had a female defendant appearing before him for sentencing following conviction of a drug offense. The Probation Department had recommended probation in conjunction with participation in a drug diversion program known as Operation Intercept. The defendant happened to be a very curvaceous young woman.

After reading the report, the judge announced to all that the defendant was sentenced to participate in Operation Intercourse. There was an immediate ripple of laughter in the courtroom and the judge angrily demanded an explanation. The attorneys approached the bench and whispered to the judge that he had said Operation Intercourse, rather than Operation Intercept. He told them they were obviously wrong and ordered the court reporter to read back his comments. The reporter read back Operation Intercourse, just as he had said it. The judge then ordered his previous comments stricken from the record and resentenced the defendant, using the proper terminology.

The color on the judge's face that day made the red stripes on the flag look pale by comparison. Certainly no one in that courtroom could claim that the judge had failed to take judicial notice, however Freudian it may have been.

Judges are a rather strange breed of animal. In some ways they are like presidents. A politician may be well known in congress or the senate and then, after attaining the presidency and confronted with the awesome power of the office, become a totally different person, unrecognizable to former colleagues. Soon after appointment to the bench, many judges assume a completely new personality. To be sure, some remain down-to-earth individuals, but many become raging prima donnas.

Just as a popular entertainer runs the risk of having an inflated ego because of the constant adulation of thousands of fans, so too must a judge guard against the temptation of assuming the role of a deity. It is not that easy to resist when everyone in the courtroom, with the possible exception of some hard-nosed criminal defendants, approaches you with an attitude of obeisance—"Yes, Your Honor." "No, Your Honor." "May I approach the bench?" "May I approach the witness?" "If the Court please, may the witness be excused?" Everyone in the courtroom stands when you enter the courtroom and everyone stands when you leave the courtroom. Is it any wonder that a judge might begin to think, "By God, I must be pretty damned special or they wouldn't treat me that way." I am not saying these things critically because I firmly believe that respect for the court is an absolute necessity for the judicial system to operate effectively. I am merely pointing out the pitfalls which can sometimes ensnare a judge along the way. After all, the respect is directed towards the institution of the court rather than the man or woman wearing the black robe. The respect for the individual must be earned.

When I started reporting in the Palo Alto Municipal Court, there were only two judges in that court and they detested each other. This really didn't hinder their effectiveness because prior to May of 1962, when a new court building was completed in Palo Alto, they rarely had occasion to be in the same building together. While one judge was holding court in Mountain View, the other judge was holding court in Palo Alto and the two courtrooms were about eight miles apart. On the rare instances when circumstances forced them to share each other's company, there was a stony silence between them.

The early court facilities in Palo Alto were located above the police station and there was no free parking provided for court personnel. The two judges, however, had a canvas bag which locked over a parking meter to allow them greater accessibility to the courtroom. The judge I worked for, who I will call Judge X (*no relation to Malcolm*), told me of the following incident which occurred prior to my employment in that court. Judge X, it seems, was fond of performing marriage ceremonies in his chambers. On several occasions, Judge Y interrupted these proceedings by barging into chambers in search of some document, without a word of apology. This of course infuriated Judge X because he was convinced it was deliberate. So one day he decided to lock the door to his chambers while he was performing the wedding ceremony and, sure enough, Judge Y showed up, trying to get into chambers. He banged on the door, rattled the lock, but was unable to gain entry so he left, steaming.

After the ceremony was concluded, Judge X had occasion to go down to his car and found that his canvas bag had been unlocked and removed from the parking meter and thrown up into a nearby tree. Members of the Palo Alto Fire Department obliged Judge X by judiciously retrieving his bag out of the tree.

Judge X was an amazingly unique individual. He was a rather portly man with a jaw that jutted forth like a bulldog's, especially when he was lecturing someone in court—which is to say it jutted forth most of the time. He was a rock of integrity and had a particular distaste for drunk drivers. If the organization called *Mothers Against Drunk Driving* had been around in the '60s, they probably would have made his courtroom a national shrine. When people pled guilty to drunk driving in his court, he would stick out that jaw, shake his finger at them and bellow, **"What you've done is about as popular as cancer and gonorrhea!"** Not exactly the recommended words to put a person at their ease in a crowded courtroom. He would then proceed to impose a very stiff fine in addition to sixty days in the county jail, suspended on three years informal probation, during which time they were not to violate any portion of the Vehicle Code dealing with reckless or drunk driving and were forbidden to drink any alcoholic beverage or frequent any place where alcohol was sold for the entire three years.

I often wondered how he expected to enforce such a provision, but occasionally he would learn that someone he had sentenced was seen in a bar or imbibing and that person would be summoned back to court. If, after a proper hearing, it was determined that the allegations were true, the defendant was ordered to serve either a portion of or sometimes the entire previously suspended county jail sentence.

I recall one preliminary hearing where the defendant was charged with felony auto theft, along with misdemeanor drunk driving. The fact situation developed as follows: The defendant had been sentenced by Judge X for drunk driving about eighteen months prior to the present charge. The last thing he wanted was to be brought back for an encore. Therefore, when he was invited to a party the night of his arrest, he dutifully took a cab and left his car at home. After spending several hours at the party and getting sloshed to the eyeballs, he wandered out the front door and there at the curb, though hard to believe, was a car identical to his own with the keys in the ignition. In his state, he thought it was his and decided to drive it home. The owner of the car soon noticed it missing and called police, who apprehended the defendant a few blocks away.

Once these facts were brought out in court, a plea bargain was entered into and the defendant pled guilty to the second drunk driving charge and the auto theft felony was dismissed. Personally, I think I would have taken my chances on a felony trial in Superior Court, rather than appear before Judge X again on an alcohol related offense.

Judge X was truly Victorian in his thinking. The so-called sexual revolution of the '60s caused him no end of travail. His court clerk was a middle-aged woman with grown children, yet whenever a case involving sex was heard in his court, he would have the clerk swear in all the witnesses in advance and then excuse her from the courtroom. When pantsuits became popular, it was almost two years before he would allow a woman attorney to wear one in his courtroom. He suffered equal consternation over miniskirts. I could never understand this since I had always agreed with that ancient holy man who said, "I never tire of admiring the Lord's handiwork."

As I mentioned before, his demeanor in court could be very intimidating and often caused strong men to tremble. One person who gave him absolute fits was a deputy public defender who came to court wearing miniskirts, pink stockings and had ribbons and flowers in her blond hair. He thought this very inappropriate for an officer of the court. He also was exceedingly vexed that, in spite of his most fearsome tirades, she refused to be intimidated and would not back down. Some years later, she was appointed Chief Justice of the Supreme Court of California.

Although my work load kept me from recognizing the full extent of the need at the time, in retrospect, the '60s and '70s were certainly times that cried out for protests and demonstrations. Not only in relation to the war in Viet Nam, but also as to the rights of minorities and women. One reporter friend of mine told me that it was routine in his court, whenever a guilty plea was entered to driving under the influence by a college student or college professor, etc., the judge in that court would lecture the defendant by loudly stating, *"What's the matter with you? You ought to be ashamed! You know better than this. You're college trained. You're not like some of these dumb Mexicans around here!"* Meanwhile, a large number of Mexican-Americans in the audience were patiently awaiting the unbiased judgment of the court. In my experience, this type of thing was extremely rare and certainly by 1990 when I retired, it would be political suicide for such words to be uttered from the bench.

Judge X vouched for the authenticity of an incident involving a judge in Fresno who was only five feet, two inches in height. Because of this it was sometimes difficult to see him on the bench, especially when he leaned back in his chair. On one occasion, two attorneys from another jurisdiction were arguing a motion before him. One attorney, who was concentrating intently on his argument, looked up for a moment from his list of citations and did not see the judge on the bench. Surprised, he turned to opposing counsel and asked, "Where did the little son of a bitch go?" "Here I am, counsel," answered a voice over his left shoulder. It seems the judge had tired of counsel's long presentation and had decided to come down from the bench and read for himself from the attorney's long list of citations. I have no knowledge of the results of that case, but I'm sure a decision was reached shortly.

As our old friend Dracula might say, in a similar vein, a local deputy district attorney encountered a slight problem while trying to get a judge's approval for a search warrant. In this county the procedure for obtaining a search warrant is for the police agency to convince the district attorney's office that there is probable cause for obtaining such a warrant and once that is done, the deputy district attorney must convince a judge of that same probable cause. After working hours and on weekends, various judges are assigned as duty judges for the purpose of granting and signing warrants, etc.

In this instance, the police officer had successfully convinced the deputy district attorney that there was probable cause. However, when the district attorney contacted the judge at his home, the judge was unconvinced and refused to issue the warrant without more evidence. Less than pleased, the district attorney had to call the officer back to break the bad news. He dialed the number and as soon as there was an answer, he blurted, "That asshole judge refused to sign the warrant!" There was a short pause and then, "This is that asshole judge, counsel, and I want to see you in my chambers first thing Monday morning!" In his anger, the deputy had mistakenly redialed the judge's number. Once again, I have no information regarding the end result of that case, but no doubt by Monday afternoon the deputy district attorney would have been interested in the services of a good proctologist.

I had occasion to work for a short while for a retired judge from a rural county in northern California. Under the law in California, retired judges are permitted to return to the bench occasionally to help out with the large backlog of cases waiting to be heard. This judge was a very kindly old gentleman, but had a distinct hearing problem and refused to wear a hearing aid. For instance, many times when counsel would make an objection during a trial, he would respond with, "Oh, you want a recess? Sure thing! Court will be in recess for ten minutes." In one case a jury was being selected to hear a trial and during the questioning of the potential jurors, one gentleman asked to be excused because his mother-in-law had been killed in Oregon and he wanted to go there with his wife to help out her father. The judge was sympathetic and excused the man from jury duty. While the man was on his way out of the courtroom, the judge called out, "I hope your mother-in-law gets better soon!"

The last judge I worked for in the Municipal Court was a man of great legal brilliance and dry wit, but whose vocabulary was sometimes rather salty on the bench. He called things just as he saw them and had very little patience with attorneys who tended to drag things out needlessly. If he felt too much time was being wasted on one subject, he might interrupt with, "For Christ's sake, Counsel, give me credit for having a few brains! Let's move on." This usually had a salutary effect on the speed of the trial, although not always on the attorney. I used to wince at some of the things he would say on the record because they would be included in any review by the Appellate Court. However, his record for being upheld on appeal was very good. He was always kind and courteous to the litigants themselves and only gave the attorneys a hard time when he felt they had earned it.

When this judge was appointed to the Superior Court, it was my good fortune to accompany him. Several years later during the jury trial of a personal injury case, many proceedings had to be held in chambers out of the presence of the jury because one of the attorneys refused to abide by the judge's rulings regarding the proper conduct of the trial. No matter what ruling he made, the attorney would proceed in a manner that was just the opposite of his ruling. Finally, he called counsel into chambers and told them he was going to declare a mistrial. The recalcitrant attorney demanded the right to make a statement on the record and the court agreed.

She started in at an extremely rapid pace and I had great difficulty keeping up with her. After about twenty minutes, the judge interrupted her and said, "Mr. Bailiff, would you get some water and pour it on the reporter's machine? It's starting to smoke." This of course was his not so subtle effort to get her to slow down for my benefit. She responded with, "I know the court does not like me, but—" The judge quickly reassured her that, "It's not that I don't like you; I just think you're nuts!" Far from being nonplussed by the judge's comment, she continued her speech on the record for another twenty minutes, after which a mistrial was declared and the matter was reassigned to another department.

The court clerk who worked for this judge was a woman in her early fifties who suffered a slight hearing loss. She would also occasionally tend to doze off during testimony that was somewhat boring. The courts in this county are designed so that the judge's bench is elevated approximately eighteen inches to two feet above the level of the floor. Immediately in front of the bench, there is a narrow walkway and then the desks of the clerk and the court reporter. In front of that is the counsel table where the attorneys sit facing the judge. The clerk sits with her back to the judge, facing the audience.

In the older courtrooms a flashing light was installed on the clerk's desk so that if the judge wanted to attract the attention of the clerk, a button was pushed and the light would flash. If the clerk happened to be looking elsewhere and did not see the light, which was rather small, there was also a buzzer the judge could press. This usually got the clerk's attention and she would turn to the judge and he would whisper that he needed a file or an exhibit, etc. The whole purpose of all this was to avoid causing any distraction during the presentation of evidence or argument, especially with a jury present.

On more than one occasion I can recall the judge trying to get the attention of the clerk while she was sneaking a few Z's. Remember, he could not see that she had her eyes closed. First, he would whisper her name a couple of times. Then he would press the flashing light. Still failing to get a response, he would press the buzzer, more-or-less negating any attempt to avoid distraction. If that failed to rouse her, he would wad up a piece of legal paper into a ball and toss it at the back of her head.

This usually did the trick, much to the amusement of the jury, which had been witnessing the whole scenario. I don't mean to malign the clerk because she was quite capable in performing her duties. She just shared the same problem the jury had with remaining attentive during something like two or three days of testimony by a C.P.A., dealing with nothing but numbers.

Another instance of this judge having fun with a different clerk occurred during a court trial (non-jury) where the clerk had occasion to leave the courtroom on several errands during the trial. This clerk was a gentleman of many years experience who tended to be somewhat officious. During one of the absences of the clerk, a new witness was called to testify. When the clerk is not present, the witness is sworn in by the judge. As is customary, the witness stated and spelled her full name for the record. A short time later, the clerk returned to the courtroom and the judge handed the clerk a note purportedly containing the name of the witness so he could enter it into the court's minutes. Later, during a brief pause in the questioning, the clerk approached the witness and said, *"Excuse me, Mrs. Hoffenschlockerdinger, but may I have the spelling of your first name?"* The witness looked at him, startled, while the people in the courtroom snickered and the judge almost fell off the bench. She had previously stated her name was Mary Brown.

⚖

In Marin County on August 7, 1970, the trial of two defendants in a San Rafael courtroom was interrupted when friends of the defendants produced guns and demanded the release of the two defendants. The judge, the male prosecutor, and three women jurors were taken hostage and placed in a van. In the shoot-out with police that followed the attempted escape, the judge was killed and the prosecutor, along with one of the women jurors, was shot. This naturally had a profound effect on other judges concerned with the security of their court-rooms and provided the impetus for the installation of metal detectors and other security devices now common around most California courtrooms.

One of our local judges at the time was more concerned than others, almost to the point of paranoia. When his court was in session, he required that all lights in the front of the courtroom be turned off, with the exception of one small light over the witness stand. The only other lights allowed to be on were those in the back of the courtroom. This made it some-what arduous for witnesses to examine documents and exhib-its, but it also made the judge a more difficult target.

Court reporters normally store their notes in boxes kept in their offices for a period of a year or so, but in time they take up so much space they must be placed in the basement of the courthouse or some other storage facility. Notes of criminal matters must be retained for at least ten years so storage rap-idly becomes a problem. One of the reporters whose office was on the same floor as that of the aforementioned judge had de-cided to send about ten boxes of notes from her office to the basement. To that end, she had stacked them in the corridor outside her office and then gone to lunch.

The judge, while strolling around that area, spotted them and knew they had not been there the day before. (*More judicial notice?*) He did not realize what they were. In those days, any unidentified box, package or even briefcase found around the courthouse might be suspected of containing an explosive de-vice. Without further ado, the judge ordered a crew to remove the boxes immediately and they were taken to the city dump and buried. When the reporter returned from lunch and found her notes missing, she was greatly alarmed and started making inquiries. Eventually, she learned what had happened and in-formed the judge that those boxes contained the official steno-graphic notes of all the proceedings in her court for the last year and a half, without which it would be impossible to prepare a transcript on appeal of any matter tried during that time.

This all happened on a Good Friday and while many devout people were cleansing their souls in church, a Superior Court judge, a court reporter, and a bulldozer operator spent that afternoon cleansing the soles of their shoes after resurrecting ten boxes of official court notes from their entombment at the city dump.

Chapter Four

Suffer the Children

MY FIRST regular assignment in the Superior Court was in the Juvenile Court division. I spent a total of four years working in Juvenile Court—two with one judge in 1970 and 1971 and two with another judge in 1978 and 1979. In 1970 the Juvenile Court had court clerks more or less permanently assigned to that department. In all other departments each judge had a clerk, a reporter and a bailiff as part of a regular staff, but in Juvenile Court the judge was assisted by a clerk whose experience was restricted to juvenile matters.

There were only two departments in Juvenile Court in 1970 and the clerk we were assigned always impressed me as having been a marine drill instructor in another life. She was a woman in her late fifties who, in spite of her small size, put the fear of God in the youngsters who came before the court by demanding, "Stand up straight! Get your hands out of your pockets! Get rid of that gum! Pay attention!" After we had been there a short while, the judge had to speak to her and suggest that she lighten up a bit because the juveniles were paying more attention to her than they were to him.

She would even bully the juvenile probation officers who came to court, even though she had absolutely no authority over them. She had just been there so long nobody wanted to cross her. Someone wrote a book a few years ago called *Winning Through Intimidation*. I often wonder if the book had been inspired by a visit to that court in the author's teen years.

The matters heard in Juvenile Court dealt not only with law violations by juvenile offenders, but also with children who had been abused, molested, or abandoned. There was also at that time a category called "beyond control" which was applied to minors who rebelled against all parental control and in some cases even used physical force against their parents. Under this section of the law, the minor could be detained in Juvenile Hall temporarily as sort of a cooling off period.

The California Legislature later decided, in its infinite wisdom, that the "beyond control" statute was a deprival of due process for the minors and it was stricken from the books. So after that, whenever a minor refused to attend school or told his parents to shove it, they had to hope he would steal a car or commit some other criminal offense that would permit them to get some help from the Juvenile Probation Department. Today, family counseling is used extensively to help work out such problems.

Our bailiff in Juvenile Court had accompanied the judge and me from Municipal Court when the judge was appointed to the Superior Court. The bailiff's name was Charley and he almost became a legend in Juvenile Court during the judge's two-year stay there. Previous mention was made of the impatience of the judge when dealing with long-winded attorneys (*talk about redundancy*), but when it came to his staff, his patience was truly remarkable. Charley had been the judge's bailiff for about a year in Municipal Court so his somewhat eccentric behavior was no surprise to him.

In adult court there is a section reserved for spectators because most adult court proceedings are open to the public. Juvenile Court matters are considered confidential because minors are being dealt with and there is no public observance allowed. The only people authorized to be present generally were the minors, their families, the prosecution and defense attorneys, and the court staff. Witnesses were excluded before and after they gave their testimony.

The physical setup was basically a very long table, about ten feet in front of the judge's bench, at which the minors, their family members, and their attorneys would be seated. The bailiff's station was a desk situated about five feet to the right and to the rear of this table. When a minor had been tried on probation a number of times and still was unable to live within the law, the only alternative left to the court was to send the minor to either the county Boys' Ranch or the Girls' Ranch or, in the more serious cases, to the California Youth Authority, a locked facility in which the minor could be held until the age of twenty-five.

When the court was required to take this action, there was, understandably, a great deal of emotional reaction on the part of the minor as well as the family. There was a lot of weeping and the court stocked a large supply of Kleenex for just such occasions.

Sometimes when this happened, Charley would be engrossed in reading the stock market reports and the judge would have to remind him to offer some Kleenex to the parties. Charley would pick up the box from his desk, go to the near end of the table and, if the person in need was sitting at the far end of the table, slide the box, shuffleboard-wise, to the end of the table, hoping it would be caught before it fell off the other end. This usually prompted some comment from the judge such as, "For Christ's sake, Charley. Be a gentleman and hand it to them!" Charley would then comply with the judge's wishes with a look on his face that seemed to say, "Gee, why didn't I think of that? No wonder he's a judge."

Many of Charley's famous foibles occurred when minors were testifying during contested hearings—especially if they involved some type of narcotics offense. For example, if the minor testified that, "Gosh, I had no intention of using any drugs. I was just having a Coke and when I set it down for a minute, I guess someone dropped some Reds into it," Charley's immediate response was to hold his ample nose with one hand, utter a loud Bronx cheer and, with his other hand, make a motion of thumbs down, thus subtly expressing his opinion of the minor's credibility.

The attorneys and family members in the courtroom would turn around and stare at Charley in disbelief, but the judge simply ignored him. His philosophy seemed to be, "Oh well, that's Charley," and not give it a second thought. Long after we left Juvenile Court, people would ask me about various incidents their friends had related to them regarding the bailiff in that court and my standard response was always, "With Charley there, anything's possible."

You might wonder why the judge would tolerate such behavior in his courtroom. I believe the reason he did was because Charley was a very loyal and trustworthy person. He worshipped the judge and would have defended him to the death if called upon to do so. He was also quite efficient in his way and very dependable as far as attendance and punctuality. He just had a tendency to act sometimes without thinking—a condition common to many of us. Besides, I think the judge was secretly amused at some of the reactions Charley's comments produced in the courtroom.

One of the matters that came before the Juvenile Court involved a minor charged with engaging in unlawful sexual activity with an adult in a public restroom. The conduct was alleged to have taken place in the men's room of a large public park in downtown San Jose. The charge was contested and the chief witness for the prosecution was a city landscape gardener who had been working in the park at the time of the alleged offense.

When the witness entered the courtroom, the clerk stood and raised her right hand as an indication to the witness that he should raise his right hand in order to be sworn in as a witness. When the witness saw her right hand in the air, he raised his hand and waved, saying "Hi! How are you?" obviously assuming she knew him from somewhere and he didn't want to appear rude. After the protocol of being sworn in was explained to him, he took the witness stand and was questioned about what he had observed.

During the questioning, the judge asked him to describe how the restroom was designed. He was unable to verbally explain to the judge the layout of the restroom, so the judge asked him to draw a diagram of the scene on the exhibit board. When he seemed reluctant to do so, the following colloquy took place:

> The Witness: I can't draw very good. Do I have to do that?

The Court: Well, I have to know what the scene looked like so I can follow what you're talking about. It doesn't have to be perfect. Just give us a rough idea.

The Witness: Well, can we just go to the bathroom?

The Court: Of course not. We're holding a trial here. We can't just go down there and look at the bathroom. Just give us your best shot at a diagram.

The Witness: You mean I can't go to the bathroom?

The Court: No, we can't. You mean you have to go to the bathroom?

The Witness: Yes.

The Court: We'll take a brief recess. Charley, show him where the bathroom is.

At this time I am not certain of the disposition of that case, but I believe the failure of the witness's recollection caused the prosecution's case to go down the toilet. As I recall, by the end of the hearing the prosecutor's face was very flushed.

The preparation of trial transcripts comprises a substantial portion of a court reporter's income. During the time of my initial service at Juvenile Court, very few transcripts were ordered of Juvenile Court matters. To help compensate for this, there was a practice of offering the reporters in Juvenile Court, as well as those in Domestic Court, first choice when an opportunity arose to work on a "daily" in a trial department of the Superior Court.

The term "daily" refers to the fact that a complete transcript is prepared each day of all proceedings held on that day and is delivered to the attorneys and the court the next morning or sometimes even late the same night. Today reporters who work with computers can do them alone. Before computers, however, it was necessary to have two reporters working together in a trial to be able to deliver a daily.

The procedure was that both reporters would sit together when the trial commenced. One reporter would record the proceedings for about three minutes and would then leave the courtroom while the other reporter took over. The first reporter would dictate the stenographic notes onto a recording tape and give it to a typist or transcriber, who was paid by the reporters. The reporter would then literally race back to the courtroom to relieve the other reporter. Timing was of the utmost importance because it takes almost twice as long to dictate your notes as it does to take them down. By the noon recess, each reporter's turn in court was at least thirty minutes. By the time the morning's proceedings were dictated, it was time to begin the afternoon session and the same procedure started all over again. Many times it was almost 9:00 P.M. before the transcript was finished, proofread, corrected and put together. These assignments can become very exhausting and stressful, especially during a long trial. Obviously, the only reason reporters are willing to take on this extra work load is that they are paid for these transcripts and in an extended trial the payment can be very rewarding.

When I was offered the chance to work on a trial in which two defendants were charged with murder and there was a daily transcript required, I quickly accepted the offer. Not only because of the additional revenue, but because it would provide a break in the puerile matters that came before the court every day in my regular assignment.

In the vast majority of cases, judges learn very early that they must control what goes on in their courtroom. When judges are first appointed to the bench, the attorneys who appear before them will invariably test them to see how far they can go as far as misconduct, before being found in contempt of court. They may argue with the court, argue with each other, engage in screaming matches, or be consistently late in their appearances. If the judge bangs the gavel and says something like, "Counsel, I will not allow that kind of behavior in this court! In this courtroom you will behave like ladies and gentlemen and if you can't do that, you can have five days to think about it in the county jail," the demeanor of the attorneys invariably is miraculously transformed.

Most judges also want the record to be as accurate as possible so they will admonish counsel not to both talk at the same time or they will ask a witness to speak up or slow down for the benefit of the reporter. This is immeasurably helpful to the reporter. Conversely, when a judge makes little effort to control the proceedings in court, the reporter's job can become a nightmare.

The two defendants in this murder trial each had separate attorneys. The prosecutor was a deputy district attorney who had previously been a police officer and a professional boxer prior to that. The trial strategy of defense counsel seemed to consist chiefly of baiting the prosecutor to the point of becoming so angry he might overlook some important part of the evidence—much as a boxer might drop his guard because of a whispered insult and then be the recipient of a knockout punch. This created a very acrimonious atmosphere in the courtroom.

When counsel approach the bench for a conference with the judge, their words are supposed to be whispered, out of the hearing of the jury. In this trial the discussions at the bench became so heated the jury could easily hear almost everything they said. When one of them said, "You're stupid!" and the other replied, "You're a son of a bitch!" I had to make parentheticals in the record that they were speaking to each other and not the judge. At one point the prosecutor offered to go outside and take on both defense counsel, one at a time or both together.

For reasons known only to himself, the judge did little to curtail this spectacle before the jury. The only way I could get any cooperation at all, when all three attorneys were shouting at each other at the same time, was to scream, **"One at a time for the record!"** This would calm things down momentarily and then the whole procedure would begin again. I developed a parenthetical that I used frequently during this trial which said "simultaneous, unintelligible screaming by counsel." The attorneys did not appreciate this, but it seemed to get their attention sufficiently to eventually restore a little bit of order.

One of the few lighter moments in this trial occurred during a hearing outside the presence of the jury. A defense motion was made to suppress evidence of a tape recording made of one of the defendants when he was a guest of the California Youth Authority. The recording had been made without his knowledge and the tape recorder had been hidden inside a telephone in the interrogation room. The tape was over an hour long and it was necessary to listen to all of it to determine whether or not it could be received into evidence.

This judge's bailiff was a retired military man (as were most court bailiffs at that time) and he would occasionally grab forty winks when things got a little dull. Needless to say, he had little opportunity for that during this trial. In this instance, however, the long playing of the tape soon had him deep in slumber. About halfway through the playing of the tape, the telephone rang on the tape and it was very loud because the tape recorder was attached to it. The bailiff was immediately aroused, grabbed his telephone and shouted, "Judge Blank's court, Bailiff Jones speaking." I guess you had to be there to appreciate how funny that was, especially in a case that had been so devoid of any kind of warmth. Even the defendants could hardly stop laughing.

The oldest person on the jury in this trial was a woman in her mid-sixties. I don't know whether she suffered from narcolepsy or had a night job, but she slept during a major portion of this trial. In most trials if a juror starts to nod off, the bailiff will usually notice and take them a cup of water, trying not to embarrass them. There was so much turmoil in this trial, I guess the condition of the jurors had a pretty low priority.

When the trial finally ended, the matter went to the jury for their consideration late in the afternoon. At that time, juries were still sequestered in this county and the members of the jury were soon taken to a hotel for the night. The next morning the jury resumed its deliberation and after only a half hour, the foreman of the jury sent a note out to the judge suggesting that the judge interview juror number six (the drowsy one) because she claimed to have heard things unheard by the other jurors.

The woman was brought into the judge's chambers, along with all the attorneys and the defendants, and she stated that she had heard defendant B talking to defendant A, saying, "You may be my buddy, but you know you did it and I didn't and I ain't taking the rap for you!" The judge asked her if this was during a recess and she stated it was not. It was during the cross-examination of the defendant by the prosecutor. She then turned to me and said, "You heard it. You were sitting there writing it all down." I assured her that I had not heard anything like that. She was convinced, however, that she was correct. After a brief discussion between the court and counsel, it was agreed the woman should be excused from the jury because she was hallucinating and an alternate juror was sent in to replace her.

I don't believe the woman was hallucinating at all. I believe during the time that defendant was testifying, she took one of her little naps and dreamed that the defendant said those things. When she awoke, he was still on the stand and in her mind there was no doubt he had said it. This was about as close as you can come to a mistrial and not have one. Ironically, the jury's verdict was that one defendant was guilty and the other was innocent. Despite the behavior of counsel, the jury reached a verdict which most impartial observers during the trial agreed was the correct one, based on the evidence received. It was almost a pleasure to get away from the juvenile performances in this trial and return to the comparative maturity of my regular assignment.

Chapter Five

Thou Shalt Not Covet
Thy Neighbor's Ass

OUR TOUR of duty at Juvenile Court came to a close at the end of 1971. It had been a real learning experience for all of us. Although amusing situations occasionally arose—especially with Charley present—the calendar for the most part was rather depressing. Each day you are witness to families that are torn apart, either through the misdirected actions of their children or the failure of the parents to exercise responsibility.

The environment at that time was similar to working in a jail. It was a locked facility and the security of minors in Juvenile Hall was uppermost in the minds of everyone. You needed a key to do anything from going to the bathroom to using a light switch. Our next assignment was somewhat like being released on our own recognizance. We were no longer in a locked facility, but we were still involved with families that were torn apart—or in the process of becoming so. Welcome to Domestic Court.

In 1970 the law in California was changed to permit no-fault divorce. Prior to that time, a divorce could be obtained by proving, among other things, adultery, mental or physical cruelty, or desertion. The testimony of the person seeking a divorce was often not sufficient, standing alone. Most judges required corroborating evidence to prove the allegations in the complaint.

My only experience in California under the old divorce

law was when the judge I worked for in the Municipal Court sat one time as a pro tempore Superior Court Judge. During this temporary elevation, he was assigned a number of uncontested divorce matters. One of the cases he heard involved a husband seeking custody of the children and the husband's corroborating witness was his mother-in-law. She testified, among other things, that her daughter was no good and was an unfit mother for the children. Since the matter was uncontested, the wife was not there and I cannot report on the sharpness of her horns or the length of her tail. I can only surmise that she must have been dreadfully late in mailing her Mother's Day card.

Many people are under the impression that all you have to do to end a marriage is to go to court, let the judge decide who gets what and who pays what, and that's the end of it. Wrong! In most cases, that is just the beginning. Inevitably, a few months after the judge makes a decision, there are motions brought for reconsideration, increase or decrease in child support amounts, changes in visitation with the children, changes in amount of spousal support (formerly alimony), or motions by one side or the other to find their ex-partner in contempt of court for not fully obeying the orders of the court.

One such motion was brought by an ex-husband who was required to pay spousal support to his ex-wife. His contention was that his former wife was now living with another man who was employed and therefore he should not be required to continue payment. His allegation was that the man was an ambulance driver who could be seen leaving the house of his former wife every morning and returning there every night. There was a vehement denial of such an arrangement and the former missus countered that her roommate was not a man, but another woman.

The ambulance driver, with a name like Terry J. Smith, was subpoenaed as a witness. When that name was called out in court, the witness who reluctantly came forward was a woman. Under questioning, she revealed that she did indeed live with the petitioner's former spouse and that she was employed as an ambulance driver. She also acknowledged that she dressed as a man during the day because the ambulance company would not hire women and she was quite fearful that if the company learned of her testimony, that would be the end of her job. Based on the evidence, the husband's motion was denied. Today we take for granted the employment of female ambulance drivers or attendants as well as a vast array of occupations formerly restricted to men. But, this was still in the early 1970s—the age of discrimination—and life could get pretty complicated.

There is a time-honored maxim about the road to hell being paved with good intentions. This was sharply illustrated in a case where a father was seeking sole custody of the children because he claimed the mother was unsuitable to raise his children. The testimony established a fact situation as follows: After being married about seven years, approximately six months prior to the divorce the husband was becoming bored with their sex life (obviously the classic symptomatology of the seven-year itch). After much penetrating consideration, he decided that the best remedy for getting the old home fires burning again was a *menage a trois*. The wife was appalled and horrified at such a suggestion and absolutely opposed to the idea.

The husband persisted, however, begging, cajoling, promising his undying love and eventually persuaded his wife to go along with the idea. The third party he had in mind was their nineteen-year-old baby-sitter. They had both known her for about five years and after relatively little effort, he persuaded her to join the party. (*I believe I may have bought a used car from this man once.*) Things seemed to progress rather nicely and he was consummately pleased with his accomplishment. He noted, with some pride, that his wife had overcome her initial reluctance to the idea and now seemed to embrace it with great enthusiasm.

After a few weeks, her enthusiasm seemed to know no bounds and he began to get the distinct impression that the two ladies felt that three was a crowd and he was the crowd. His fears were soon realized when his attempts to socialize were rebuffed by both of them and they declared they no longer wanted any part of him—especially *that* part. Now it was

his turn to be appalled at the monstrous situation he had created. He immediately ordered the baby-sitter to leave and his
wife stated that if the baby-sitter left, she would leave with her.

That is exactly what happened. The wife left, taking the
children with her, and rented a house with the baby-sitter. The
frustrated husband suddenly decided it was a moral outrage to
have the children exposed to such a situation and thus the
matter came to court. Evidently it was not morally outrageous
for the children as long as hubby was part of the action. Once
again, the social tolerance of the '90s was twenty years down
the road. The wife was granted custody of the children, only
by agreeing to renounce the baby-sitter and to seek therapy.

An interesting footnote to that case was that both husband
and wife were members of the super-intellect group known as
Mensa. I don't know what significance that has except perhaps to illustrate that where raging hormones are concerned, a
near genius can demonstrate the same questionable judgment
as that of a person whose I.Q. may be closer to room temperature.

One day on a crowded domestic motions calendar, a case was
called for hearing. In most instances, when the case is called,
the attorneys come forward with their clients, the husband
and wife. In this matter, the attorneys were accompanied by
two women, both wearing modified miniskirts, high heels and
full makeup. One of the attorneys asked if he might approach
the bench. The judge stated, "I think you'd better." The discussion at the bench was not on the record, but the gist of the
matter was that the husband had chosen to have a sex change
operation in the near future and, pending that, had decided to
be a woman until the surgery could be performed. The rock
group Aerosmith did not release their song, "Dude Looks Like
a Lady" until 1987, but it would have made appropriate background music under the circumstances.

The judge came very close to finding him in contempt for
appearing in court that way. He also had a few choice words
for his attorney about client control. Aside from however sin-
cere the gentleman's sexual preferences may have been, the
most obvious conclusion was that he would later claim inabil-

ity to maintain the same level of employment and therefore not be able to pay as much spousal support or child support. This was a motion for temporary support and the trial of the matter was assigned to another department so I have no knowledge of its ultimate conclusion. All I know is that when they left the courtroom, we could hear loud whistling in the corridor. Since we were on the third floor, I think it's safe to assume no one was hailing a cab.

The termination of domestic relations usually brings out the worst in all of us. There is generally a great feeling of betrayal and a strong desire to "get even" by one party or the other. Giving in to one's emotions can often be costly under any circumstances, but allowing your good judgment to be clouded by feelings of hatred or spite in a divorce can become one of the most expensive mistakes of your life. It is undeniable that divorce is a very painful and emotional process and people are hurting. However, adding an unnecessary additional financial burden only makes it worse.

Many people spend thousands of dollars in attorney fees trying to regain property that is only worth a fraction of the amount they pay their attorneys. By far, the wisest people are those who settle their cases before they ever get to trial. They are, after all, much more familiar with their own lives and needs than some strange judge, no matter how well intentioned he or she may be. Statistics show that cases that end in settlements rarely come back to court with disputed matters, as opposed to those that wind up in long, contentious trials.

I have reported cases involving murder, rape, kidnapping, assaultive behavior of almost every type, but I am convinced there is a greater potential for violence in a Domestic Court than any other. The hatred that leaps from the eyes of some people involved in domestic disputes makes you wonder how they could ever have cared for each other. Whenever there is a report in the newspaper about a shooting at a courthouse, nine out of ten times it involves a domestic matter where someone is seeking revenge against an ex-spouse or their attorney. In this county, all persons entering domestic court must pass through a metal detector identical to the one that scans people going to criminal court.

Often, the property that people want to claim in a marital dispute ranges from the ridiculous to the pathetic. In addition to the division of community property, many personal items must be equitably divided by the court such as family photographs, books, records, trophies, etc. I have seen vigorous arguments over who gets to keep the children's baby teeth as well as one case where they actually fought over who should receive a leg of lamb in the freezer. One woman called her young daughter as a witness to help prove that a customized toilet seat had been a birthday gift and should not be awarded to the husband. If my memory serves me correctly, the wife stated her husband only required half a seat anyway.

Family pets are also often the subject of hotly disputed cases. One of our local judges, who was later a distinguished Associate Justice of the California Supreme Court, once made a very structured order regarding the husband's visitation rights with the family dog. I wondered at the time if noncompliance with the order would have resulted in an illegal beagle.

⚖

Our assignment to Domestic Court only lasted about six months, but a domestic angle was involved in one of the major civil jury trials we were assigned. This trial concerned a general contractor who was suing a school district over construction of a large auditorium at one of our local junior colleges. It was an extended trial, lasting about twelve weeks. There was a huge exhibit, weighing over a ton, used for the purpose of illustrating to the jury the various types of construction involved. There were also hundreds of documentary exhibits including maps, plot plans, architectural drawings and the building plans.

Because of the expected length of the trial, three alternate jurors were selected in addition to the regular jury. An alternate juror is somewhat like a spare tire. If one of the regular jurors becomes ill or incapacitated, the alternate replaces that juror and becomes a member of the main jury. As it turned out, we could have used a fourth alternate.

The plaintiff in this case was seeking an award involving many millions of dollars. There were four or five lawyers representing multiple clients and there had been a great deal of time and money invested in both the prosecution and defense of this case. One of the most important exhibits in the matter was the building plans. When not being used, they were rolled up into a tube shape and held with several rubber bands. In this condition, they were about five feet long and awkward to manage. In order to have more room on her desk, the clerk decided to store them temporarily in the wastebasket between her desk and mine.

One evening, when the trial was about a week away from its conclusion, she forgot to remove the plans from the wastebasket at the end of the day. The janitor came in that night and routinely emptied the wastebaskets. The next morning the clerk was frantic. Without the building plans, the case would surely end in a mistrial and the huge expenditure of time and resources would be in vain. It is very likely as well the clerk would be seeking employment elsewhere.

Never one to leave a damsel in distress, Sir Charles rushed in to the rescue. Rushed into, that is, the Dempster Dumpster. It isn't often one sees a man in the uniform of a deputy sheriff flailing his way through a mountain of trash, but that is exactly what Charley did. Fortunately for all concerned, he was able to retrieve the missing building plans and the case proceeded to its conclusion. None of the attorneys were aware of the slight mishap or how narrowly disaster had been avoided.

By the end of the trial, it had been necessary to use all three of the alternate jurors. At the time there was a particularly virulent flu bug going around and additionally, I believe there was a death in one juror's family. Just prior to closing arguments in the trial, one of the remaining twelve jurors became violently ill and had to be excused. This meant either the case would end in a mistrial or the attorneys would have to stipulate to a jury of eleven members instead of twelve. Because of the tremendous investment at stake, the attorneys agreed to stipulate to eleven jurors deciding the case. Such a stipulation would have been unlikely in a criminal case where a unanimous verdict is required, but in a civil case a verdict is reached when nine out of twelve jurors agree, or in this case, eight out of eleven.

⚖

Oh, the domestic angle? In jury trials, especially lengthy ones, jurors often become very friendly with each other during the course of the trial. There is a special camaraderie that develops among them because they are sharing a very unique experience. It is quite common for them to go to lunch together, share coffee breaks, etc. In this case, juror number one was a handsome young man who was unmarried. Juror number seven, who was seated immediately in front of juror number one, was a very attractive young woman. She, however, was married. During the course of the trial, the two became very good friends. Towards the end of the trial, they were no longer joining the other jurors for lunch and could be seen holding hands when they returned to court.

About two months after the trial, juror number seven was on the court's domestic calendar seeking a divorce. It would be foolish to assume her marriage was not troubled prior to her jury service, but one can only speculate as to how much of a catalyst that service had been and what may have been her fate, had she not been selected as a juror in that case.

Chapter Six

In the Beginning Was the Word

PEOPLE WHO come to court, either as jurors or litigants, often are fascinated by the reporter's Stenograph machine. Many times they look upon it as being almost magic. I have attempted on many occasions to explain to people the workings of the machine and the complexities involved, but they still seem amazed when either a recent question, or something that was said two hours earlier, is read back.

There is nothing magic about the machine and the reporters are not magicians, although many times they wish they were. The fact that untold numbers of fast-talking attorneys and witnesses have not vanished into thin air is proof positive that reporters possess no magical skills. They do possess some unusual skills, developed over a long period of time, such as the ability to concentrate intensely on every word, handling a great deal of stress and controlling natural functions when working for some judges who rarely take recesses because they have the bladders of camels.

The Stenotype system can be basically defined as machine shorthand. The keys on the machine can all be struck consecutively. The keyboard does not contain all the letters of the alphabet so that combinations of letters are sometimes necessary to form other letters. All the punctuation is in the form of letters. For example, a period is FPLT. A comma is RBGS and a question mark is STPH. There is a tired old joke among reporters about a worried female reporter who was late with her FPLT.

There is a number bar which gives access to the numbers

one through ten. However, many reporters prefer to write the numbers out to ensure greater accuracy. Words are written phonetically on the machine. The word "phantom," for example, would be spelled with an "F" on the machine. There are initial letters and final letters. The word "dead" would be written TK-E-D, the initial "D" being comprised of the letters "T" and "K", all done in one stroke. The system is similar to written shorthand only insofar as the use of briefs and phrases in both systems.

The phrase "do you recall?" would be written out as TK-OU-RL. There is no letter "I" on the machine so "I" is a combination of "E" and "U." Thus, the brief for Salt Lake City would be written out as S-HR-A-EU-BG-S, which translates to S-L-A-I-K-S. If this sounds like a foreign language to you, maybe it's because that's exactly what it is. The process requires instant translation from English to Stenotype and then instant translation back to English when it is read back. Further, the brain must be trained to permit you to write down the last sentence, while listening to something new being said. In other words, the reporter is almost always one sentence behind. In this instance, a split personality comes in very handy, which may explain why a lot of reporters sit there with a goofy look on their faces.

It gets sort of spooky when you begin to think your fingers are taking over the function of your brain. The first time I was aware of this was when I had reported a preliminary examination in the Palo Alto Municipal Court involving the theft of an automobile. During the testimony of the police officer, he stated the license number of the stolen vehicle. The next day in my office when I was dictating my notes, my recollection of his description of the license number was entirely different from what was in my notes. I called the police department and had them check the police report of the case and they verified that the license plate number in my notes was correct. I knew the telephone company wanted me to let my fingers do the walking through the yellow pages, but this was ridiculous.

The level of concentration and the extent to which your subconscious can be trained to take command is really quite remarkable. When I was a court reporting student in San

Francisco, there were two advanced students in my class who could take down everything the instructor was dictating, while engaging in a whispered conversation with each other without dropping a word of what was being dictated. I never quite reached that level of skill, but years later in court I would often catch my mind wandering and have to read back my notes later to find out what had happened during that time.

The question most often asked by jurors of reporters is, "Why don't they just use tape recorders?" Many reporters are rather touchy about this question because reporters have been battling the promoters of electronic audio recording for almost forty years. It is, however, a legitimate question. People ask, "If they can put a man on the moon and transplant hearts, why can't they replace court reporters?" The answer is rather complex and may be open to the charge of being self-serving, but basically it is need for the human factor.

Many times during a trial, someone may sneeze or cough, covering up an answer, or a plane or siren from outside may make a question impossible to hear. The reporter simply asks that the question or answer be repeated and nothing is lost from the record. A tape recorder, on the other hand, often lulls one into a false sense of security with the assumption that everything will be on the tape. In most instances when it is played back, that sneeze, cough, or backfire will be very clear, but the question or answer is blotted out and lost forever.

The sophistication of the recording machines can sometimes work to their own disadvantage. They are so sensitive they pick up the sounds of papers rustling, throats being cleared, and, in some cases, comments not meant for the record. For example, if an attorney makes an objection and the judge overrules it, I may hear the attorney mutter under his breath, "This judge could use a brain transplant," but I would certainly not include that remark in the record anymore than I would an overheard confidential remark between attorney and client. The recording machine, however, might very well include the remark as part of the record since it is not designed to exercise human judgment.

In most cases, court administrators are urged to install electronic recording equipment with the goal of no longer having to pay the salaries of court reporters. When this is done, it has generally proven to be false economy. Court reporters traditionally supply their own equipment. They pay the transcribers who type the transcripts, they pay for the transcript paper and other supplies and the majority of the reporters today use computer aided transcriptions and they invest many thousands of their own dollars for that equipment.

They are not paid overtime or given compensatory time, as are the clerks and bailiffs, for staying late at night with a jury. The only regular expenditures chargeable to the courts are the pads of paper required for the Stenograph machine. Conversely, each of the advanced tape recording machines costs several thousand dollars. There must be one for the courtroom, one for the Judge's Chambers, and one for the jury room in case the jury wishes to rehear testimony. Additional staff must be provided to monitor these machines and typists must be hired to prepare transcripts. All of these things taken together represent a cost to the county or state which actually exceeds the salaries paid to reporters and for a final product that is far less accurate than what is presently available. So, as that sweet old lady used to say on television, "Where's the beef?" There is, of course, a lot more to this never ending debate, but enough said now.

(Note to author: Stop! Do Not Pass Go! Get Off Soapbox!)

Some of the greatest unsung heroines of the judicial system are the court transcribers or legal transcribers, as they prefer to be called. (If they didn't do court work, would they be illegal transcribers?) While a few men perform this function as well, the vast majority of legal transcribers are women, married to long-suffering husbands who must tolerate their wives typing sometimes until two or three in the morning. Most transcribers work out of their homes, so they are not required to cope with the problems of child care, parking and commuting which beset the rest of us. However, this generally means that the transcribing must be fit into the precious spare time between family needs.

Until recently, the procedure for creating a transcript involved the reporters dictating their stenographic notes into a recording machine, such as a Stenorette, then delivering the tapes to a transcriber's home. The transcriber would play back the tapes and type them into a transcript which would then be delivered back to the reporter. After proofreading and making any corrections necessary, the transcripts would then be filed or mailed to the attorneys who ordered them. In addition to the tapes, the reporter would also furnish the transcriber with a list of proper spellings of unusual names or medical terminology or anything else that might be confusing.

Transcribers are expected to be excellent typists and to be able to spell exceptionally well. Dependability and reliability are equally important. If a transcript absolutely has to be filed by a certain date, it must be delivered to the reporter on that date even if it means the transcriber has to work all night to get it out. This does not often happen, but a good transcriber must be able to deliver when it does. As previously mentioned, transcribers are paid by the reporters. The fee varies in different areas, but generally it amounts to something between a third and forty percent of what the reporter is paid for the transcript. Since most transcribers work for several different reporters, their incomes can be very attractive considering the fact that they rarely have to leave their homes.

In spite of every precaution, some mistakes can still occur. I reported the deposition once of an attorney who was getting divorced. His wife was present, along with her attorney, who was taking the deposition. During one of her husband's long answers, she interrupted sarcastically with, "Oh boy! T.S. Eliot, here we go again." The transcriber was not used to my dictation (or with poetry, evidently) and when I got the transcript back, that portion read, "Oh boy! T.S.L.E.F., here we go again."

In Washington, D.C., congressional reporters often strap on their Stenograph machines, much as one would an accordion, and follow the congressmen around to record their speeches. Prior to computers, they would utilize the services of note readers, rather than the more time consuming practice of dictating. Note readers are transcribers who have trained themselves to read Stenotype notes, but not to operate the machine. They earned a higher fee because of the time saved by the reporter.

As noted, combinations of letters are used to form other letters on the Stenograph machine. The form for the final "M" is "PL." The abbreviation for Americans is "A-PL-S," or AMS. Many things are written the same way on the machine, but the reporters know by the context which word is applicable. The word "apples" would also be written on the machine as "A-PL-S." Thus, a note reader's error enriched the congressional record one day with entry of the eloquent phrase, "It just takes one bad apple to make a whole barrel of rotten Americans."

One local transcriber, who had evidently been formerly employed by a gynecologist, must have been unfamiliar with a large Silicon Valley company named Varian Associates. She delivered a transcript containing the following bit of testimony:

Q: What sort of work do you do?
A: I'm a tube technician.
Q: How long have you done that kind of work?
A: Twenty-four years.
Q: Is that in a hospital or something?
A: No. I work for O'varian Associates.

In a somewhat similar incident, a transcript dealing with the answer to a question about a nurse's responsibilities in a hospital was supposed to read, "Her duties were restricted to a very circumscribed area of the hospital." The transcriber (who may have been married to a rabbi) submitted the transcript with that answer reading, "Her duties were restricted to a very circumcised area of the hospital." Fortunately the error was uncovered and excised. Otherwise it may have been interpreted as a very cutting remark.

If given the opportunity, I am certain that most transcribers could fill several volumes with some of the dumb mistakes and instructions that reporters have given them. A capable and hard working transcriber is a very vital part of the judicial system. The reporter usually gets the credit for a neat and accurate transcript. But, just as attorneys in court almost always blame their secretaries for their own mistakes, if an error is discovered in a transcript, then surely it must have been the fault of the transcriber.

Most transcribers today have made the transition from typing tapes dictated by reporters, to performing the equally valuable service of "scoping" rough drafts of transcripts for reporters who have adopted the system of computer aided transcription. This, of course, has required the purchase by transcribers of computers which are compatible with the software of the computers used by reporters. When the same stenographic brief is used for several different words, the dictionary of the computer simply causes all the possibilities to be printed out. Therefore, it is necessary for the transcriber/scopist to select the proper word, based on the context, and this requires proofreading every line of the transcript as it appears on the video terminal.

The fatigue of endless typing has been replaced by the exhaustion of spending countless hours before a video terminal. However they accomplish it, the work they perform is a priceless service to the court and has, for the most part, gone completely unrecognized. So, for whatever it's worth, transcribers of the world, I salute you!

Chapter Seven

What Gain Has the Worker From His Toil?

IN DECEMBER of 1975 a motion for enforcement of a temporary restraining order was brought before the court for the purpose of preventing a video game manufacturer from doing business, based on the allegation that the manufacturer had pirated not only the employees, but the ideas and trade secrets of another video game company. Nine attorneys were involved in this litigation, including one who was a New York attorney admitted to the bar in California. This hearing was estimated to last five days and actually took eighteen days, which is about par for the course for attorney's time estimates.

There were also five very large video game machines which were brought into the courtroom as exhibits and they were rigged so they could be operated without the need of putting in quarters. (Too bad you can't do the same thing with attorneys.) These machines attracted a great deal of attention in the courthouse because this was at a time when video arcades were first making their debut. At recesses and during the noon hour, we could have sold tickets to all the clerks, bailiffs, reporters, and even judges from other departments who wanted to try their luck and test their skills.

I must admit that I also brought our children to the courthouse in the evening after court was adjourned and they greatly enjoyed playing these machines without charge—a child's fantasy made real. Compared to today's technology, they were very basic (the machines, not the children), but they were quite awe inspiring at the time. This was also my first introduction to the world of gravity algorithms, roms, rams, comparator motion circuits, bits, bytes, etc.

The testimony in this case revealed that in the world of video games, the Pentagon could learn a thing or two from these manufacturers about security and safeguarding secret plans. The evidence showed that the "think tank" of the original company was located in a remote part of northern California on considerable acreage, which was bounded by heavy chain link fencing topped with barbed wire. There was electronic surveillance as well as observation towers, where guards would watch someone through binoculars from the moment they passed through the gate until they entered the building, and then be admitted only with a coded card.

The rationale for all this seeming paranoia was that competition was so great in that industry and information leaks were so common, that by the time a new idea was formulated and planned, another company might jump into production with it before the first company ever got it off the ground. The company president who testified to all these security measures was a very serious, intense man who was not prepared for the droll wit of the judge, which passed right over his head. Because of that, the record was enriched with the following colloquy:

The Court: So you have barbed wire and...
The Witness: Yes, Your Honor.
The Court:...observation towers and...
The Witness: Yes, your honor.
The Court:...binoculars and...
The Witness: Absolutely, your honor.
The Court:...moats with alligators...
The Witness: Yes, Your Honor. They are watched every minute.

The evidence in this case, provided by many different witnesses, was that when workers would ask their new employer if they weren't likely to be sued when they released a new game which had been on the drawing board of the original company, they would all receive the same standard response from the employer: "We'll just say: Fuck 'em. We thought of it first." The first warning to the court about the use of this language and the court's somewhat whimsical response, taken from the actual court transcript, was as follows:

> Mr. Jones: Your Honor, in this connection, I know what the witness is going to testify and it involves the use of an obscenity...
>
> The Court: All the ladies put their fingers in their ears. If there ain't no ladies, then don't.

This was rather shocking language for a courtroom the first time around, but after numerous witnesses said the same thing for several days, there was no longer any reaction to it.

Because the case had aroused so much interest, the spectator section was almost full when it came time for the attorneys to make their final arguments. Many in the audience had not been able to attend the main part of the hearing, but dropped by to see what all the action was about. During the final argument of the attorney for the plaintiff, in support of his argument he cited a certain precedent-setting case we'll call *Cowpie vs. Whiteshoes*. When it was time for the attorney from New York to respond with his argument, he stood up and said, "Well, I was afraid Mr. Jones, the plaintiff's attorney, stole some of my thunder because I was going to cite *Cowpie vs. Whiteshoes* as part of my argument. But, then I decided to refer to it anyway and just say: Fuck 'im. I thought of it first."

The judge never batted an eye and the court staff and the lawyers registered no reaction, other than an appreciative smile for his humor. The people in the audience, however, were in shock. Especially those who had not witnessed any part of the hearing previously. They were astonished that an attorney could make such a remark to a judge in court, apparently with complete impunity. Obviously, if it had not been for the repetition of that phrase during the presentation of the motion, the attorney would never have used. it. If he had, he would have been an immediate guest of the local Hoosegow. The reactions on the faces of the audience that day were truly a sight to behold.

⚖

The verdict in the first trial of the four Los Angeles police officers charged with beating Rodney King was unique, only insofar as the allegation of racism and the subsequent protests it engendered. What I mean by that is it is impossible to accurately predict what any jury verdict will be until it is rendered. I have reported hundreds of jury trials, some lasting only a day and some lasting several months and I learned early on that you can never be sure of the result until it is announced and the jury is polled. I have seen cases where the evidence for conviction was overwhelming and the defendant was still acquitted. (Sound familiar?) I have also seen cases where the prosecutor was almost embarrassed by the lack of convincing evidence and I wondered why the defense did not move for dismissal and yet a guilty verdict was returned. The importance of the jury selection process known as *voir dire* examination cannot be overemphasized. No matter how many questions a prospective juror satisfactorily answers under oath, it is impossible to know what is really in that juror's mind until they get into the jury room.

When I was still working in the Municipal Court at Palo Alto, I was involved in a case where a jury was being selected and one of the men on the jury looked very familiar to me. I could not quite place him, but he answered all the questions of counsel and the court satisfactorily—including assertions that he had no prior criminal history. Just before the jury was officially sworn in, I remembered who he was. When I had worked for Judge X two years earlier, this man had been adjudged to be a mentally disordered sex offender and was convicted of child molesting.

I requested a recess of the judge because I wanted to inform him of this fact before he dismissed the remaining portion of the jury panel. He told me to be patient and we would take a recess in a minute, but first he wanted to swear in the jury and dismiss the remaining panel members. I did not want to whisper the information to him while court was in session because it would cause unnecessary embarrassment for everyone concerned. The jury was sworn in and the remaining panel members were thanked and excused.

When the recess was taken, I informed the judge and counsel of the juror's history in another court. The deputy district attorney checked his office files and verified that I was correct. The juror was called into chambers and, when asked about the prior conviction, readily admitted it. He was then excused from the jury and another panel had to be summoned to court to select one more juror. There had been no selection of an alternate juror because these trials usually only lasted a day or two. For some reason I never seemed to have a problem getting a recess from that judge after that.

I had occasion some years ago to report a trial of attempted murder in which a woman was accused of poisoning her husband with arsenic by adding a little ant poison each day to his dinner. He would grow progressively ill, weak, and lose weight until he weighed less than one hundred pounds and had to enter the hospital. The doctors there were unable to diagnose the cause of his illness, but under their care and nourishment he gained weight and recuperated sufficiently to return home. In a matter of several weeks, the process was repeated. He would again enter the hospital, very ill and emaciated, without a clue as to what was causing his problem. The doctors still were unable to figure out what was wrong with him, but as soon as he got better they would send him back home to enjoy more of that good home cooking. Finally, after the fourth hospitalization, someone decided to test his blood for arsenic. Bingo!

An investigation was launched which resulted in the charge against his wife for attempted murder. One of the strange aspects of this case was that she remained free on bail and they continued living together, with her preparing his dinner every night. The day he testified against her at the preliminary hearing, he went home with her and ate the meal she prepared. During the trial, three of her coworkers testified that the subject of poisoning one's husband had been discussed as a result of a newspaper article relating to a woman's conviction for murder in Florida. The defendant in our case was alleged to have stated that the woman in Florida was stupid for getting caught. She stated that she was certain that she could accomplish the same thing without ever being convicted.

Further, the jury heard a tape recording which had been made without her knowledge while she was still in jail before posting bail. On the tape, an officer had begun to question her when he had to leave to receive a telephone call. He left the formal complaint with her, suggesting she might wish to read the allegations her husband had made against her. At first, there was nothing but the sound of pages being turned and then very clearly she stated, "*I hope you die, you son of a bitch!*" There was also evidence their domestic life had been rather violent and that he had locked himself in the bathroom at one time while she repeatedly stabbed at the door with a butcher knife.

I do not mean to portray the husband as a Caspar Milquetoast because there was ample evidence that he used his fists to beat not only his wife, but his children as well. As usual, the children were the innocent victims of this domestic warfare. The two boys, ages ten and twelve, were called to testify during the trial. They were handsome and bright and seemed amazingly well adjusted for children who lived in the home from hell. They knew if they testified one way, their mother might go to prison. If they testified the other way, their father would likely beat them when they returned home. Fortunately their questioning was brief and discreet and they were not required to say anything incriminating.

There were two or three small bottles of ant poison containing arsenic which were exhibits in evidence in the case. They were dark green in color and were referred to and handled frequently during the trial. At one point, the defendant's attorney even opened one of the bottles and tasted it, presumably to show the jury how little concern he had for the dangerous contents therein.

For some reason the elderly parents of the defendant took a real liking to me during the trial. They were very solicitous about my well being at recesses and expressed concern several times about my looking tired. Except for a slight cold, I was fine both physically and—well, I was fine. During the deliberations of the jury, there was a request to have the testimony of the husband read back. This request was granted and I was required to read aloud his testimony for almost an entire day.

Near the end of the day, my voice was growing quite hoarse so the judge took a short recess to enable me to compose myself. As soon as the recess began, the defendant's parents came up to me and very kindly offered me a soothing remedy for my throat. I have no idea what it was, but it was contained in a small, green bottle. I politely declined their offer and I doubt if they ever understood why.

The jury resumed deliberations for two days and then informed the judge they were hopelessly deadlocked eleven to one. The judge brought them back into the courtroom and gave them what was then known as "the Allen instruction." In essence, it instructed them that they had heard all the evidence any other jury could hear in the case and they were just as capable and intelligent as any other jury and they should go back into the jury room and reach a verdict. That jury instruction was later declared illegal in California on the theory it was too prejudicial against defendants.

Ten minutes later, the jury returned to the courtroom and delivered a unanimous verdict of not guilty. With the possible exception of the defendant and the jury, everyone else in the courtroom was in a state of shock. When they had previously announced they were deadlocked eleven to one, the assumption was that it was eleven to one for conviction.

So, once again. the prophets were proven wrong as far as predicting the jury's verdict. My own personal theory was they thought the husband and wife deserved each other, but only the jury and their hairdresser knows for sure.

⚖️

When I was still working for Judge X in the Palo Alto Municipal Court, we had a drunk driving trial which proved to be quite interesting. A woman had been waiting for a signal light to change in a left turn lane, when a police officer pulled up behind her. The light changed and she made a legal left turn, drove one block and then turned into the carport of her apartment. To her surprise, the officer followed her, stopped behind her, and informed her that one of her taillights was out. He proceeded to write her a "fix it" ticket, which means as soon as the light is replaced, the ticket is dismissed.

She became enraged and started berating the officer in no uncertain terms, even suggesting his mother was registered with the American Kennel Club. At that point the officer detected the odor of an alcoholic beverage on her breath and decided to arrest her for driving under the influence of alcohol. By that time, three other officers were at the scene as they had been monitoring the vehicle stop on their car radios.

In these cases the prosecution must prove (1) that the defendant was driving the vehicle; (2) the driving was done on a public roadway; and (3) the defendant was under the influence of alcohol. The first two aspects are usually not even contested. The third, however, is the most difficult to prove and generally requires testimony by the officers regarding the defendant's weaving in and out of a lane, inability to successfully perform roadside sobriety tests—such as walking a straight line, heel to toe, etc.—slurred speech and bloodshot eyes. Additionally, a sample of blood, breath, or urine is taken to prove the level of alcohol in the defendant's blood. That was not done in this case because at that time it was not mandatory.

In this case all the prosecution had to go on was the odor of an alcoholic beverage, which could be acquired by drinking one beer, and a considerable attitude problem on the part of the defendant. The three officers who had been present at the arrest were subpoenaed by the defense attorney. They all reluctantly testified that she had done well on her field sobriety tests. They also stated her speech was profane, but not slurred and that if it had been their case, they would not have arrested her for driving under the influence. Getting three officers to testify against another officer is even more difficult than finding a doctor to testify against another doctor in a medical malpractice case.

At this point most defense attorneys would make a motion for a directed verdict of acquittal, which would probably be granted, based on the evidence in this case. None was forthcoming. Defendants in criminal cases obviously have the constitutional right not to testify because their testimony might incriminate them. Nevertheless, the defense attorney decided to put his client on the stand so she could "have her day in court." With his encouragement, she proceeded to berate all police officers in general and the arresting officer in particular. In response to questioning, she blithely admitted she had consumed five or six highballs about two hours prior to the arrest.

In addition, the defense attorney was extremely sarcastic with the prosecution witnesses and seemed to go out of his way to alienate the jury. The jury was out approximately fifteen minutes and returned with a verdict of guilty. Because this was the first conviction for the defendant, she should not have had her driver's license suspended under the law at that time. However, due to a clerical error, her license was suspended for six months in addition to a stiff fine and a suspended jail sentence.

A deputy public defender told me she had once received a thank you note from one of her clients, sincerely praising her for being "the best *district attorney* I ever had." The judgment used by the defendant's attorney in this case gives new meaning to an old adage, which might be paraphrased to read: *With defense attorneys like that, who needs prosecutors?*

Chapter Eight

To Whom Has the Root of Wisdom Been Revealed?

IN WILLIAM Shakespeare's *Henry VI*, Part II, Act IV, Dick the Butcher says, "The first thing we do, let's kill all the lawyers." I think if he was alive and that point was pressed, even old Bill would admit that might be overreacting just a tad. On the other hand, a potential juror, who had made a date with a friend for lunch and at 12:30 P.M. was being asked very intrusive questions about his or her personal life, might think that was a marvelous idea.

A jury is the quintessential example of a captive audience. The jurors are commanded by the court to be there and may not leave until excused by the court. They are subjected to interminable delays while the court hears motions and makes decisions which must be done out of the jury's presence. Yet, when the trial is ready to resume, they are expected to be there promptly. Through no choice of their own, some juries must be *regaled* by a judge who considers himself to be the world's most gifted undiscovered comedian, while they are collectively praying for a remote control that would change the channel.

In all fairness, most judges and attorneys do make an effort to be considerate of the jury, but their intentions are sometimes misguided. For example, an attorney might suggest that the testimony of an expert witness might be better absorbed by the jury if it is completed with just a few more questions before taking the noon break. He then proceeds to a new subject with the witness, which is certain to produce further time consuming cross-examination and by the time the witness is excused, it is 12:45 P.M. The fact that some of the jurors may have planned to meet someone for lunch either does not enter into the attorney's thinking or it is not of sufficient importance for him to alter his trial plan. Such actions, of course, do not endear one's cause to the jury.

Lack of consideration for others is inexcusable in any circumstance, but if practiced in court it can blow your case right out of the water. Even though most juries—and judges, for that matter—try diligently to reach a decision on the facts, they cannot help but be influenced by actions or comments of counsel which are arrogant or rude. An attorney who adopts this style is not acting in the best interests of the client. On the other hand, some young lawyers create great empathy with a jury by apologizing for their nervous mistakes because they have never had a jury trial before. Sometimes this is so successful, they try *their first jury trial* about a dozen times.

Occasionally, judges can unwittingly be the cause of great distress, not only to the jury, but the court staff as well. I worked for one judge who never learned to take an attorney's time estimate for a trial with several grains of salt. If the attorneys stated the trial would be concluded in four weeks, the judge expected it to be completed in four weeks or less. He would then promise the potential jurors the trial would be over in four weeks. Invariably, he would leave one or two people on the jury who either had surgery scheduled or a wedding to attend in Kansas in five weeks.

The trial almost always took longer than expected, either because of the unavailability of witnesses, the difficulty of laying a foundation for the admission of evidence or unexpected motions by one side or the other. The foot dragging of counsel often played a part as well in the delay. At the end of two weeks it would become obvious to the judge the trial was not likely to be completed in four weeks at its present pace. He would then exhort counsel to keep in mind the important appointments the two jurors had and that he had promised them the trial would only last four weeks.

To underscore his resolve, he would order the jury to report an hour earlier in the mornings and stay at least an hour later in the evenings. On some days the usually extended lunch period would be restricted to twenty or thirty minutes. This hurried atmosphere usually produced some anxiety and resentment on the part of the attorneys, who felt they were not being given adequate time to present their case. The tense environment this caused could not help but be transmitted to the jury.

To his credit, the judge's pushing generally resulted in the trial being finished pretty close to schedule. It would have been so much easier for everyone involved, however, if he had simply announced at the outset that the trial could last four to six weeks. Then anyone with a justifiable scheduling conflict could have been excused. I never could understand why one of the alternate jurors could not have been used in a case like that, but then I never got past the fourth grade. They didn't want to put me ahead of my old man.

Near the middle of one non-jury trial in Palo Alto, at the end of the day the plaintiff's attorney announced that he planned to call the defendant as his first witness the following morning. The next day the defendant was not present when court convened. When the judge inquired of defense counsel as to the whereabouts of his client, the attorney stated that he had no idea. The court then reminded the attorney that plaintiff's counsel had stated his intention to call the defendant as his witness as the first order of business in the morning. Defense counsel replied that he was not his client's keeper and he had no idea where he was or when he might show up.

The judge paused for a long minute, waiting for the smoke to stop coming out of his ears, and then told the attorney matter of factly, "You know, Counsel, you always have rubbed me the wrong way and I never have liked you. Now, we're going to take a fifteen minute recess and see if you can't get your act together and get your client in here. If you don't and if he isn't here, I'm going to grant sanctions against both you and your client."

When the recess was ended, both attorney and his client were present and ready to go. The first thing defense counsel did was to make a motion for a mistrial, based on the fact the judge was prejudiced against him and his client could not receive a fair trial. The motion was denied and at the conclusion of the trial, the defense attorney appealed the court's judgment. The Appellate Court upheld the judgment of the trial court with the special comment that because of the behavior of counsel, the remarks of the court were deemed to be not only appropriate, but rather restrained under the circumstances.

The well intended remarks of counsel in court often provoke a great deal of unintended levity. Near the conclusion of one domestic trial, the husband's attorney was sworn as a witness so that he might testify as to the amount of attorney fees it had been necessary for his client to incur in the defense of the case. When his testimony was completed and he was preparing to resume his presentation of the case, he paused and asked the court very sincerely, "Your Honor, may I be relieved of my oath now?" He seemed genuinely puzzled at the mirth his request evoked, apparently not realizing it sounded as if he was requesting permission to start lying again.

Near the beginning of a jury trial in San Jose, it became painfully apparent that the attorney for the plaintiff was very inexperienced, to say the least. When his client was cross-examined by defense counsel, he was asked an improper question. The young attorney objected and the court sustained his objection, however, the attorney persisted as follows:

> Mr. Schwartz: But, your Honor…
> The Court: I said sustained!
> Mr. Schwartz: But that question, Your Honor was improper and…
> The Court: Counsel, I sustained your objection!
> Mr. Schwartz: Well, I don't think…
> The Court: Counsel, please approach the bench.

There was then an off-the-record discussion between the court and counsel, out of the hearing of the jury as follows:

The Court: Counsel, when I say, "sustained," that
   means you win.

Mr. Schwartz: Oh. Thank you, Your Honor.

⚖

In the early 1960s the District Attorney's Office of Santa Clara
County might have been accused of "tokenism" along with a
great number of other organizations. I am not aware of the ra-
tio of other minorities, but I know of only one woman and
one black man who were deputy district attorneys at that
time. Now, of course, the percentage is considerably higher,
not only in the district attorney's office, but the office of the
public defender and county counsel as well.

The black D.A. was a hard-driving prosecutor, but a man
of considerable wit who often spoke in folksy colloquialisms.
To this day, I know of no one who can tell a funnier story. I
am sure it was just coincidence, but his services seemed to be
utilized ninety-five percent of the time in the prosecution of
black defendants. Why, it was almost as if there was an attempt being made to persuade the jury the black defendant
must be guilty or there would not be a black man prosecuting
him. Occasionally the D.A. was not above suggesting that very
thing to the jury, which would get him into trouble with the
Appellate Court.

He would often tell the jury in his opening statement that
he *understood these people* and spoke their language because
he was raised in the ghetto himself. This might be considered a
slight exaggeration because actually he grew up on a farm in
Arkansas. I reported one murder trial he prosecuted which involved the testimony of about eight black witnesses in their
late teens. I was going out of my mind trying to keep up with
their rapid speech and street talk, while this man, who *understood these people*, leaned over and asked me on several occasions, "What did he say?"

During one trial in which a black defendant was being
tried on a rape charge, the district attorney cross-examined
him on his reputation for being sought after by the ladies because of his romantic prowess. A portion of the questioning
was as follows:

Prosecutor: So you admit you had a relationship with
    Mary Harding and Sandra Moore?

Defendant: That's right. I also made it with Sandra's
    sister, Virgie.

Prosecutor: Then you said you was living, off and on,
    with three other ladies about that time?

Defendant: Sure. They all knew about it too.

Prosecutor: Sounds like you're a real lady killer.

Defendant: I gets my portion.

Prosecutor: Sounds to me like you been gettin' my por-
    tion too.

In the mid-1970s indictments were brought against a number of people who were charged with the theft of trade secrets from the giant I.B.M. complex in San Jose. Most of the defendants were employees of I.B.M. and hired their own attorneys to defend them in court. One defendant could not afford private counsel so a public defender was appointed to represent him. In the practice of criminal law in this state, one of the first things an attorney does—after writing down the client's name and the charges filed—is to begin planning the presentation of a 1538.5 motion or a 995 motion.

Section 1538.5 of the Penal Code of California is a motion to suppress evidence based on the grounds it was obtained illegally. Section 995 of the Penal Code is a motion to set aside the Indictment or Information, alleging improper procedure in the filing of the charges. These two motions are the basic steps in the preparation of a defense against almost all criminal charges.

In the I.B.M. trade secrets case the private attorneys hired by most of the defendants were competent lawyers, but their previous experience had been limited to civil litigation almost exclusively. The first thing the presiding judge did was to set a date for hearing 995 motions or 1538.5 motions. As soon as all the parties left the courtroom, all the private attorneys converged on the deputy public defender and asked him, "What the hell is a 995 motion? And that other—1538 something or other?"

The public defender patiently explained to them the procedures involved in both motions and subtly suggested that some perusal of the Penal Code might not be out of order. During the entire case, the private attorneys uniformly looked to the public defender for leadership in defending the case. The supreme irony of all this was that the private attorneys were earning annual incomes in six figures, while the man they were looking to for guidance was an employee of the county and earned a fraction of the amounts they were paid. Prior to this case, if they had encountered him at a Bar Association function they probably would not have given him a friendly nod. None of the attorneys was named Hormel, but he really saved their bacon.

Many times people look with disdain upon a public defender, saying things like, "Too bad Joe couldn't afford a *real lawyer!*" The fact of the matter is that in spite of their tremendous work load and the paucity of time allowed for each client, they generally achieve the best results possible for their clients. They are in court every day and are made aware of the latest Supreme Court and Appellate Court rulings as soon as they come down and their clients often fare better than they would if they had private counsel at $150 an hour.

The value of the experience they gain from spending so much time in court is incalculable and their presence before a jury is very commanding. This is not to say that there are not a great many extremely capable private attorneys who limit their practice to criminal law or that occasionally a public defender doesn't show up who should have been a plumber. On the whole, however, at least in this county, ninety-nine percent of the criminal defendants I have seen represented by the public defender have had excellent representation.

⚖️

One of the most formidable tasks facing a prosecutor in a drunk driving trial is overcoming the feeling on the part of some jurors who look at the defendant and say to themselves, "*There, but for the grace of God, go I.*" Although juries are uniformly instructed by the court that they are not to let personal feelings, bias, prejudice or sympathy enter into their deliberations, many jurors remember times they have driven home from social affairs after a few drinks when they probably shouldn't have been driving.

One of the deputy district attorneys who practiced in the Palo Alto Municipal Court in the 1960s had a unique and effective way of accomplishing this task. Because the people have the burden of proof in criminal trials, they are granted two closing arguments to the jury. Their first argument usually covers about two thirds of their allotted time, then the defendant's argument is presented, followed by the final argument of the prosecution.

In almost every case, this prosecutor would quote the ancient Grecian leader Pericles regarding the paramount importance of doing one's duty as a citizen, no matter how difficult it might be. He would somehow manage a tear in his eye and a catch in his voice and tell how the young Athenian men had gone off to war to be killed while the old men and women tilled the fields and tended the flocks at home because to do anything less would have been shirking their duties as citizens and an Athenian citizen did what was required of him, as it were from instinct. This story rarely failed to have a profound effect on the jury and the attorney's record for convictions was very high.

On one occasion he failed to relate this story to the jury in his opening argument, probably because he felt he had sufficiently proven his case without it. The defense attorney, however, took particular note of it and when it was his turn to speak he commented to the jury in a rather cavalier manner, "Ladies and gentlemen, you've been deprived of a dramatic performance by Mr. Swift. He usually gets up here and tells juries about some ancient Greeks doing their duties and he gets a tear in his eye and a catch in his throat and he has us all almost in tears." He then proceeded with the rest of his final argument.

When it was time for the district attorney to make his final summation, he stood up slowly, thanked defense counsel for his comments and told the jury the same story he had related to dozens of other juries, delivering it with a tear in his eye and an emotional catch in his voice. Fifteen minutes later the jury's verdict was guilty.

Chapter Nine

Thou Shalt Not Kill

IN SEPTEMBER of 1971 I began working on what was probably the most interesting and challenging criminal trial of my entire career. The defendant was charged with the murder of a police officer in San Jose. The defendant's father and brother were police officers in another city. The charges alleged that while the victim was issuing a traffic citation to a motorist unknown to the defendant, the defendant walked up to the officer and shot him to death. A plea of not guilty by reason of insanity was entered by the defendant, who claimed also that at the time of the homicide he was under the influence of L.S.D.

Under the law at the time, that type of defense potentially required the trial to proceed in four different phases. First, a jury had to decide whether or not the defendant was sufficiently competent to aid and cooperate with his counsel in his defense. If that jury found that he was competent, a second jury was selected to determine the guilt or innocence of the defendant. That portion of the trial was known as the guilt phase. In the event the defendant was found to be guilty, he was then entitled to a third finding by jury, the sanity phase, to determine whether he fit the legal definition of insanity. If he was found to be sane, the jury then had to determine whether he should receive the death penalty or life imprisonment. This was known as the penalty phase.

The case was prosecuted by a rather soft spoken, but very thorough and capable, deputy district attorney. The defense attorney was an imposing man who exuded remarkable charisma and animal magnetism. His booming voice would have been equally suitable for a fundamentalist revival tent. The judge in whose courtroom this case was tried had the reputation for being one of the toughest and most conservative judges in the county, whose manner could be very intimidating, not only to attorneys appearing before him, but to many other judges as well.

At the 1968 Summer Olympics held in Mexico City, athletes Tommie Smith and John Carlos raised their clinched fists in a salute to Black Power during the playing of the national anthem. By the fall of 1971 when this trial commenced, there were considerable numbers of advocates of Black Power at some of our local universities. The defendant, who was black, had been a student at a local university prior to his arrest. Media coverage of the case generated a lot of interest, not only among the general public, but the college community as well.

Just prior to jury selection, a court employee had occasion in the men's room to overhear plans being made for a demonstration inside the courtroom intended to disrupt the trial. This information was given to the judge and he immediately ordered additional deputy sheriffs to provide greater security during the trial. The trial transcript reveals that, excluding the potential jurors, the judge made the following comments to the people in the audience:

> The Court: Bailiff, have the man take the hat off, please. All right. May I have it quiet, please? Let the record show the defendant and the jury are absent. The attorneys are here and we have a number of visitors in the audience.
>
> Ladies and Gentlemen, I have called this session to talk to you, to try to explain to you some of our procedures. We are now conducting a trial involving a charge of murder against a Mr. Mark Johnson. He is entitled to a fair trial and our entire procedure is concerned with that. Now, everything else is incidental, including your own presence here. You are welcome here. We are glad to have you here. You are welcome to come in here and listen, but if your presence interferes with giving Mr.

Johnson and the district attorney, both sides, a fair trial, you will not be permitted in here.

Now, this is one reason I said that no small children can come in because they might be quiet when they start out—all right, let's close the door and let the last lady in and nobody else. We are not going to have small children in here because they interrupt our proceedings. We are not going to have packages brought in. If we have to, we will search everybody that comes in, or we might decide to keep everybody out.

There are not going to be any demonstrations in here. We are going to have it quiet and there are not going to be any demonstrations in the hall. There are not going to be any demonstrations in the courtroom. I have instructed the deputies not to permit it and I urge you not to start anything in here because there will always be a number of deputies in this courtroom. They are all equipped with weapons, the weapons are loaded and you are apt to get shot if you start something.

We don't want any of this to happen. I don't even want people to get scared. I don't want people to worry about it. If something happens, we are going to take appropriate measures.

The trial lasted almost three months and there were no demonstrations and, with one exception, everyone stood when the judge entered the courtroom.

The first jury determined, based on the evidence presented, that the defendant was competent to cooperate with his attorney in the defense of his case. Subsequently, another jury was selected to determine his guilt or innocence. The defendant's behavior before this jury was extremely bizarre. I am obviously not qualified to judge whether the defendant was mentally ill or merely posturing before the jury. I would comment, however, that if he was playing a role for the jury's benefit—that lasted almost three months—he should receive the mother of all Academy Awards. (His language alone would have guaranteed him star status in a Spike Lee movie.)

Throughout the trial he would interrupt the proceedings with unsolicited comments or shouts; he would curse the jury; he refused to change out of his jail clothes into a suit and tie which had been provided for the trial; he escaped from the courtroom one day and was apprehended almost immediately. After that he was manacled and handcuffed to his chair and his feet were hobbled. His comments continued to disrupt the testimony to the extent he had to be gagged. Despite the gag, he still created such a disturbance he had to be removed to an adjacent holding cell with a speaker in it so he could hear what was going on in his trial.

So you may experience the true flavor of the trial, I am going to reproduce some excerpts from the trial transcript, except that the names of the players are changed along with certain addresses referred to. In the first instance, a police officer is being questioned by the prosecutor regarding the search for the defendant immediately prior to his arrest:

Q: And what was the nature of that duty?

A: I was instructed to pair up with another officer and start making a yard search of the area on 96th Street.

Q: All right. And who was the other officer?

A: The other officer was Officer Brown.

Q: And did either of you have a dog?

A: Officer Brown had a dog.

Q: All right. Is this a regular police dog?

A: Yes.

Q: Or a dog that is assigned for police duty; is that correct?

A: Yes, sir.

Q: And in connection with the...

(Whereupon the defendant made an inaudible remark.)

Q: (By the prosecution)...in connection with the search, do you know if you were the only officer assigned to search, or was some kind of systematic search being made of the area surrounding the 300 block of North 96th Street?

A: It was a systematic search comprised of a skirmish line going through each individual yard.

(Whereupon the defendant made inaudible remarks.)

Q: I take it that involved quite a few police officers then, is that correct?

A: Yes.

Q: When you talk about a skirmish line, you moved forward to minimize the possibility that anything might be overlooked, is that correct?

A: Yes.

Q: In connection with your search duties, did you arrive in the vicinity of a backyard or the yard in the residence at 324 North 98th Street?

(Whereupon the defendant made inaudible remarks.)

A: I did.

Q: And that would be approximately what—North 98th would be two blocks east of 96th Street, is that correct?

A: Yes. sir.

Q: And the 300 block on North 98th Street...

(Whereupon the defendant made inaudible remarks.)

Q: ...would be directly east of the 300 block on 96th?

A: Would you repeat that, please?

Q: Don't answer the question if you can't hear it. The 300 block on North 98th would be directly east of the 300 block on 96th Street?

(Whereupon the defendant made inaudible remarks.)

The Court: Just a minute. Mr. Johnson, you are going to have to keep quiet.

The Defendant: Yes, Your Honor. Policeman, are you aware that a policeman has to go back to the streets and my brother is sitting back of him? It is pretty funny, huh—that is my father, man.

Q: (By the prosecution) Upon your...

The Defendant: I want him to think about it. He is a
   police officer, Your Honor.
The Court: Go ahead, Counsel.
Q: (By the prosecution) Upon your arrival at this vi-
   cinity of 324...
The Defendant: I can't talk, Mr. Officer.
Q: (By the prosecution)...North 98th, did you have
   occasion to go into the backyard of that residence?
A: I did.
Q: And that would be a typical dwelling house for
   that particular area of town, is that correct?
A: Yes, sir.
Q: And after getting to that location, was your atten-
   tion directed to something unusual?
A: Yes. sir.
Q: And what was that?
A: As I was checking out the rear yard at 324 North 98th...
The Defendant: Mister...Mister...Your Honor, I have
   had a court appointed psychiatrist.
The Court: Be quiet, Mr. Johnson. Go ahead.
Q: (By the prosecution) What did you observe?
A: I observed the defendant lying between a...I believe
   it was a garage and a fence.
The Defendant: The dog bit me in the head, Your
   Honor. The rest I don't remember.
A: At this time I was standing on top of the barbecue.
The Defendant: I had several bone fractures, Your
   Honor. At the time my head was bleeding quite
   badly and I couldn't remember.
The Court: All right. Just be still.
Q: (By the prosecution) You indicated you were stand-
   ing at the time?
The Defendant: I believe I was molested by a police-
   man, Your Honor.
The Court: We didn't ask you. Now, just keep quiet.
   Go ahead, Counsel.
Q: (By the prosecution) At the time you observed the
   defendant, you were standing on a brick barbecue?
A: I was.

The Defendant: I think it was him and seven other policemen, Mr. D.A. My father was...

The Court: We will take a recess for ten minutes.
Please bear in mind the same admonition. The jury
is excused. I will ask the attorneys to remain.

Defense Counsel: Now...

The Defendant: Be quiet?

Prosecution attorney: I think you can step down from
the stand.

(Whereupon the witness left the stand and the jury
left the courtroom.)

The Defendant: A police officer's rights...

The Court: All right. The jury has left the room; the
defendant and his attorney and the District Attorney remain. Mr. Johnson, you are going to have to
keep quiet if you want to sit in here and watch
what is going on. This is your trial and they are
talking about you. I should think you would want
to listen.

The Defendant: I was arrested at the scene of the
crime by several officers.

The Court: You are not helping yourself.

The Defendant: I was brought to the Santa Clara
County Jail. I have been waiting for a phone call
from another officer.

The Court: All right. Put the defendant back in his cell
for the rest of the morning.

The Defendant: Your Honor, if...if there is anything
else done with an officer's son, I will speak to him.
They beat me up, Dad.

(Whereupon the defendant was removed from the
courtroom.)

The Court: Mr. Jerque, would you come up here,
please?

(Whereupon Mr. Jerque, a newspaper reporter, approached the bench.)

My experiences with members of the news media were positive for the most part, but this trial was covered by a reporter

for a local newspaper whose overzealousness almost landed him in jail. He was sitting in the courtroom when the judge ordered that no one was to approach the jurors or talk to them during a recess. As soon as the recess was taken, the reporter approached several jurors outside the courtroom to ask them their opinions on the death penalty.

This was observed by the bailiff and the reporter was brought before the judge. The judge read him the riot act and told him if he did it again, he'd better bring his toothbrush with him because he was going to spend some time in jail. This seemed to make at least a temporary impression on the reporter, but later in the trial he had to be reprimanded once again.

If I had the time, I didn't mind reading back some small portion of the record if it would help someone out. One day the defendant's father arrived in court after proceedings had already commenced. When the defendant saw him, he cried out, "Daddy, help me!" The newspaper reporter came in after that and at the recess he asked me if the defendant had called his father a pig. I told him he had not and I also read back that portion of the record to him. That evening the headlines on the newspaper read: *"Murder Defendant Calls Father Pig!"* Obviously, I never did any favors for that reporter or even spoke to him again. I don't know whatever happened to him, but he's probably a very successful politician somewhere.

The trial judge was not noted for his patience. In fact, just the opposite was true. This case challenged his self-control to the utmost limit as may be perceived by the following excerpts from the transcript of the afternoon session, which followed the portion previously referred to:

> (Pursuant to the noon recess, court reconvened and the following proceedings were held:)
>
> The Court: The defendant and his attorney and the district attorney are present. The jury is absent. Anything before we proceed?
>
> Mr. Blanca: Only, Your Honor, that I would like the record to reflect—I think we can reach agreement on that—on this, that during the morning session, and the record will reflect when that occurred, when he

was placed in the holding cell, where there is a—
where testimony is being transmitted or piped in—it
appeared during the examination by Mr. Smith of
the witness Verdi, who is presently on the stand, and
during my cross-examination, that there was a constant sound emanating from the holding cell, that
from my point at the counsel table, I could hear.

I couldn't make out what he was saying, but I'm
satisfied the jury heard the noise or the—the talking. In addition to that, the record can reflect of
course that he has been returned to the courtroom
for the purpose of the afternoon session. I have had
one brief discussion with him in which I informed
him as to where we are and that the witness is
about to be further cross-examined by myself. I requested of him and he gave me his assent that he
would remain quiet. That's the size of it.

The Court: Okay.

Mr. Blanca: I of course have informed him, and I think
he knows, that he is not to be—at least I know he's
been informed constantly, that if he does have another outburst, that we will have to—the court will
have to remove him again because he's disruptive
of the examination.

The Court: All right. I think the defendant understands that. This morning while the defendant was
in the holding cell, I could hear him shouting, notwithstanding the soundproof door. And, if necessary, if it happens again, I guess I'll have to put a
gag on him in there. But it looks as though we can
proceed.

The Defendant: Are these American people in the
courtroom now?

Mr. Blanca: Wait a minute now. Wait a minute!

The Defendant: American citizens?

Mr. Blanca: I thought you said you would be quiet.

The Defendant: I am. I am.

The Court: We are going to proceed with this trial. We
are not going to have any interruptions, whether

it's by the defendant or other people. Now, I don't want anybody, whether it's newspaper reporters or people in the audience, interviewing witnesses around this courthouse. The people who testify on the stand, when they leave, they're free to go. But attorneys and their investigators can interview witnesses all they want. But I don't want other people interviewing witnesses around this courtroom. And nobody comes up beyond this barrier, on this side of it, except the attorneys and the defendant and the people employed by the court in this case. Nobody else. Anybody else comes up here, Mr. Bailiff, you take them into custody. Whether it's in a recess, before we're in court, or afterwards.

Another thing, we have a custom in court—people stand up when the judge comes in the courtroom. I didn't start it, it's not going to end with me. But, we do it. So the young man in the back on the left side, Mr. Bailiff, take him out. Young man in the back. Outside. Stay out.

The Defendant: What's wrong with him?

(Whereupon a young man in the spectator section left the courtroom.)

The Court: All right. Mr. Blanca, you think the defendant can keep quiet this afternoon?

Mr. Blanca: Yes. That's the assurance that he's given me, Your Honor.

The Court: All right. Bring in the jury, please.

Later that same day, during cross-examination by the defense counsel of the police officer on the stand, the following events occurred:

The Court: Excuse me, Mr. Verdi. Would you stand up? We have a problem with the board. Okay. (Referring to exhibit board.)

The Defendant: My father said he would kill everybody on this jury.

The Court: Now, Mr. Johnson, just quiet down.

The Defendant: He has got a .45 on his hip.

Cross-examination resumed by Mr. Blanca:

Q: Officer, I will show you People's 62 now in evidence and ask you whether or not you recognize what is depicted there? I mean can you tell us what is depicted there?

A: Yes, I can.

Q: And very briefly, what is that a picture of?

A: It is a picture of where the defendant was located in between the garage and the fence, also the barbecue pit that I was standing on.

The Defendant: He hit me.

Q: (By Mr. Blanca) There is an officer in that picture. Do you know who that officer is? That is all right.

A: No, I don't.

Q: That picture appears to be taken in the nighttime or early daytime, I should say, and...

(Whereupon a small child made an inaudible remark from the spectator section of the courtroom.)

The Court: Young lady, you are going to have to take the child outside. I am sorry. You have to take the child outside.

Unidentified woman: We have been sitting here...

The Court: Take the child outside! We don't have children in here.

The Defendant: Hey, I think I better leave too. Man, I ran yesterday and boy, they beat me up. I got out that door. They kicked my ass.

The Court: All right. Take the defendant out.

The Defendant: I want that baby to run.

(Whereupon the deputies began to escort the defendant out of the courtroom.)

The Defendant: Hey, Man. Hold it a minute. Don't put the kid in jail!

(Whereupon the defendant was escorted from the courtroom.)

Chapter Ten

A Time to Live
and a Time to Die

BECAUSE THIS was a capital case—that is, the prosecution was seeking the death penalty, a daily transcript was ordered and the law required an automatic appeal of any conviction that might result. My partner in the production of the daily transcript was a petite woman court reporter, a little over five feet tall.

The trial judge required that all bench conferences between the court and counsel be done on the record. When it was my turn in court and a bench conference was called for, I detached my Stenograph machine from its tripod, placed the machine on the edge of the judge's bench and, while standing, took down the whispered colloquy which the jury was not meant to hear. When the other reporter had to assume this task, she was not tall enough to reach the top of the judge's bench so she took her machine on its tripod in back of the bench and leaned over to report the proceedings.

On a number of occasions when I came into the courtroom to relieve her, she would be in back of the bench reporting the discussion and would signal me to let her finish that portion before I resumed my part of it. As I sat at my machine waiting for the conference to end, the defendant would continue his constant muttering to the jury. Since court was officially in session, I decided to take down his remarks so that any reviewing court would have a better picture of exactly what was happening in the trial.

I don't know if two court reporters ever covered different aspects of the same trial before, but it was done in this case. Even though by this time the jury had grown somewhat used to the behavior of the defendant and his obscene remarks, and even though they would later be instructed that they were to consider only the evidence that came from the witness stand and any documentary evidence, it is difficult to imagine they could ignore the following:

(Whereupon, the following comments by the defendant were made while the other reporter was reporting a conference at the bench between the Court and counsel:)

> The Defendant: What you want me to scream out right now? I'll say anything. Yeah, I murdered the motherfucker. Killed him in cold blood. And I'm a drug addict and treated very badly. Some things I didn't have to wait for.

The judge and the attorneys, engrossed in their bench conference, were often not aware of all the defendant's remarks until they read the transcript later. The defense attorney's ability to concentrate on the proceeding was sorely tried because of the almost constant interruptions by the defendant when he was present. If he wasn't shouting out, then he was continuously muttering in his attorney's ear. Finally, when the defendant began bragging to the jury about how well endowed he was—using his hands to indicate—his own attorney requested that he be taken out.

One of the male alternate jurors had been a member of the German army during World War II and one of the female alternates had been a member of the French Underground at the same time. While the jury was deliberating the fate of the defendant, these two almost rekindled the war. The gentleman insisted that he had been drafted and was never a Nazi. The lady didn't buy that for a minute and made accusatory comments, such as "That's what they all say." He countered that he didn't believe she had really been a member of the Underground because she was too stupid to have survived that long. It's probably just as well they were not required to serve on the main jury or there might never have been a verdict. A war, maybe, but not a verdict.

The jury found the defendant guilty of first degree murder and adjudged him to be sane under the law. After the penalty phase, they recommended life imprisonment as opposed to the death penalty.

The final arguments of the attorneys had not been included as part of the daily transcript. I was required to transcribe them later as part of the automatic appeal. During the trial, I could not help but feel that the prosecutor was somewhat outclassed in contrast to the dynamic, electrifying performance of defense counsel. When I dictated the final arguments, however, it was apparent that such was not the case. The prosecutor's argument was right on point, with complete sentences, proper syntax and covered all the evidence presented in a logical and cogent fashion.

The defense argument, on the other hand, while it covered the evidence, was replete with half sentences, incomplete thoughts and more than a little rambling. At the time it was presented to the jury, it seemed very compelling and the delivery was that of a great orator. In plain, unemotional black and white, however, it lost some of its luster. Still, attaining life imprisonment for the defendant as opposed to the death penalty was no small accomplishment for the murder of a police officer.

Many years later the prosecutor in this case was elected district attorney of this county and is now retired. The attorney for the defendant was appointed to one of the Appellate Courts in northern California. At this writing, the defendant is still serving a life sentence at the California Medical Facility at Vacaville, California.

⚖️

In 1976, the judge Charley and I had accompanied to Superior Court developed a severe case of laryngitis. He was an ardent golfer who spent a lot of time outdoors and was the picture of health. The laryngitis caused him no pain, but he could barely speak above a whisper. He was determined, however, to conduct business as usual in his courtroom.

During this time we had a court trial in which the plaintiff's attorney was quite deaf—even with the aid of a hearing aid. Each time the judge made a statement, I was asked to read it back for plaintiff's counsel because he could not hear the judge's whispered comments. I even had to tell him whether objections were overruled or sustained. I was considering buying a black robe for myself, but the trial didn't last that long.

We began to be somewhat concerned when the judge's voice did not improve after three weeks. He finally went to a throat specialist who told him he had a benign growth on his vocal cords. The growth was removed and his voice seemed to be returning a little bit at a time. He had been a pipe smoker for many years, but had given up smoking some years earlier. He looked good and handled his calendars just as efficiently as he ever had and he said he felt fine. We were therefore optimistic about his recovery.

Our optimism was short-lived, however. Not long after that, further testing revealed he had lung cancer. He began a long and debilitating series of treatments involving both radiation and chemotherapy. In spite of the weakness produced by the treatment and the loss of most of his hair, he remained in good spirits and was determined to vanquish the dread disease. As is the case with most victims of cancer, some days were better than other days. On some of his good days, he would come into court and hear short matters that did not unduly physically tax him. It was apparent, however, that he was very fatigued by the end of the day.

At one point, he evidently pushed himself too hard while on a weekend trip and had to be hospitalized again. I went to visit him in the intensive care unit of Stanford Hospital when he was allowed to have visitors. I have spoken earlier of his sense of humor and since I had discovered a "laughing box" in a novelty shop, I thought he would get a kick out of it. It was a recording of maniacal laughter in a small, square box and the more it was shaken, the louder the laughter. As long as it was not shaken, there was no sound.

As I was walking down the corridor of the hospital in search of his room, I accidently jostled the package containing the box of laughter and peals of insane cackling immediately filled the somber halls of the intensive care unit. I was instantly admonished and chastised by the medical staff, but once the laughter began, it had to run its course before it would stop. Probably the only worse place this could have happened would have been at a funeral. Fortunately, I found his room at that point and closed the door to help muffle the sound. The judge thought it was highly amusing and seemed to enjoy my discomfort even more, so I guess it accomplished its purpose.

Over a period of several months, there was no noticeable improvement in his condition and he continued to go downhill. He still maintained a cheerful facade and I never heard him complain about anything except that he could no longer play golf. The judge, the clerk, the reporter, and the bailiff had been a team together for a number of years. We had shared some wonderful experiences and many pleasant memories. I think the judge handled this tragedy better than any of us.

One night Charley, the clerk, and I decided to visit the judge at his home in Los Altos Hills. The clerk baked him a cake, I took along my guitar to play a few songs for him, and Charley brought with him his supply of jokes. The judge's wife was a very gracious and genteel lady who had, I suspect, led a rather sheltered life. She had certainly never encountered anyone quite like Charley.

After a little music, some cake, and polite conversation, Charley decided to tell the judge his latest joke. It was a real experience to hear Charley tell a joke. He would become so amused by his own joke, he would almost be rolling on the floor before he ever got to the punch line. On this occasion he told a joke about a first grade teacher asking the students about their fathers' occupations:

The teacher asked little Timmy what his father did and Timmy said he was a fireman. She asked Mary what her father did and Mary said he was a bus driver. When she asked Michael, Michael replied, "Nothing. He's dead." The teacher expressed her regret and asked, "What did he do before he died?" Michael's response was a loud, death-rattling shriek.

The judge's wife turned about three shades lighter than white and she almost dropped her coffee cup. There may have been a more inappropriate joke, under the circumstances, but you would have had to travel to the moon to find it. The judge, however, thought it was hilarious and had a good laugh. Knowing his sense of humor, he was probably a lot more amused by the situation than the joke itself. We departed soon after that, much to the relief of the judge's wife.

That was the last time we saw the judge. He died about a week later in April of 1977 at the age of fifty-nine and the family held a private funeral. He had graduated from Stanford Law School in 1947 with the highest scholastic ranking in the class and that superior intellect served him well during his years on the bench. His dedication to making certain that the most important things were handled first was best exemplified by the time he was still in the Municipal Court and there was great speculation that he would be elevated to the Superior Court.

We were in the process of finishing a jury trial when the bailiff approached the bench and told the judge that then Governor Ronald Reagan was on the telephone. The judge told Charley, somewhat irritably, "I'm in the midst of instructing the jury. Tell him I'll call him back!" It was only after the jury was fully instructed and was deliberating in the jury room that the judge called back the governor to be notified of his appointment to the Superior Court. His death was a great personal loss and a very real loss to the public as well.

About one year elapsed between the time the judge first became ill and the time his replacement was appointed to the court by the governor. During this time period our former "team" was broken up. Charley returned to the Municipal Court as a bailiff, the clerk was assigned to another judge, and I was sort of a *floating reporter*, assigned to fill in for vacationing or ill reporters or visiting judges who had no staff of their own. I rarely worked for one judge for more than one week at a time.

The appointment of a new Superior Court judge to fill the vacancy created by the death of my former judge was made in August of 1977. I was assigned to that judge as the Official Reporter and he selected a new court clerk and a new bailiff.

I was the *old man* on the new team, not only chronologically, but in terms of experience. When new judges are appointed, they often are given calendar assignments which are not exactly fought over by the more senior judges. Rarely does a senior judge opt for assignment to Domestic Court or Juvenile Court. So, in January of 1978 I packed my things and headed back to Juvenile Court. Déjà vu.

Chapter Eleven

A Time to Weep
and a Time to Laugh

MY SECOND assignment to Juvenile Court was different from the first time around in two respects. Number one, the policy of permanently assigned Juvenile Court clerks had been discontinued and each judge was now accompanied by a complete staff. Number two, the department to which we were assigned had a tiny office which had to be shared by the clerk, the bailiff, and the reporter. It also served as a *waiting room* for people who wanted to see the judge in his chambers.

Just as it is essential to eliminate personality conflicts among seamen living together aboard a submarine, it was very necessary for the three of us to be compatible or we could not have worked together effectively. As it turned out, that was the least of our worries. The clerk and the bailiff soon became two of my very best friends (so far, anyway). At first blush, this may have seemed odd because I was twenty years their senior. (If my math is correct, there's an even chance I still am.) We all shared, however, a distinctly distorted sense of humor.

The character of the clerk was best illustrated by the fact that even though she was a two-pack-a-day smoker, she gave it up *cold turkey* because neither the bailiff nor I were smokers and she knew we would be distressed in a small office filled with smoke. All of us who are former smokers know that was not an easy thing to do. As an alternative, she began jogging and soon persuaded me to join her, thus establishing a habit for me which has probably added considerably to my longevity. The bailiff was also into running and years later in 1991 successfully completed the Los Angeles Marathon.

The bailiff was a young deputy sheriff who had just completed a three-year assignment working inside the county jail. Such assignments are usually very difficult because of the constant climate of hostility from the inmates towards anyone in authority. Because the deputy was a man of moderate size, his jail experience taught him to be a master of diplomacy which was a great asset to him in dealing with people in court. His calm, assured demeanor could usually diffuse any potentially disruptive situation. (If that failed, he would simply take off his shoes and the courtroom would be instantly evacuated.)

The judge had a sense of humor as well, but insisted on proper decorum being observed in the courtroom. One day a surly fourteen-year-old boy appeared in court with his parents and he was wearing an old fashioned undershirt—not the T-shirt variety—and the judge refused to hear his case until he was properly dressed. The boy protested that he had no other clothes with him so the judge told him to borrow a shirt from someone else in the waiting room.

About fifteen minutes later the boy and his parents returned to the courtroom and he was wearing a man's shirt about six sizes too large. He was small for his years to begin with and the sleeves of the shirt hung down at least six inches below his fingertips. He was absolutely seething and it was very difficult for all of us to keep a straight face because he looked so ridiculous. If looks could kill, the judge would have most certainly been vaporized on the bench. The boy was there for a relatively minor offense and received probation. Presumably, he learned a valuable lesson about dressing for the occasion.

One young gentleman, who was a frequent guest of Juvenile Hall, had established a distinguished career for himself as a thief by the age of thirteen. He had been given many opportunities to straighten out on probation, but could not seem to keep his hands off other people's property. It was therefore decided by the court that he should become a resident for a while at the County Boys' Ranch. That facility had a limited number of beds available, so when the court ordered the boy to the ranch, the probation officer requested the order be stayed until a space was available. The court agreed and stated, "All right, I'll make the order now, but the execution will be stayed."

Evidently the minor had not been paying attention to the proceedings, but when he heard the court's comment, he stood up with his eyes wide and shouted, "*Execution?*" His attorney calmed him down with an explanation of the term, but it certainly got his attention for a moment. I often wondered how he evolved as an adult, but with his natural talent he probably holds a public office of some type today.

In another instance, a boy about twelve years old admitted the truth of a petition charging him with the theft of a vehicle. While the judge was reading the probation officer's report, he observed that the theft had occurred at 4:00 A.M. He then asked the boy, "What in the world were you doing out at four o'clock in the morning?" With a look of utter exasperation at such a question, the boy replied, "*Stealing a car!*"

During my Juvenile Court assignment in 1970 and 1971, by far the most prevalent offenses were drug offenses. One of the most tragic cases I witnessed involved a fifteen-year-old boy who was addicted to glue sniffing. Even at that time, it was common knowledge that sniffing glue destroyed brain cells. When he was first brought before the court at the beginning of the year, he appeared bright and alert. During that year he was returned to court about five different times for the same offense and each time the deterioration of his mind was more obvious than the last time. At his final appearance near the end of the year, he had to be committed for private institutional placement in a mental hospital.

In 1978 the offense of burglary easily surpassed all charges made against juveniles in this county. It is conceivable, of course, the burglaries were committed in order to obtain money for drugs, but burglary charges far outnumbered drug charges, nonetheless. It was amazing that none of the minors got shot or injured during the commission of these crimes, considering their lack of sophistication. One of the minors accused was so small that he could wriggle through a swinging pet door and then unlock the main door to allow his older co-participants to enter the premises.

One of the Juvenile Court judges had to disqualify himself from hearing a case when he realized the burgled premises were his own. His home had been burglarized about a month earlier and he had been unaware the culprits had been apprehended until the facts of the case were presented to him. I can only surmise what the odds are against such a thing happening, but they must be astronomical.

They were probably similar to the odds in a drunk driving trial I reported once in Palo Alto. As each prospective juror was questioned, they were routinely asked if they knew anything about the case or the attorneys or the defendant. One woman in the jury box stated she knew the defendant. When asked to describe how well she knew him, she said he was her husband. It would have been interesting to learn how she voted, had she been allowed to remain on that jury.

⚖

For reasons unknown to either of us, the new bailiff and I at Juvenile Court could become convulsed with laughter simply by looking at each other. I could be having a serious conversation with the clerk and the bailiff would enter the office—without saying a word—and we would both dissolve into helpless paroxysms of laughter. The clerk would then begin to giggle at what idiots we were making of ourselves until the judge was forced to admonish us to knock it off. He did not feel it was proper for people who were in the waiting room, worrying about their child going into custody, to hear all this laughter just on the other side of the office door. He was correct, of course, but even then it was so difficult to control ourselves that we took turns waiting inside the supply closet until we could better restrain ourselves.

I sometimes wondered if nitrous oxide was being pumped into the air conditioning system, but since only the two of us were affected it seemed unlikely. In retrospect, it seems silly for two grown men to act that way (in my case it was probably the beginning of my second childhood), but it certainly provided a release from the stressful and depressing matters we all had to deal with on a daily basis.

⚖

One cold, rainy morning a hefty young man of sixteen years was being sentenced to the County Boys' Ranch. As an indication of his reluctance to accept the county's hospitality, he bolted from the courtroom into the waiting room area and headed for the exit door, which was kept locked. But, as luck would have it, someone had just opened it to enter the waiting room area and he was able to force his way through. Our trusty bailiff immediately gave chase. The young fugitive left the building, ran across six lanes of an expressway and headed for the rain-swollen creek nearby.

He plunged into the creek, swimming and wading across, with our bailiff in hot pursuit. (Perhaps in this case, *shivering pursuit* would be more appropriate.) The boy emerged from the far side of the creek, jumped someone's backyard fence and made it out to the street, where he was apprehended by the San Jose Police Department. By the time the bailiff reached that point, the boy was already being transported back to Juvenile Hall. The bailiff walked back to the juvenile facility, this time using the bridge in lieu of a backstroke.

When he returned to court, he looked like a lost little boy. He was very wet and dirty, his uniform was torn and his knees were bleeding. Instead of receiving the praise he deserved for his valiant effort, he was greeted by howls of laughter from his peers. (One clerk + one reporter = two peers.) It was not a total loss, however. He was given the rest of the day off, when the sheriff sent over a replacement. The final straw was the report of the incident in the newspaper the next day, giving exclusive credit for the capture to the S.J.P.D., with no mention of his involvement.

Earlier I commented on the fact that Juvenile Court was not very productive of reporter's transcripts during my previous assignment. During the intervening years, this situation had changed to the extent that about ninety percent of the contested cases that were adjudged to be true were appealed. I am not sure whether that was because of new changes in the law or the infusion of new public defenders, but there was a dramatic increase in demands for transcripts.

In the great majority of cases, the minors were represented, at least initially, by public defenders. One of those public defenders was a lady attorney who possessed a unique ability to get under the skin of everyone else in the courtroom, including the judge and the parents of the minor she was representing. In many instances the parents, who were unfamiliar with the criminal justice system and the rights of the minor, knew the minor had committed the offense and they just wanted him to admit his guilt, take his punishment (usually probation), and get on with his life.

"*Au contraire,*" sayeth the public defender! In her zealousness to protect the minor's rights to due process, she would contest the charges with various motions and then a subsequent trial that might last several days. The evidence was usually so overwhelming there was little doubt of the outcome. After the final disposition of the matter, the parents would be referred to the finance department to arrange for reimbursement to the county for the legal fees paid to the public defender.

Many parents were angered at the amount they were asked to pay because the fees would have been much less had the case been uncontested. If the case was appealed, the fees were even higher because of the cost of the preparation of the transcript. From the standpoint of the public defender, she was representing the minor, not the parents, and cost should not be a consideration. If she was successful in having the minor's case dismissed because of a legal technicality, she was satisfied she had done her job well.

Some of her tactics in court are worthy of comment. She would often tweak the prosecutor's dignity by deliberately mispronouncing his name. For example, we had one prosecutor named Sprought (rhymes with brought) and she would refer to him as "Mr. Sprout." She might pause during a caustic argument to smile sweetly and say, "God bless you," if someone sneezed—including the prosecutor—and then resume her pejorative comments. On one occasion she was representing a sixteen-year-old shoplifter who had a young child and she was asking the court to release the teenager so she could care for the child.

Because of the minor's extensive record, the court declined to release her from custody. The public defender expressed her vexation by shaking her head and stating to the man on the bench, "I wish the Court could be a mother." On another occasion, when she had exhausted the patience of the court and the judge was shaking his head in exasperation because of her endless objections, she stated, "Let the record show there is a smirk on the Court's face." I did not have sufficient skills to determine whether the Court's face revealed a smirk or betrayed unbearable agony, but I would be inclined to opt for the latter. On the other hand, he may have had a large bowl of chili for lunch.

One incident that left an indelible impression on my mind was a case involving two brothers, aged sixteen and seventeen respectively, who were charged with disturbing the peace, inciting a riot, and failure to disburse, to name a few. They were alleged to have been part of a confrontation between the police and an unruly crowd of teenagers. What set this case apart from others was the fact that one of the brothers had been cut on the arm by a very large knife held by a police officer.

During the contested hearing, the police officer testified that he had taken the knife away from another teenager, but before he could dispose of it he was called to render aid to another officer during the arrest of the two brothers. He attempted to keep the knife tucked between his arm and his body, but during the scuffle he accidentally cut one of the brothers. The two brothers were extremely agitated in court and the one who had been cut appeared to be very hyperactive, alternately screaming and sobbing and had to be restrained on several occasions by his parents and the bailiff.

The brothers were represented by their own counsel. When it was time for the defense portion of the case to begin, the first thing the defense attorney did was to call to the stand the brother who had been cut during his arrest. The brothers' lawyer was an elderly attorney who proceeded with great deliberation. That is to say, he deliberately proceeded to pick up the knife, which was an exhibit in evidence, and hand it to the highly agitated witness, saying, "Now, Tommie, will you please show us how the police officer cut you?"

I was seated at my machine about three feet from the witness with nothing between us, but a lot of air and prayer. I fully expected him to lunge out with the knife, which was only slightly smaller than a machete. The judge was astounded that counsel had done such a thing, but recovered quickly enough to calmly state, "Tommie, just put the knife down; and Counsel, you take it back to the Clerk's desk." Fortunately the minor complied and a brief recess was taken during which the judge held a short seminar with defense counsel concerning the proper handling of weapons in court.

Obviously, the minor was not a mass murderer, but it was still a very stupid thing for an attorney to do under the circumstances. It was almost tantamount to handing a loaded Uzi to a defendant charged with being part of a terrorist attack. The allegations against the minors were found to be true and they were both placed on probation and sent back home with their parents. Hopefully, defense counsel devoted himself to becoming at least partially as sharp as the knife he had handled so carelessly.

During a period of time when my regular judge had a few days off, another judge was sent out to preside over his court. I had never worked for this judge before and my first impression was that he was rather pompous and cold. I had no doubt he was cold because he brought along his own electric heater and covered his legs with an electric blanket. One of the contested matters on the calendar involved the testimony of a witness who was hospitalized and unable to come to court. In real life, sometimes the mountain goes to Mohammed. The judge decided that he and the staff would go to the hospital and take the testimony of the witness from her hospital bed.

When we all met at the hospital, we entered the room of the patient and I set up my machine and headed for the only chair in the room. Court reporters always work seated, with the exception of reporting an occasional bench conference. The judge beat me to the chair with the admonition of, "You've got to be kidding!" He seated himself with great aplomb, as if to say, *"I am the Judge, by God, and if anybody gets a chair, it's going to be me!"* I had no choice but to adjust the tripod of my machine to it's fullest extent and report the testimony standing up. Fortunately, it only lasted about twenty minutes.

Some years later I became pretty good friends with this judge and discovered that his aloof appearance was merely a façade that covered up a weird sense of humor. I worked for him during a lengthy jury trial and, as is often the case, many things had to be put on the record out of the presence of the jury in the court's chambers. There were four attorneys involved in the prosecution and defense of this case and they were all from out of town and had never appeared before this judge before.

During one of the in-chambers proceedings, the judge was making a ruling on the record and he stated something incorrectly. He realized it immediately and turned to me and said, "Strike that, Mr. Reporter," while simultaneously flipping me the bird with his middle finger. The attorneys' mouths dropped open and they all stared at me, as if seeking some confirmation of what they had seen. I sat there with my usual deadpan expression, giving no indication that anything unusual had occurred and the judge went on with his ruling.

They never quite seemed to know how to approach the judge after that, but the trial soon ended and I'm sure they all went back to San Francisco with wild tales about the strange judge they had encountered in the hinterlands of Santa Clara County.

Chapter Twelve

Out of the Mouths of Babes

BEFORE DEALING further with proceedings in Juvenile Court, I should point out that Juvenile Court is considered a quasi-criminal court and, therefore, the terms "plaintiff" and "defendant" are not used as they would be in the adult court.

In the adult court, charges are brought against a defendant in either a Complaint or an Information. In Juvenile Court the charges against the minor are contained in a petition. If the allegations are found to be true, there is not a finding of guilty, but rather a finding that the facts in the petition are true. The results are the same, however, much like the entry of a plea of *nolo contendere* instead of guilty in the adult court. End of lesson.

One of the prosecutors we worked with at Juvenile Court was a deputy district attorney who had a fiery disposition in the courtroom, tempered by an irrepressible sense of humor. In later years he became one of the most successful prosecutors in the District Attorney's Office and was ultimately appointed a judge of the Municipal Court.

Most people visualize the minors dealt with in Juvenile Court in terms of being children. While this may be true in the literal sense, it is not unusual to find *boys* of sixteen or seventeen years of age who are over six feet tall and weigh more than two hundred pounds. Many of the female minors of that same age group could as well pass for twenty-one—a fact that has threatened the liquor license of more than one cocktail lounge.

One such well-developed young man appeared before the

116

court on a charge of participating in the gang rape of a four-teen-year-old girl. He denied the charge and the trial of the matter was assigned to the previously mentioned deputy district attorney. During the proceedings, the minor admitted being present during the rape, but denied that he had participated and testified that he had remained in the back seat just to "watch." During the minor's cross-examination by the district attorney, the following interchange took place:

Q: So you admit that you were part of the group that assaulted this young lady, but you didn't have sex with the girl?
A: That's right.
Q: You've had sex before, haven't you?
A: Yes.
Q: You like sex, don't you? You think it's pretty great?
The Witness: Your Honor, do I have to answer these questions?
The Court: Yes, you do. Answer the question.
Q: (By the prosecution) You like to have sex, don't you?
A: I guess so, if you say so.
Q: Well, I'm not the one that's saying so. Do you enjoy having sex or not?
A: Yes.
Q: But, on this night, even though your buddies were all having sex with this naked girl, you weren't interested?
A: I was interested, but I didn't have sex with her.
Q: Were you too tired?
A: No.
Q: What's the matter—didja have a headache?

The prosecutor's sarcasm went right over the minor's head—at least he pretended it did—but the rest of the people in the courtroom found it difficult to stifle a chuckle. Obviously, there is nothing laughable about the crime of rape, but sometimes the testimony of an accused person is so imaginative that it borders upon the absurd. Based upon the victim's identification and contradictory description of the minor's actions, the petition was found to be true and the minor was placed in the County Boys' Ranch for a lengthy period of time.

Another memorable occasion involving the same district attorney occurred when he was prosecuting a young man of seventeen years of age for the felony of first degree burglary. As previously indicated, the judge does not see the file or history of the minor unless the petition is admitted or is adjudged to be true. Occasionally, however, if the minor has a particularly violent history, the probation officer may suggest to the bailiff that extra security might be in order. In this case the P.O. let it slip to the staff that the minor had been involved in a homicide in Chicago.

The matter proceeded to trial and, based on the evidence, the petition was found to be true. Once the truth of the petition is established, the court then reads the probation report which includes the history of the minor. Prior to the disposition portion of the trial, both sides are given the opportunity to argue as to what they consider to be the appropriate disposition of the matter. The only options addressed by both the prosecutor and the defense attorney were the California Youth Authority or the County Boys' Ranch. At the conclusion of the arguments, the following exchange took place.

> The Court: Well, Gerald, the Court has read the Probation Officer's report and has decided to place you on probation in the home of your parents.
> The Prosecutor: Oh, shit!
> The Court: Did you have a comment, Mr. Papparazzi?
> The Prosecutor: That is the worst decision I have ever heard!
> The Court: You may sit down, Mr. Papparazzi.
> The Prosecutor: Even defense counsel didn't ask for...
> The Court: Sit down, Mr. Papparazzi!

Later on, the clerk told me she had already begun filling out the form for finding the district attorney in contempt. Fortunately for him, the judge had known him for some time and was familiar with his volatile nature and let him off with a stern warning. As the minor was being escorted from the courtroom, he turned to the prosecutor and sneered, "I'm gonna get you, sucker!" About three months later, the minor was arrested on a more serious charge and was subsequently placed in the California Youth Authority.

One of the deputy sheriffs who served as a bailiff in another department of the Juvenile Court resided in a town about twenty-five miles south of San Jose. He commuted every day on a big Harley-Davidson motorcycle, wearing black leather pants, biker boots, and a black leather jacket. This was prior to the mandatory helmet law and with his wrap-around sun glasses and hair blowing in the wind, he was often mistaken for a Hell's Angel, minus the insignia.

On one weekend, he was visiting the coastal town of Santa Cruz, which is, oddly enough, in Santa Cruz County, immediately adjacent to Santa Clara County. Santa Cruz is famous for its boardwalk and surfer dudes. While he was strolling down the street, he was approached by a roving reporter for a local newspaper who stopped him and asked him if he had an opinion on what could be done to improve the criminal justice system. Without hesitation, the deputy told the reporter that he agreed with Shakespeare when he said, "The first thing we do is kill all the lawyers." The deputy was dressed in civilian clothes and when the reporter asked him his occupation, he simply said, "deputy sheriff."

When his picture and his comments appeared in the *Man in the Street* portion of the local newspaper, the president of the local Bar Association took great umbrage at such a remark by a deputy sheriff and demanded that the sheriff take disciplinary action against the deputy. When the sheriff consulted his personnel files, he discovered that he had no deputy with that name in his department. The sheriff then contacted the sheriff of Santa Clara County, who disclosed that he did indeed have a deputy by that name.

The incident was not deemed of sufficient importance to merit a reprimand by the Santa Clara County Sheriff's Office. However, fellow deputies of the Santa Clara County Sheriff's

Office concocted an elaborate hoax to convince the court deputy that he was facing an investigation by the Internal Affairs unit of the Sheriff's Office. He was very concerned about a possible suspension and it was not until he had hired an attorney to defend himself that his cohorts admitted it had all been a gag.

As noted earlier, our court clerk was an athletic young woman whose pastimes included jogging, scuba diving, and bicycling. She was also very quick-witted and intelligent and earned a bachelor's degree by attending night school at a local university. In spite of these gifts, she occasionally had problems with the correct pronunciation of certain words when she was required to read aloud the petitions in Juvenile Court. No doubt nervousness was the primary cause of this, but it occasionally resulted in some very creative and amusing prose.

One of the minors before the court was charged with the theft of an automobile. The vehicle alleged to have been stolen was an automobile imported from Sweden known as the Saab. When the clerk read the lengthy petition, she was not familiar with foreign cars and momentarily hesitated before reading the name of the vehicle. Finally, she blurted out, "did steal a motor vehicle, to wit, a *Say-yab*."

On another occasion a young man was charged with the crime of grand theft, under the subheading of rustling. He was alleged to have stolen two calves from a local ranch. Even in the far West, this is an unusual charge to encounter in this day and time. Evidently, when the clerk read aloud the petition, she did not connect the rustling charge in her mind with the object of the grand theft. When she got to the end of the petition, she stated, "did take and steal property belonging to another, to wit, *two cal-ves*." She may possible have been influenced by the ghost of Elvis, but more likely she thought these were two more foreign cars with which she was unfamiliar. In any case, she provided some of the lighter moments that were so precious in Juvenile Court.

The first thing that happens to a minor when commencing a Juvenile Court hearing is to be placed under oath by the clerk. Prior to entering the courtroom, most minors' parents or attorneys have drilled into their heads the importance of saying, "Yes, Sir" or "No, Sir" to the judge, assuming of course the judge is a man. Many times the nervous minors, when asked by the female clerk, "Do you swear to tell the truth, the whole truth and nothing but the truth, so help you God?," would answer, "Yes, Sir."

Even though the clerk knew this was unintentional and somewhat amusing, she was mildly perturbed. But, when they corrected themselves and said, "I mean Ma'am," she was really pushed out of shape. Today, women under fifty are offended when they are called Ma'am because they believe it to be a term reserved for the elderly. This is a generational development because when I was young, back in the covered wagon days, I was taught the word was a mark of respect for a woman of any age. I heard a television *comedienne* state recently that a woman should not be called "Ma'am" until she has had her first mammogram. We learn something new every day. (Well, in my case maybe every other day.)

An interesting scenario developed in another department of the Juvenile Court when a hearing was held to determine whether or not a minor should be released from custody so that he might help support the child he had fathered. He was in custody because he had beaten up his girlfriend, the mother of the child. The position of the prosecution was that he should remain in custody because of his violent nature, while the defense was seeking his release on the theory he could then help pay child support.

One of the witnesses called by the prosecution was the girlfriend of the baby's mother. The purpose of her testimony was to show how many times Celia, the baby's mother, had visited her with bruises and abrasions on her face. Even though the witness was of the same ethnic background as the parents of the child, she spoke English with a very thick accent. Her initial testimony created quite a stir, as indicated by the following:

Q: (By the prosecution) Did you see Celia shortly after the baby's father, Manual, was brought into Juvenile Hall?

A: Yes.

Q: What can you tell us about that? About her condition?

A: Well, she came over to my house with this big black guy and...

(Defense counsel): Objection to any testimony about some black guy. Absolutely no relevance to this issue.

(Prosecution): Your Honor, I believe the witness can...

The Witness: Your Honor, can I say something?

The Court: Just a moment, please. I have to rule on this objection.

The Witness: But, I meant...

(Prosecution): Your Honor, I believe the witness has a right to explain her answer.

The Court: But, not before I make my ruling.

The Witness: Your Honor, can I just...

(Defense counsel): Your Honor, my client feels very strongly that...

Manuel: I'd like to know who this black guy is she's running around with while I'm stuck in this joint!

(Prosecution): Your Honor, that is entirely out of order and I request the Court to admonish the minor not to speak out in court when he has counsel representing him.

The Court: Just a moment, counsel. I am going to sustain the objection and order the comments of the witness stricken. Now, ask another question.

Q: (By the prosecution): Do you remember my original question?

A: I just want to say, I never said she was with a black guy. You asked me her condition and I tried to tell you she came over by herself with a real shiner. A very big black eye.

When her testimony finally sank in, the only people in court without a red face were the imaginary black guy and the witness, who seemed very disillusioned by the whole colorful spectacle.

⚖️

It is a generally accepted fact that the majority of child abusers were themselves abused as children. This of course does not excuse their aberrant behavior, but it emphasizes the need for extensive counseling before they have the opportunity to extend the cycle to a new generation of innocent victims. One of the things I found to be mind-boggling in Juvenile Court was the propensity on the part of some mothers, whose children had been molested by their fathers, to enter into a new marriage or new relationship with a man who ultimately molested her children as well.

I can recall at least five instances of this during my assignment to Juvenile Court, so those cases might have been the tip of the iceberg. One woman was married three different times and each husband molested her children. There was no suggestion that she encouraged or participated in the molestation because she quickly divorced each man as soon as she learned of the abuse. Evidently some mysterious chemistry caused these women to be attracted to men whose character was flawed in this particular manner. I don't know what the psychologists would say about this, but I'm sure the children would have been inclined to dial 911 the next time she brought home a new daddy.

When the subject of child molestation is brought up, most people assume the perpetrator is a man. Surprisingly, this is not always the case. Although rare, there were instances in Juvenile Court where the minor had been molested by a grown woman or a teenage girl. Usually the accused was a baby-sitter or a neighbor, but in some cases the minor had been victimized by a relative. There have even been some cases where mothers have allowed their children to be violated for payment so the money can be used for drugs.

Part of the job of being a court reporter is to remain completely objective and unbiased so there is no suggestion of anything but a true and accurate record of the proceedings. Further, there must be no indication of any opinion formed by the reporter by the look on their face or any body language which might conceivably influence a jury. This is one of the reasons most reporters maintain a poker face—in addition to the extreme concentration involved in doing their jobs.

Reporters are, however, human (*contrary to the belief of some judges and lawyers, who consider them robots*) and cannot help but form opinions and be affected by what they see in court each day. If I may be forgiven a completely gratuitous comment, my personal feeling is that the offense of child molestation is right up there at the top of the list of the most heinous crimes. The physical and emotional damage done to innocent children—often by someone they trust and look to for protection—is incalculable.

I have reported many sentencing calendars where group after group of inmates in chains are brought into court from the county jail for sentencing after either a finding or a plea of guilty. They are usually garbed in the routine jail coveralls, colored either orange or red, depending upon the seriousness of their crimes, and seated in the jury box until their case is called. Then, in a separate part of the courtroom, are seated prisoners in brown-colored coveralls which are an indication of protective custody.

While a small percentage of the protective custody inmates are transsexuals, the vast majority of those in protective custody are child molesters. The reason they are kept in protective custody is that a large portion of the regular inmates are parents and, while they may not set a high standard for respecting the law, they are no more sympathetic to child abuse than anyone else. If the molesters were not housed separately in the jail, it is doubtful many would be around by the time of the sentencing calendar.

I often thought it might have a very salubrious effect on the community if the child molesters were mixed in with the general jail population. County officials, however, were more concerned with matters of liability and their responsibility for the safety of inmates.

Before leaving this subject (*finally!*), I just want to relate one more instance of a Juvenile Court hearing involving a thirteen-year-old girl who had been touched indecently by her uncle. When dealing with minors over the age of twelve, most prosecutors try to use the proper medical terminology in describing various sexual organs. In this case, the prosecutor was either an incredibly naive young man, or had been studying geography during his anatomy classes. Although admittedly hard to believe, the following partial examination of the minor actually took place:

> Q: (By the prosecution) Would you tell the Judge just where your uncle placed his hand?
> A: Right there. (indicating)
> Q: Well, I know it's kind of embarrassing, but you have to be specific for the record. Can you tell us what part of you he actually touched?
> A: Right down here. (indicating)
> (The prosecutor): Your Honor, if I may lead the witness slightly...
> Q: Did he put his fingers in your Virginia?
> A: In my *Virginia*? (witness begins to laugh)
> Q: Just tell us where he touched you?
> A: (Witness still laughing)
> Q: Please try to control yourself.
> The Court: I believe Counsel meant to use the word, vagina.
> The Witness: No, he touched me on my pussy.

When the hearing was concluded, it was decided to place the minor under the protection of the court and she was made a ward of the Juvenile Court. I don't know if the prosecutor is still a member of the district attorney's office. It is entirely possible he may have accepted a position teaching sex education at one of our local high schools.

One of the judges sent out to Juvenile Court to fill in for a judge who was ill was a very idealistic man who had little experience in dealing with criminal or juvenile matters. One of the minors appearing in court before this judge was accompanied by her legal guardian, who was also her older sister. The older sister was in a wheelchair. After the minor's case was completed, the judge gave a rather lengthy, inspiring talk to the older sister. He tried to impress upon her the fact that just because she was in a wheelchair did not mean she could not hope to succeed in life.

He told her about a personal friend who had conquered her disability and become a flight attendant for a major airline. He encouraged her to keep on trying and said he was certain she would not fail if she did. The sister thanked him for his encouraging comments and assured the judge she would keep working hard to excel professionally. After the judge left the bench and the courtroom was cleared, the probation officer told us the older sister was a prostitute and was in a wheelchair only because her pimp had recently shot her in the leg.

Chapter Thirteen

Be Not Righteous Over Much

IN THE Old West, hired guns were gunslingers employed by people of means who found them sometimes useful for removing any obstacle to the success of their nefarious plans. In more modern times, the label of hired gun might well be applied to specialists in many fields who supplement their incomes by testifying as expert witnesses in court. These experts cover a wide range of disciplines, which include medicine, psychology, engineering, criminology, accident reconstruction, rehabilitation and real estate, just to name a few.

To be qualified in court as an expert witness, convincing evidence must be presented as to the formal education, training, experience, and practice of the person seeking such qualification. Once the applicant's curriculum vitae has satisfied counsel for the defense and the prosecution, as well as the court, the court will declare the witness qualified to give expert testimony.

The biggest problem facing jurors in trials involving expert witnesses is deciding which expert to believe. In civil cases, an expert for the plaintiff may have impeccable credentials and give very assertive and convincing testimony as to the cause of an accident or the results of a surgical procedure. But then, just as the juror is almost persuaded by the plaintiff's expert witness, lo and behold, the defendant brings forth a defense expert with an equally impressive background, who testifies to the complete opposite. Mercy, what is a juror to do?

In murder trials where there is a plea of not guilty by reason of insanity or diminished capacity, both sides routinely present a battery of psychiatrists whose testimony is diametrically opposed. The experts for the prosecution will usually testify that the defendant was completely lucid and knew the difference between right and wrong at the time of the commission of the crime. Then, equally qualified psychiatrists will testify in the defense part of the trial that the defendant had the cognitive ability of a grapefruit and had no knowledge of the consequences of throwing the victim out of a twentieth-story window.

Fortunately there is a jury instruction that is given by the court whenever expert testimony is offered during a trial. The jury is instructed basically that the testimony of experts may be given whatever weight the jury deems appropriate in relation to the case, but they are not required to consider it at all if they determine that the testimony is unreasonable. While this instruction, no doubt, is of help to the jury during its deliberations, the jury is still faced with an awesome task if the experts for both sides have been equally impressive.

Sometimes expert testimony has been known to backfire on the litigant who has called the expert to testify. In one medical malpractice case brought against a local orthopedist, the plaintiff was alleging the doctor's surgery had failed to alleviate her back pain. The evidence revealed the woman had a number of psychological problems, not the least of which was the fact she was a world-class hypochondriac. She had apparently been so insistent about her back trauma that, in spite of a number of tests that showed nothing wrong, the doctor agreed to perform an exploratory laminectomy.

During the surgical procedure, visual inspection confirmed the findings of the earlier tests that there was no damage or herniation to the intervertebral disk. Therefore, the doctor simply closed up the incision and proceeded no further. About a year later, the woman consulted a neurosurgeon about her back problem. Upon examining the woman's back, he noted the telltale scar of the previous laminectomy—a scar that is apparently identifiable to any physician. He immediately concluded her problem was caused by the fact her previous doctor had *failed to remove all the disk material* during the earlier operation. He subsequently scheduled her for surgery, discovered the disk he thought had been removed previously and did indeed remove it this time.

On cross-examination by defense counsel, the neurosurgeon was asked if he had read the operative notes of the previous surgeon or had attempted to contact him. He answered that he had not looked at the notes because he considered them irrelevant. (The notes were offered in evidence and clearly indicated the first doctor's finding that the disk had not only been visually examined, but had been tested with a saline solution as well and proven completely normal.) The neurosurgeon explained that since he had determined the pain of the woman was caused by the first doctor's failure to remove all the disk material, he did not contact him because he did not want to embarrass him or tarnish his reputation in the medical community.

He further stated that he could sympathize with the other doctor because the first doctor's level of skill was not as great as his own. His thinly veiled arrogance was not lost on the jury. He was then asked why he had removed the disk which appeared to be healthy and his response was that because this was the second time the patient's back had been opened up and the disk probed, it was likely the disk would cause problems in the future so he decided to take it out.

After rendering a verdict in favor of the defendant, some of the jurors stated they felt the wrong doctor was being sued. A number of them drew an analogy to some of the old Perry Mason stories where, at the last minute, someone stands up in the back of the courtroom and confesses to the crime.

In divorce cases where it is stipulated the wife will receive the family home so there will be less disruption in the lives of the children, the husband has a right to be compensated for his half of the value of the home. To this end, the husband's attorney will bring expert real estate appraisers into court to testify to the value of this beautifully landscaped, charming, and well cared for property in an upscale neighborhood. There will also be testimony relating to comparable sales of other properties in the same area—all of which add thousands of dollars to the potential worth of the subject property.

Another squad of expert real estate appraisers then march to the witness stand to testify, in the wife's behalf, that the same property is just this side of being condemned. The roof leaks, several windows are broken, the toilets overflow and the front yard has been officially designated as the local rain forest. The comparable sales in the area testified to by these experts are worth approximately half the amounts stated by the husband's experts and the neighborhood is described as lower middle class, at best.

Fortunately, this is not an issue which must be decided by a jury. It is up to a judge to decide these cases and an experienced judge is in a better position to determine the credibility of the witnesses testifying. Even so, the court may ask both sides to stipulate that the judge may personally view the property or that an independent appraiser be called in before a decision is reached. At the risk of being labeled repetitious, I will attempt to paraphrase the first sentence of this chapter: *In the New West, hired guns are employed by people of means, who find them sometimes useful for removing any obstacle to the success of their nefarious plans.* And, just for the record, I believe a prostitute is the only lay person qualified to testify as an expert.

⚖️

The testimony of police officers in court can sometimes be very vivid and occasionally entertaining. In the mid-1960s, when police nationwide were grumbling about having to comply with the United States Supreme Court decisions in the cases of *Miranda vs. Arizona* and *Escobedo vs. California* (which focused on advising suspects of their right to counsel before being questioned, among other things) occasionally very picturesque scenarios were presented from the witness stand.

During one preliminary hearing concerning a police raid on a building where illicit drug dealing was alleged to be taking place, one of the arresting officers testified to the following:

Q: (By the prosecution:) Tell us now, Officer, what happened as the five of you entered the apartment?

A: All of the suspects fled in different directions. Some headed for bedrooms, others for the bathroom. I caught one of the suspects as he was attempting to jump out of the window.

Q: I take it this was a ground-floor apartment?

A: No, sir. This was a second-floor apartment.

Q: And the suspect was still trying to jump out of the window?

A: Yes, sir.

Q: I take it you were able to prevent his escape?

A: Yes, sir. I grabbed him by the back of his collar and held him there.

Q: Then I presume you brought him back inside the apartment?

A: No, sir. I was holding him by the collar, while he was still outside.

Q: Why didn't you bring him back in immediately?

A: Because I was advising him of his rights.

One of the most identifiable signs that a police officer witness is a rookie is the use of the stilted language and vernacular which is apparently drilled into the cadets at the police academy. For instance, when a question may be answered with a simple yes or no, the rookie cop will invariably say, "That is affirmative," or "Negative." Once, when a witness answered a question with "negatory," the judge asked him if that was the same thing as "no." The witness responded with, "That is affirmative," which only made the answer more confusing. The bad guys are always "suspect number one" or "suspect number two." If the witness really wanted to impress the judge, he might say, "The alleged perpetrator proceeded to perilously pummel the professor on the pavement." Most judges are not amused by and become very impatient with these kinds of responses. Fortunately, after about eighteen months service, coupled with good training by the prosecutor, this type of "cop talk" gradually disappears.

Even after their testimony has been polished and raised to a higher level of understanding, many police officers still resort to the same style of language in preparing their police re-

ports. In the early 1970s, there was a heroic effort mounted by the police departments of this county to stamp out the deadly scourge of massage parlors, which surely must have threatened the very existence, if not the pristine image, of this county. Two of those establishments were located within a block of the courthouse in Palo Alto.

One of the perquisites of being a court reporter is that you get to see things such as police reports, which are usually not available to the public. On one of the forays into the trenches of a local massage parlor, an undercover policeman described in his detailed police report the perils he faced while pursuing this hazardous assignment in a noble, upright, and erect fashion, as follows:

> This officer entered the establishment at 2200 hours and was immediately approached by the suspect, who inquired of this officer whether he wanted a straight massage or the special massage. This officer replied that he wanted the special massage. Suspect then asked this officer for fifty dollars, which this officer paid in marked currency, and the suspect then escorted this officer into a back room of the establishment. Suspect then disrobed and had this officer disrobe and climb onto a padded table. Suspect then placed her hand on this officer's penis, and this officer then removed her hand (gently). This officer then advised suspect of her Miranda rights and placed suspect under arrest.

I always wondered whether the police officer actually used the word "gently" in parenthesis in his report or the police typist was just having a little fun.

The subject of being advised of one's constitutional rights soon became very popular in the media, as well as every cop show that was portrayed on television. This was brought home to me when a young friend of my daughter's, during a biblical quiz, listed as one of the Ten Commandments, "You have the right to remain silent." During this period of time, I was employed in the Municipal Court and the process for advising the people in court of their rights soon became a very time consuming endeavor that at times approached the ridiculous.

Initially, the judge would read a prepared statement of rights to the people in the courtroom, which required at least twenty minutes to read. As time went by, attorneys for people who had been convicted began alleging that their clients had come into the courtroom late, had not understood their rights, or did not understand English and thus their convictions were not constitutionally valid. To counter these allegations, the judges then began inquiring of each defendant who entered a plea of guilty, whether or not they had been present, heard, and understood their rights. If, God forbid, they said no, then the entire twenty minute advisement would be repeated on the spot.

If the defendants did not speak or understand English, the court would hire interpreters to read them their rights in their native language. Today, court interpreters are employed daily in the courts, with the major language demands in this area being Spanish or Vietnamese. In the 1960s, the court's proximity to Stanford University was very helpful because of the many foreign language classes available there and the University's willingness to aid the court in translating some obscure dialect spoken by a defendant from some Middle Eastern or Asian country. I might add parenthetically, at that time all traffic offenses in California were considered misdemeanors (*most are now called infractions*), but if you were accused of running a stop sign, you were advised of the same rights as an accused murderer.

One of the perennial residents of the local jail was an amazingly well-preserved (pickled?) man in his sixties, who would get himself arrested for being drunk in public within a day of his release from jail. He was nicknamed Ivan because he always indicated to the court he could only speak and understand Russian. The court would, therefore, summon a Russian interpreter from Stanford—at county expense—and the proceedings would be translated into Russian for Ivan. The local police agencies, as well as the jail personnel, all claimed

Ivan could speak and understand English as well as anyone, but this was his little joke on the court.

Just about the time the court felt it had covered all the bases regarding advisement of rights, defense attorneys hit upon the idea that their clients had not had sufficient education to enable them to make an intelligent decision regarding the waiver of their rights. It then became necessary for the court to question all defendants, before a guilty plea was entered, as to the extent of their academic achievements and to determine whether they possessed the requisite intelligence to waive their rights and enter a plea of guilty to the charge.

Defendants today who offer a plea of guilty are examined by the judge, who uses a fairly standard litany of questions which have been developed after many, many revisions over the years. These inquiries cover not only the constitutional rights of the defendant, but are designed to determine his or her educational background; that the plea is voluntary; the defendant is not under the influence of any drug at the time of entering the plea and the defendant fully understands the consequences of making the plea. If a state prison sentence is involved, these guilty pleas are transcribed and the advisement usually covers at least four full pages of the transcript.

Because of the fact that a second conviction for driving under the influence results in much more serious penalties and serving a jail sentence, attorneys for second offenders would often ask court reporters for transcripts of the arraignment and plea of their clients at the time of the first offense. This was to determine if they had been properly advised of their rights and the charge of a prior offense was constitutionally valid. If the transcript revealed some discrepancy at the time they were informed of their rights, the prior conviction could not be charged against them and the penalty was less severe.

For several years after I went to work in the Superior Court, I continued to get requests from attorneys for transcripts of drunk driving pleas made while I was in the Municipal Court. This was a common occurrence for any court reporter who had formerly worked in the Municipal Court. On one occasion a young woman reporter, who was just working temporarily, told me she had been requested to provide such a transcript of a prior plea made in another county. She showed me her stenographic notes and she had recorded everything up to the point of a response to the question, "How do you plead?" At that part of her notes there was a long blank portion, followed by the cryptic remark, "I *sneezed*." I'm glad I didn't have to respond to the request in that case.

During the time of my service in the Municipal Court, three armed robbers accosted the crew of a Brinks truck while they were picking up bags of cash from a large drug store in Mountain View. One of the Brinks employees was killed during the robbery. Two of the suspects were later captured, but the third one eluded the police. On the day scheduled for the preliminary hearing of the two suspects in custody, the deputy district attorney casually mentioned to the bailiff at noon that there was evidence the three suspects had made a pact that if any of them were captured, the ones remaining free would come into court with a machine gun and liberate those in custody.

The bailiff, charged with courtroom security, almost flipped out over the fact that he had not been informed of this earlier. He immediately contacted the Palo Alto police, the Sheriff's Department and other police agencies in the area. The preliminary hearing was scheduled for 2:00 P.M. By 1:45 P.M., the area was an armed camp. I doubt if a suspected presidential assassination could have produced much more security. There were police in all the corridors, all the stairwells, all around the building and on the roofs of adjacent buildings. The entries and exits of the courthouse were all guarded by police with shotguns.

For the sake of this tale, let us say the name of the suspect who remained free was Joe Green. At 1:55 P.M., with two of the suspects safely in custody inside the heavily guarded courtroom, a gentleman walked into the supercharged atmosphere of the bailiff's anteroom with some papers in his hand. He was immediately challenged as to his purpose for being there. He was somewhat taken aback and mumbled something to the effect that he was there to help out his friend, Joe Green.

He was instantly thrown against the wall and handcuffed. He protested loudly that he was only there as a witness in a

Small Claims action. The papers he carried verified that he had indeed been supoenaed as a witness in a Small Claims action titled Smith vs. Green. The court clerk's office ascertained this case was scheduled in a different courtroom on a different floor and the man was released with an apology. The third suspect never did show up. Perhaps he tried, but did not like the looks of his welcoming committee. I don't know whether or not the Small Claims witness was an opera buff, but if he was he probably went home and destroyed all his records by Giuseppe Verdi.

⚖

By the end of the 1960s, the two-judge Palo Alto Municipal Court had expanded to four judges. One of those judges was an accomplished raconteur with a devilish sense of humor. One day a defendant appeared before him charged with ignoring about two dozen parking tickets. The man entered a plea of guilty and the judge told him to be seated until the end of the calendar, at which time he would be sentenced. About two hours later, when he was the only defendant remaining in the courtroom, he was summoned before the bench. Because of the imposed delay, he was nervously considering what kind of penalty the judge had in mind for him. The judge looked the defendant in the eye and announced, in a very solemn voice, "*It is the judgment of this court that you shall be hanged by the neck until you are dead.*" The man grew pale, not believing what he had heard. The judge then continued, "I just always wanted to say that. Penalty suspended. Next time, pay your parking tickets."

Chapter Fourteen

Spare the Rod

WITH CREDIT for time served, we were released from our Juvenile Court assignment in December of 1979. The judge I worked for then lived nearer to the courthouse in Palo Alto than the courthouse in San Jose, so he volunteered to preside at the Palo Alto facility. In January 1980, we reentered the adult world. At that time the Palo Alto branch of the Superior Court did not handle any criminal matters, but it handled most matters in the civil category, be it domestic, law and motion, probate matters, or contested trials. Civil jury trials were referred to San Jose.

About midway during our Juvenile Court sojourn, prior to our Palo Alto assignment, the bailiff I spoke of earlier was transferred to patrol duty. His replacement was a super macho deputy sheriff about twice the size of the first bailiff. Fortunately for all of us, he also had a good sense of humor. One day, unbeknownst to me, he plastered the rear bumper of my car with stickers proclaiming such philosophies as "sex instructor: first lesson free." This was initially brought to my attention when my pre-teen children, seeing the car in the driveway, asked me how long I had been a teacher.

A few days later, I went to a printing shop and had about two dozen bumper stickers made up with the logo, "Support Gay Rights For Deputy Sheriffs." At the first opportunity, I affixed several of the bumper stickers to the front and rear bumpers of the deputy's Jeep. I don't know how long it took for him to notice them, but several days later as I passed the parking lot on the way home, I saw the deputy searching every inch of his jeep, looking for any other stickers that he might have missed. Revenge was sweet. He never bothered my car again.

The clerk, the deputy, and I commuted by train to Palo Alto from San Jose, which made the trip much more pleasant than fighting the traffic on the freeway. The court calendars in the Palo Alto court were quite varied. While in San Jose, whole departments were set aside for specific matters such as domestic cases or probate matters, the judge in Palo Alto handled a little bit of everything because the case load was so much smaller than it was in San Jose.

My previous experience with probate matters was very limited and I found the daily probate calendar, though usually brief, quite interesting. Probate matters deal primarily with determining the validity of wills (splitting heirs?), but they also include all proceedings related to the administration of estates, guardianships, and the sale of estate property. Whenever an attorney representing an estate would petition the court to approve the sale of some real property, the law required that the attorney turn to the people in the audience, give a brief description of the property and the sale price and then ask if there were any other bids. Frequently, there was very spirited bidding by various groups in the audience and the judge had to act as an auctioneer. Occasionally, this bidding would last for ten or fifteen minutes, with the court finally approving a sale of the property to the highest bidder at many thousands of dollars more than the original amount asked for in the petition.

The probate calendar had its seamy side as well, when the purported love of some people was overshadowed by their greed. Many times a petition was brought before the court on behalf of an elderly relative confined to a nursing home, who was in need of basic necessities, such as a robe, slippers, or clean underwear. These petitions were usually brought by grandchildren, whose parents were the legal guardians of the grandparent in the nursing home. The parents were often penurious concerning the expenditure of estate funds and the grandchildren could not bear to see the extent of their grandparents' neglect.

Despite the protests of the guardians, the only conclusion to be drawn was that they were more concerned with the solvency of the estate they would ultimately inherit than they were with providing some comfort to their elderly mother or father in the nursing home. In the more aggravated of these cases, the judge would revoke their guardianship status and appoint the Public Guardian to administer the estate.

For the most part, the attorneys in the Palo Alto area were a little more laid back than their colleagues in the rest of the county. One of them told me of a golf tournament they staged at a local country club in which they named the tournament after one of their local brethren, whose performances in court made him somewhat less admired than most. The second prize awarded in the tournament was a large, poster-size picture of the aforementioned attorney. The first prize was a wallet size version of the same picture. Needless to say, great care was taken to ensure the absence of the tournament's namesake because he probably would have been very teed off.

Civil law and motion calendars are proceedings where attorneys make legal motions for temporary restraining orders, injunctions, discovery, continuance of cases, attorney's fees, and just about everything else their fertile little minds can come up with. The law and motion calendar was always the most difficult proceeding for me to report. This was because the attorneys were restricted to a short amount of time in which to make their motions and, therefore, talked as fast as they could to cover all the points they wished to make within their allotted time.

The attorneys had usually lived with the case for six months to a year and the judge had read the file before taking the bench. They were, therefore, familiar with all the terminology used and the citations referred to, whereas the court reporter had never heard any of it until they walked in the door. Ideally, in maybe one out of one hundred cases, a proceeding would take place as follows:

Mr. Lude: Good morning, Your Honor. Larry Lude of
Lude, Lecherous and Lascivious, appearing for the

moving party, the defendant in this case. We are prepared to submit the matter on the moving papers, with particular emphasis to the cases cited therein of *Haught vs. Frigid*, at 23 CAL.APP. 3rd, 243, and *Canine vs. Feline*, at 34 CAL. 2, 978 [fictitious citations]. We are further requesting attorney fees, as authorized by the Smythe case, S-M-Y-T-H-E, in the Supreme Court review, Volume Ten, Article Fifteen.

In that illustration, everything was done in a manner that made the reporter's job very easy. The attorney clearly identified himself and his firm, the cases referred to were stated with their full citation numbers and locations and the Smythe case was spelled out, so as not to be confused with Smith. If a transcript was ordered, which was more often than not, the reporter usually had access to the law books in the judge's chambers to check the citations and verifying spelling of names and cases, such as Haught rather than Hot, to attain greater accuracy in the transcript.

Unfortunately, in the majority of cases, this was the exception rather than the rule. In most instances the following example would be more typical:

Mr. Witless: G'morning, Your Honor. Willard Witless of Witless, Snarf, Grumnflgh, Phrumph and Snotworth appearing for the petitioner—actually, I guess we're the respondent—and the moving party of this motion. Well, in one of the motions, I guess we're the responding party, but—whatever.

I think there can be little doubt as to what your ruling must be in this case, based on the doctrines of Caveat Emptor, Res Ipsa Loquitur and Sic Transit Gloria Mundi. I think this case is on all fours with the theory expressed so eloquently by Justice Flatulent in his article in the West Poughkeepsie Law Review, wherein he stated—and I quote:

"Thefecundityofthesowisofgreatrelevancetothe-

corpulenceoftheneighbor'sboarbecauseofthe-
constructionofthenarrowgateofFarmerBrown.
Anyotherconstructionwouldbecastingpearlsbefore-
swine."

I think that states it very clearly, Your Honor, and with that, I would submit the matter. By the way, Mr. Reporter, I'd like an expedited transcript of this by to-morrow morning.

At that point, I would usually exercise tremendous restraint and refrain from hitting the attorney in the head with my ma-chine. But, as I grew older and more crotchety, I developed a few pat phrases to get the attention of fast-talking attorneys, such as, "Counsel, would you mind slowing down to the speed of sound?" Another attention grabber was, "Counsel, what part of this would you like on the record?" Most of the time the attorneys were genuinely surprised they had been talking too fast. After all, they were there to win their case and the reporter might well have been another piece of court-room furniture as far as the object of their concentration was concerned.

Occasionally, attorneys would tell me of transcripts they had received of law and motion matters in other departments (never *my* transcripts, of course) and they swore they had nev-er said anything similar to what was in the transcript. Even though people rarely remember everything they have said after the fact, it is not unreasonable to suppose that some bedrag-gled reporter might have become somewhat inventive while at-tempting to transcribe the notes of a chaotic hearing in which three or four lawyers were all trying to talk at the same time. Evidently, my assessment of the difficulty of reporting the law and motion calendar was not exclusive.

⚖

Our stay in the Palo Alto Superior Court facility was relatively brief and we returned in the early summer to the courthouse in San Jose. As Monty Python used to say, "*Now for some-thing completely different.*" It was time to take the bulletproof vests out of mothballs and order a new supply of Kleenex. Our next assignment was a return to the domestic court calendar. Nothing seemed to have changed much since the last time, except there were a lot more cases and a lot more attorneys involved. The same old hurt, hate, and hubris were still very much in evidence. The paperwork had increased. The paperwork always increases. One of the Domestic Court forms dealing with the incomes and expenses of the parties in the dispute was initiated in this county during the mid-'80s and it was referred to as a 17.1 statement. Over a period of time it was modified, amended, and adjusted and by the time I retired in 1990 it was called a 17.4 statement. By this time it may be up to 17.17, given the skill and imagination of its designers. And that's just one form.

One of the more notable domestic cases to come before the court involved a highly volatile couple who had been married many years and had raised a fine family. Presumably, after raising the family, they decided to raise hell with each other for a period of years. Various portions of their domestic case were heard in many different departments of the court (as well as one portion in the Criminal Department) and were presided over by a variety of judges over a span of several years. Because of the religion of the parties, divorce was not an option they chose to exercise. In the never-ending quest for some semblance of domestic harmony, one judge ruled that they could both live in the same house, as long as they remained segregated in separate quarters. The wife was to occupy the main house and the husband was to live in a previously remodeled basement apartment.

This arrangement proved to be something less than auspicious when the husband allegedly drilled holes in the floor of the house for the purpose of (1) spying on his wife and (2) sticking wires up through the holes to puncture her bare feet. In a series of counterattacks, the wife reminded him that staring was impolite by pouring hot water in his face each time she spotted him gazing through the holes in the floor. The level of spitefulness and violence gradually increased to the point where one night the wife answered the front door and was shot six times in the abdomen. Amazingly, she survived and the husband was arrested for attempted murder.

During the trial of the husband, his attorney questioned the victim's ability to adequately identify her assailant in the darkness of the front porch. When she admitted she had not actually seen the face of her attacker, the jury was unable to make a finding of guilty beyond a reasonable doubt and the husband was acquitted of the charge and released. New temporary living arrangements were initiated for the husband and mutual restraining orders were issued in an attempt to keep husband and wife away from each other. Inevitably, there were violations of the restraining order which brought the matter back to court time after time after time.

Each time the matter returned to court, the parties would be accompanied by their grown children, who would sit between the parties and act as referees. The adult children were very calm, refined, and cultured and gave one the impression that perhaps there had been a mix-up at the maternity hospital and they had been given the wrong parents.

After a while, the hearings were more comparable to a soap opera than a court session. In spite of the efforts of their attorneys and the judge to maintain order, both husband and wife were continually shouting accusations at each other, sometimes turning around to the people in the audience as if to enlist their aid in proving a point. After the shooting incident, the wife would raise up her blouse to show the audience the scars she claimed were a result of her husband's marksmanship. On one occasion the exasperated judge took a recess, after listening to a long speech by the husband, and the husband turned and continued making his point to the audience for at least another ten minutes after the judge had left the bench.

After the expenditure of thousands of dollars in attorney fees and countless hours of court time and recrimination and frustration over a very extended period, the parties reconciled. I have no idea what finally brought this about, but it certainly reinforced my belief in miracles.

⚖

There are few things more chilling than the potential violence that may be committed against innocent victims by a person convinced that his or her interpretation of the Bible divinely authorizes such violence. One of the contested matters that appeared on the domestic calendar graphically illustrated this problem wherein the wife was challenging the husband's right of visitation with the children, unless he promised not to inflict corporal punishment upon the children during the visitation. The children were three boys under the age of ten. The father was six feet, four inches tall and weighed approximately 230 pounds.

The father acted as his own attorney and was adamant that no one could stop him from exercising discipline over his children. In previous hearings, he had quoted extensively from the Bible and stated that, not only *God's law*, but the constitution guaranteed him the right to exercise corporal punishment. The following excerpts from the trial transcript may prove enlightening, with the usual caveat that the names have been changed—we will call the father Delbert Dreck:

Mr. Dreck:...If I go after my child with a paddle, or after any child, it is not to injure him, but to show him love and turn him around and make him hate what's bad. And I have never used it in a way that abused them in any way, Your Honor. And I feel that my authority now has been taken away from me as a father.

I feel that I...I used my hand for quite awhile, just to..I used my hand...I used to use a stick, but it would break on him and then I got a bigger stick and the boys would hide it. And I spanked...you know, I spanked their rear ends. It's about that big around and I hit him and it hurt my hand. Am I supposed to get the same punishment? So I got a paddle and I cut it out...it has a handle on it about that long, about that thick. Nice and wide. It's about that wide and when I hit them...

The Court: Indicating about three inches wide?

Mr. Dreck: It's about that wide, yeah. I like it better than I do a rod because a rod usually leaves marks...this doesn't make marks on him. I tried it on myself and it has a little bit better sting than a switch does.

I also...when I do it to him, I tell him, "You just hang on to that right there and you hold on." I grab hold of his rear end this way and I...if he struggles, I say, "Will you hold still? I'm going to hit your rear end. If you don't hold still, you're going to get hit more." I make sure I get the right spot with the paddle...I can control them. In fact, the paddle has helped me to calm myself because I have to go get the paddle. I know that it's a good-sized paddle and I have to calm myself because it could...if I hauled off and hit them, it would cause injury to them probably, so I calm myself down.

I do it in a way it's not going to cause any injury to them or any marks to their rear ends. My hand sometimes...if I get really upset and shake them, your hands can be more detrimental if it's not done the right way. And even a stick...I think you know that it depends on the way a person handles it or a paddle. They both can be a lethal weapon, if they're used in a state of violence, and I have not used my hands or the paddle, Your Honor, in such a way. Okay? That I meant to kill my kids or cause them battery.

And so my feeling is that the United States Supreme Court gives the schools throughout the country the right to use corporal punishment. The United States of America gives me the right to follow my religious beliefs and to express them in the Court as to why I carry on these principles the way I do.

The Bible provides the basis for sound discipline. All persons are in need of discipline and correction. These are our beliefs. Accept discipline as evidence of loving concern. Take it seriously. Keep in mind the benefit that can result from it. Profit from reproof administered to others. Discipline yourself to apply the counsel of God's words and the results to those who reject discipline. Okay? And I could read some of those, but I won't bring those up, which my boys have done. They rejected the law of my house and my discipline.

Parents who love their children discipline them. It brings out here...the one holding back his rod is hating his son, but the one loving him is he that does look for him with discipline. The reason for the discipline...

Mr. Brown: Excuse me. May I...it's not so much an objection, but you have limited our time, Your Honor, and I just...

Mr. Dreck: I'm almost through. This is my last part.

Mr. Brown: Well, I'll leave that up to the Court.

Mr. Dreck: Young boys have a lot of wildness in them. Discipline calms them down. Seriously, we have...when I first had my kids come over to my house, they were wild. They jumped on the bed, they jumped on the couch and everything else. I told them to go to bed, it would take them an hour to go to bed at night.

Are you familiar with King Solomon at all? Do you know who King Solomon was?

The Court: Just make your statement, all right? Rather than asking any questions.

Mr. Dreck: Okay. King Solomon was one of the wisest men that ever was on the earth. There's written proof of his wisdom. People all over know about him. Even Mr. Brown commented to me about his wisdom in a court matter.

When a child was stolen by another woman and he told them...he says, "Cut the child in half and give half to her and half to him (sic)." That was a real strong statement, Your Honor. A shocking statement. Everybody must have been just shocked, but he did it out of wisdom and out of teaching ability. And of course he found out who the right mother was and he...he also counseled us...he says, "Use the rod on your children." You aren't going to harm them; you're going to turn them around, if anything.

So I decided to do that. The first night I told them to go to bed, I whipped their rear ends real hard. It went on for two weeks almost. And I said to myself, "Man, what kind of parent am I? I'm beating these kids every night." And my good sense says, "Keep going, Delbert, because they've been away from you for two years. They're out of hand...just keep going and do it in a calm manner and you'll see fruit." So I kept it up and sure enough, about the end of two weeks, I went in the room after I told them to go to bed and all three of them were out like a light. Because of my consistency, I've never had to use it again.

Then I used the paddle for some other problems. I have sat my boys down before I do it and I say, "Listen, boys, this is what has to be done. This is why I have to do this. I won't even tell you my reason for your punishment. Let's go to a higher source than mine." I say, "Let's go to God's words and see what He has to say about this." I told them, "Somebody higher than me has given me the permission to do this." I says, "If you don't listen to me the first and second times, boys, then you're telling me you want me to spank you." And this is how you deal with them.

...So Solomon was right and he is right all the way. He's a smart individual and he's given wisdom to us all, Your Honor. I have done nothing and I am guilty of nothing but following God's word and disciplining my children. I am not guilty of any crime whatsoever. I have also been given freedom from the United States Constitution...also from the Constitution of my religion, that I can follow freedom of religion.

The Court: All right. The Court has listened to you for approximately fifteen minutes and I have allowed you to introduce hearsay evidence, just so you can make your statement as complete as possible. The Court is even more concerned today than the

Court was concerned previously. I am concerned
that you see your children essentially as inanimate
objects to be trained, as though they were essentially some sort of mechanical device or animals,
based on the strictest discipline, strictest construction of the Bible and inability to see any sort of human response that these are just children. They will
make mistakes...

Mr. Dreck: I told you, I talked to them before...

The Court: Excuse me. You've had your chance to
speak and now I'm going to comment.

Mr. Dreck: Okay. Go ahead.

The Court: This isn't a Constitutional issue. This is an
issue just of pure and plain consideration for the
feelings of other people. And an inability to understand that your children are human and they are
not essentially things that you can train, as though
you were training a lion in a cage.

Mr. Dreck: (Smiling broadly)

The Court: Or lions in a cage. So if you are not prepared at this time to indicate to this Court that you
are willing to refrain from the use of corporal punishment...

Mr. Dreck: Your Honor, you are going against the
Constitution.

The Court: Are you prepared at this time, Mr. Dreck,
to agree...

Mr. Dreck: You can't take my paddle away, Your Hon-
or. You don't have any authority.

The Court: Then I'll take your children away.

Mr. Dreck: Okay. You can do that, but you can't take
my paddle away.

The Court: If you want to see them...

Mr. Dreck: You're out of line, Your Honor. I'm sorry.
It's unjust, what you are doing.

The Court: Okay. Apparently...

Mr. Dreck: There's absolutely...

The Court: Apparently you aren't willing to agree then
to...

Mr. Dreck: Of course I'm not.

The Court: Then the order of the Court will be that you will not have any visitation rights with your children. All right? Until two conditions are met. One is that you will agree in writing that you will not exercise corporal punishment and that all...

Mr. Dreck: On what basis, Your Honor?

The Court: Just listen. And all punishment that you impose will be reasonable. And two, that you undergo a psychiatric evaluation by a person designated by the Probation Department.

Mr. Dreck: I have to undergo psychiatric care?

The Court: Just listen.

Mr. Dreck: Har-har! I don't believe this. Beautiful. Can I take this off calendar? I think you're prejudiced, Your Honor. I'd like to get another trial.

The Court: If you don't remain silent, you're going to be in jail. You sit right down and listen and do not utter another word.

Mr. Dreck: You are very unfair, Your Honor.

The Court: Okay. You are remanded to the custody of the Sheriff at this point right now.

Mr. Dreck: You want me to go to jail?

The Court: Yes, Sir.

Mr. Dreck: Great. Let's go.

The Court: Just go sit over there in the jury box. You will go to jail for a period of twenty-four hours for your insolence.

Mr. Dreck: For what? Because I said that it's unjust? What's going on?

The Court: Just sit down.

Mr. Dreck: Your Honor, I'm not a lawyer..

The Court: Sit down, please.

Mr. Dreck: I'm not a lawyer. You shouldn't treat me like one.

The Court: All right. The order again is that Mr. Dreck will be essentially not permitted to visit with his children until he has agreed in writing not to use corporal punishment on his children and to use reasonable discipline at all other times. Two, that he undergo a psychiatric evaluation by a person designated by the Probation Department. That the evaluation be submitted to the Court and the Court approve any further visitation by the father and the children.

Mr. Dreck: Your Honor, I deem it a privilege to be persecuted in Christ's name. A privilege. Rutherford (a religious figure referred to earlier) was sent away for eighty years and he served on the Supreme Court because of it. And you are doing the same thing, Your Honor, and I deem it a privilege to be persecuted in Christ's name...even before a Jew.

Based upon the last remark of Mr. Dreck, he apparently was under the impression that Jesus was a Presbyterian. This matter was heard in November of 1981. Hopefully, with the passage of time the children have developed sufficiently and learned the art of self defense to the extent that they may now visit their father without an armed guard.

Chapter Fifteen

The Centurions

AS MAY BE apparent by reading this far, a fairly close relationship or camaraderie usually develops between court reporters, court clerks, and bailiffs. Part of the reason for this is the fact they work together in relatively close quarters every day, but the major reason is that they share a common goal of keeping the judge in a good mood. Things seem to go well for everyone when the judge is happy. On those days when the bench is burdened with pique, the staff might well be better off having root canal surgery.

For example, during my Municipal Court experience it was pretty common for attorneys to engage in "judge shopping" on behalf of their clients in criminal matters. In this state each defendant has the right to file an affidavit of prejudice against one judge, claiming they cannot receive a fair trial before that judge and the judge is then disqualified from hearing their case. Most judges do not look kindly upon these affidavits because they consider them a reflection upon their character and ability as a judge. When an attorney chooses to file such an affidavit, he or she must accept the probability that there will be very few future appearances before that judge because judges have long memories.

Previous reference has been made to the propensity of Judge X in Municipal Court to be very tough on drunk drivers. Because of that well-known fact, many attorneys would disqualify him so their clients could appear before another judge whose sentencing procedures were a bit more lenient. Quite often, if the blood alcohol reading in a drunk driving case was not much above the legal limit, the judge in the other department would agree to reduce the drunk driving charge to reckless driving.

The fine would be the same, but the defendant's driver's license would not be as greatly affected and, most importantly, it would not count as a prior conviction of drunk driving in any future charge. Whenever Judge X would learn of another such reduction of a drunk driving charge, he was definitely not a happy camper. His displeasure inevitably ricocheted around the staff making life more difficult for everyone.

Judge X took a great deal of pleasure in performing wedding ceremonies. No matter how busy he was, he was always happy to join a happy couple in wedded bliss. He performed many marriage ceremonies on his own time on weekends as well. One of the adult probation officers at that time, who enjoyed a very good rapport with Judge X, decided to get married. For reasons of his own, however, he engaged the services of Judge Y for that purpose. When Judge X found out about it, he was quite hurt. The bailiff comforted him with the observation that, "Judge, he probably feels that if the marriage doesn't work out, he can always go back to that department and get it reduced to an engagement."

This bailiff asked me once if I had ever had a tour of the North County Jail located in the basement of the court building. At that time, I had been employed there about four years, but had never had occasion to view the jail. When he invited me to the grand tour, I accepted. As soon as we entered the facility, I realized I was in for a hard time. None of the jail personnel had any idea of my identity or occupation and when they asked the bailiff if he wanted to book me, he grabbed my arm roughly and said yes. I went along with the gag and endured the fingerprinting and the mug shots, but I broke out in a cold sweat at the desolate sound of the metallic gate shutting after me. Finally, he told them who I was and I was released. They even gave me my mug shots to take with me.

The next day, on my way to work, I stopped off at the dry cleaners to leave several suits and jackets to be refurbished. When I got to work, I realized I had left my checkbook in the inside coat pocket of one of the suits I had left at the cleaners. I called the cleaner immediately, so the checkbook could be retrieved before the processing of the suit began. I told him I would pick it up that night on my way home. When I stopped in that night and asked for my checkbook, I was handed an envelope containing my checkbook, along with a strip of photographs sticking out of the envelope. The photographs were my mug shots taken in the jail, all clearly stamped "Santa Clara County Jail." The clerk gave me a rather quizzical look, but I didn't even try to explain. Needless to say, I never attempted to cash a check in there again.

Bailiffs, as a group, have changed considerably over the period of time I have been involved with the court system. When I worked in the Montana District Court, the only time a bailiff was in attendance was during the trial of a jury case. Even then, it was a civilian instead of a deputy sheriff unless it was a criminal matter, in which case there were members of the local police in the courtroom. The gentleman who acted as bailiff during civil jury trials was seventy-eight years old. He was officially designated as the poet laureate of that section of Montana. He would amuse jurors with such statements as, "I stopped by the police station and beat up six cops this morning, so I feel pretty good." When the judge took the bench, the bailiff would make the official announcement that court was in session and then promptly go to sleep until the morning recess.

When I began my service in the Palo Alto Municipal Court in October of 1961, Judge X had a bailiff who was a grizzled old veteran of the San Francisco Police Department. He had retired from that department after many years of service, some of which had been during the last days of prohibition. He was a real old style cop with a vocabulary to match. He had a way of handling difficult defendants which would be considered very inappropriate today.

I can recall one instance where a very irate young man was becoming very threatening towards a court clerk over a traffic fine until the bailiff barked, "Get your ass down those stairs or you'll be picking your teeth up off the floor!" The young man complied very quickly. Today, that sort of thing would result in a law suit alleging police brutality. At the time, it was simply an extension of the bailiff's previous experience on the streets of San Francisco. Strangely enough, despite his obviously advanced years, his demeanor was so authoritative he was rarely challenged by even the most disgruntled citizen.

At the conclusion of each jury trial, the bailiff is sworn by the clerk to take charge of the jury during their deliberations to ensure there is no jury tampering and to relay any questions or requests they may have to the judge. This bailiff had a partial upper plate and delighted in letting it drop down during the time the clerk was seriously attempting to administer the oath. To her credit, she only lost her composure about twice that I can recall, but he still made the attempt every time he was sworn.

For her revenge, she would sneak into the courtroom when court was not in session and unscrew the hammer portion from the handle of the bailiff's wooden gavel to the point where it looked secure, but when he next banged it to call the court to order, the hammer portion would fly across the courtroom creating quite a sensation. This bailiff added a lot of color to the courtroom (especially to the judge's face when the bailiff did something to anger him), but he retired about a year after I started working there and he was greatly missed by all of us.

Fortunately I had a fairly good relationship with all the bailiffs I had occasion to work with, but there were a few bailiffs in other departments of the court over the years whose performance was something less than admirable. One young bailiff in the Superior Court in San Jose was practicing his fast draw one morning before court and put a bullet through the wall of the judge's chambers. Luckily for the judge, he had not yet arrived. The deputy apologized to the judge and convinced him it was an accident and he retained his position until about two months later when the same thing happened. Once again, it happened before the arrival of the judge, but that was the end of that deputy's assignment as a court bailiff.

As earlier indicated, the majority of bailiffs in this county twenty years ago were retired military personnel. Of that group, the most prevalent were Chief Petty Officers retired from the navy. One judge had a bailiff who was a retired army colonel and that bailiff never let you forget that he outranked all others. With all due respect to army colonels, this particular retiree was really quite insufferable. He had a miserable disposition, he refused to take any messages for the judge and he maintained a haughty attitude that displayed great disdain for all those around him.

For reasons unknown to others, the judge evidently found his services quite satisfactory and the two were almost inseparable. Some observers felt the bailiff exerted a bad influence upon the judge, especially in light of a very unpopular situation the judge created for himself during an assignment to Juvenile Court in 1969. One of the cases that appeared before him involved a young man who had impregnated his sister. The minor was from a Hispanic family. The public defender assigned to defend him was also Hispanic. The comments of the judge during this hearing were quite astonishing, to say the least.

A partial transcript of the hearing was ordered and copies were made and distributed to all metropolitan areas of the state by various ethnic groups, such as Confederacion de La Raza. Ironically, a Juvenile Court judge can deny a request for a transcript of any juvenile matter, except on appeal, because the matters are confidential. In this case, the judge gave permission for the reporter to prepare the transcript with the names of the parties blanked out. That transcript of the hearing on September 2, 1969, is reproduced as follows, with the name of the public defender changed:

> The Court: There is some indication that you more or less didn't think that it was against the law or was improper. Haven't you had any moral training? Have you and your family gone to church?
> The Minor: Yes, Sir.
> The Court: Don't you know that things like this are terribly wrong? This is one of the worst crimes that a person can commit. I just get so disgusted that I

just figure what is the use? You are just an animal. You are lower than an animal. Even animals don't do that. You are pretty low.

I don't know why your parents haven't been able to teach you anything or train you. Mexican people, after thirteen years of age, it's perfectly all right to go out and act like an animal. It's not even right to do that to a stranger, let alone a member of your own family. I don't have much hope for you. You will probably end up in State's Prison before you are twenty-five, and that's where you belong, anyhow. There is nothing much you can do.

I think you haven't got any moral principles. You won't acquire anything. Your parents won't teach you what is right or wrong and won't watch out. Apparently your sister is pregnant, is that right?

The Minor's Father: Yes.

The Court: It's a fine situation. How old is she?

The Minor's Mother: Fifteen.

The Court: Well, probably she will have a half a dozen children and three or four marriages before she is eighteen.

The county will have to take care of you. You are no particular good to anybody. We ought to send you out of the country—send you back to Mexico. You belong in prison for the rest of your life for doing things of this kind. You ought to commit suicide. That's what I think of people of this kind. You are lower than animals and haven't the right to live in organized society—just miserable, lousy, rotten people.

There is nothing we can do with you. You expect the county to take care of you. Maybe Hitler was right. The animals in our society probably ought to be destroyed because they have no right to live among human beings. If you refuse to act like a human being, then you don't belong among the society of human beings.

Mr. Mendoza: Your Honor, I don't think I can sit here and listen to that sort of thing.

The Court: You are going to have to listen to it because I consider this a very vulgar, rotten human being.

Mr. Mendoza: The Court is indicting the whole Mexican group.

The Court: When they are ten or twelve years of age, going out and having intercourse with anybody without any moral training—they don't even understand the ten commandments. That's all. Apparently they don't want to. So if you want to act like that, the county has a system of taking care of them. They don't care about that. They have no personal self-respect.

Mr. Mendoza: The Court ought to look at this youngster and deal with this youngster's case.

The Court: All right. That's what I am going to do. The family should be able to control this boy and the young girl.

Mr. Mendoza: What appalls me is that the Court is saying that Hitler was right in genocide.

The Court: What are we going to do with the mad dogs of our society? Either we have to kill them or send them to an institution or place them out of the hands of good people because that's the theory...one of the theories of punishment is if they get to the position that they want to act like mad dogs, then we have to separate them from our society.

Well, I will go along with the recommendation. You will learn in time or else you will have to pay for the penalty with the law. Because the law grinds slowly, but exceedingly well. If you are going to be a law violator—you have to make up your mind whether you are going to observe the law or not. If you can't observe the law, then you have to be put away.

⚖

With the release and dissemination of the transcript, a great many demonstrations were held across the state and pickets protested by surrounding the courthouse in San Jose for a number of days. This judge was subsequently censured by the State Judicial Council and was restricted from hearing any further juvenile or criminal matters until the time of his retirement several years later.

⚖

One deputy sheriff I used to work with in the court told me of an incident that happened after he had left his court assignment and gone back out on patrol duty. One night in the early morning hours he encountered a young man of seventeen loitering around a closed business establishment. When he approached the young man and inquired as to his purpose for being there, the young man's response was, "Get out of my face, pig! I haven't done nothing. You can't do anything to me 'cause I'm a juvenile. I'm a minor and you can't touch me, so bug off, pig!" The deputy was touched by compassion and felt heartsick that the young man had evidently been denied the nurturing care and concern which surely would have endowed him with much better manners and a more socially acceptable attitude.

Determined to do what he could to be of aid to this deprived young man's development, the deputy gently assisted the young man into the trunk of his patrol car. He then drove about twenty-five miles from San Jose to a remote area of the county and invited the juvenile to disembark. At that point, it was 3:00 A.M., with very little public transportation available. As the deputy drove off, he could hear the young man shouting, "Hey, you can't leave me here like this, pig!" This saddened the deputy because he realized the extra concern he had shown the minor had still not been fully appreciated. No account was given as to how or when the minor made it back to San Jose, but presumably he showed a great deal more respect the next time he visited a pig farm.

I spoke earlier of the deputy sheriff who was a bailiff in another department of Juvenile Court who commuted to work on his big Harley-Davidson, wearing black leathers and looking as if he were a member of a motorcycle gang. After his Juvenile Court assignment, his judge served for a considerable time in the Domestic Court. One of the departments of the Domestic Court dealt with what was known as the district attorney's contempt calendar. This was a calendar for dealing primarily with fathers, and sometimes mothers as well, who were delinquent in child support payments which had been ordered by the court.

If the evidence adduced at the hearing found they had not paid the amounts ordered, even though they had the ability to do so, they would be found in contempt and sentenced to some jail time. This jail time was usually suspended on condition they start making monthly payments, as well as payments towards their arrears. While it is unseemly to generalize, a large segment of the people on this calendar were not exactly identifiable as the cream of society. Many times when the aforementioned deputy would come roaring up before court on his souped up Harley, with his wild hair blowing in the wind, sporting his black leather and dark glasses, he would be approached by defendants clad in a similar fashion, inquiring if he had any idea where the courtroom was to which they had been summoned.

He would readily oblige them and give them directions to the proper department and they always seemed pleased they had found someone to empathize with, who seemed to know his way around the court. The deputy would proceed into his own area of the courthouse to change clothes and come out wearing his sheriff's uniform. Quite often many of the defendants, who had chatted with him earlier outside the building, looked as if they had been betrayed. On more than one occasion, he would be told, "We thought you were one of us!"

One Monday morning, the day after daylight savings time went into effect, this bailiff decided to set the courtroom clock to the correct time. This was in the oldest courthouse in San Jose and the courthouse had been built in the late 1800s. The ceilings were very high and the clock was high up on the wall. Court was in session, having convened at 8:45 A.M. and the bailiff attempted to reset the clock at about 9:00 A.M. He did not have a ladder immediately available so he was using a

"SORRY, JUDGE. JUST CHECKING THE COURT'S MINUTES."

long pike-like pole, designed for opening and closing high windows which were out of reach. The pole had a hook on the end and he intended to lift the clock off its hook on the wall and then bring it down to reset it. Unfortunately, his plan failed when the clock came crashing down, startling everyone in the courtroom. When the judge asked him what he was doing, his response was, "Sorry, Judge. Just killing time."

One evening when I was scheduled to report a Grand Jury hearing, the assistant district attorney instructed the elderly bailiff to give special care to one particular witness who was scheduled to testify because there was credible information that there was a contract out on the life of the witness. The bailiff was admonished to make sure the witness remained safely inside the courtroom while waiting for the hearing to begin.

About twenty minutes later, the district attorney discovered the witness sitting outside in the corridor. He was furious and demanded to know why the bailiff had not followed his instructions. The bailiff righteously explained that he had indeed seated the witness inside the courtroom, but had come back later to find the witness smoking a cigarette. He further explained that, "Nobody was going to smoke in Judge Knumbskull's courtroom, so I kicked him out!" I guess we all have our priorities.

When I would occasionally fill in for a reporter in another department, I would often realize how fortunate I was to work with the court clerk in my own department. There was general agreement that the clerk in one department suffered some severe mental problems. As long as he took his medication, he could function properly in his job. If he went several days without his medication, his behavior was really very strange. After a civil service employee has completed a six month probationary period, the person must almost commit a felony before firing may be justified.

Whenever the judge in that department would take a recess, the clerk would remain in the courtroom until one minute before the recess was to end and then he would disappear for at least fifteen minutes. The judge would have to start without him, but that meant exhibits could not be marked or identified until he returned. His handwriting was so undecipherable that he was the only one who could read the entries he made in the court minute book. Whenever bailiffs or clerks are required to use the telephone during the time court is in session, they whisper into the telephone so as not to interrupt the court proceedings. When this clerk used the telephone, everyone in the courtroom could hear his end of the conversation.

Once, during the selection of a jury in a criminal trial, the clerk was talking to his auto mechanic on the telephone and his end of the conversation, stated very distinctly, was as follows:

> The Clerk: Yeah, we're picking a jury now. What? Oh, attempted murder, assault, and false imprisonment. What? Oh, yeah. He's guilty as hell.

This was clearly heard by everyone in the courtroom and resulted in an immediate mistrial. The entire jury panel had to be dismissed and a new one ordered. The clerk was suspended for three days without pay for that little indiscretion, but it really didn't seem to alter his behavior that much in the future.

Another clerk worthy of mention was a middle-aged gentleman of very high standing in the community. He was well respected and was an elder of his church and had been married for many years. At the same time period, a lady who was a clerk in another department was tragically diagnosed with cancer. For her own reasons, she resolved not to avail herself of any treatment. Whether it was misguided pity or true compassion, the gentleman was greatly attracted to this lady and a close relationship soon blossomed between them.

They spent all their free time together and were obviously very much in love with each other. Meanwhile, her condition continued to grow worse and with each passing day her appearance deteriorated. The gentleman's wife divorced him after a marriage of more than twenty-five years and the two clerks decided to share an apartment. The cancer continued its ravaging effect until she could no longer work. She finally succumbed to the disease about fourteen months after its inception and the gentleman clerk was, of course, devastated. After a lengthy period of mourning, his demeanor gradually returned to what it had been prior to this affair. Eventually, his former wife was persuaded to forgive him and they were remarried. Now, *that*, for all intents and purposes, is a mid-life crisis.

No doubt a multi-volume treatise could be created pertaining to all the weird, wacko, and goofy court reporters that have graced the courts over the years, but I will leave the compilation of that to others. I would not want to jeopardize my number one position on that list.

Chapter Sixteen

And Thine Age Shall Be Clearer Than the Noonday

IN 1978 the voters of California approved the famous (or infamous, depending on your point of view) Proposition 13. This proposition was welcomed by the majority of voters because its intended purpose was to greatly lower California property taxes. What was not so welcome to everyone was the resultant necessary reduction in government services available to the public. As a result of the successful passage of Proposition 13, there were many instances throughout the state of greatly reduced hours of libraries, parks, social services, and cutbacks in police and fire protection, to name a few.

In the Superior Courts in this county, people who were accustomed to being able to file papers and conduct other business with the clerk's office from eight to five, now found the clerk's office open to them only from nine to four o'clock. The employees were still working from eight to five, but public access was restricted to two hours less each day. Many citizens acquired bruised knuckles from banging on the locked doors in frustration until the fact of the new hours was finally realized. When I bade the courthouse adieu in 1990, those hours were still the same.

Inside the courtrooms, it was decided that the continued payment of deputy sheriffs as bailiffs was now a luxury in many civil departments where violence was not anticipated and they were replaced by civilian personnel known then as

---

court attendants. The men and women who were court attendants were not trained as peace officers, were not armed, and did not wear a military uniform. Their only uniform consisted of a blue blazer with the decal of Santa Clara County on the sleeve in addition to blue trousers or skirt. The male court attendants were encouraged to opt for the trousers.

The duties of the court attendants were similar in many ways to those of a bailiff, but they had no police authority. They would call the court to order at the commencement of proceedings, they would answer the telephone, take messages, fill the water pitchers, attend to the needs of jurors, and generally try to keep things running smoothly in the courtroom. They were also charged with the security of the jury during its deliberations. In the mid-'80s, sandwiched in between domestic and criminal assignments, our department had several different court attendants assigned to it, but the one who was there for the longest period of time was a lady whose life could have been scripted by the writers of *I Love Lucy*.

She was quite efficient in the performance of her duties in court, but outside the courtroom it was a different matter. When she drove her car into a gas station, she would most often wind up with at least one wheel embedded inside the brick planter. When she would pay a social call to her friends, she would carefully park her car—about four feet from the curb. She wore contact lenses, but was always misplacing one of them so she would come to work with her vision corrected in just one eye, which no doubt caused her to view the world from a slightly different perspective. She enjoyed patronizing fast food establishments and must have caused the premature aging of many young attendants when they saw her barreling down upon them in the drive-through lane.

One day the court clerk and I went to the office of the court attendant to invite her to lunch. She was gone and the judge told us he had asked her to take his Mercedes down to the car wash to be cleaned. We both looked at each other in shock. He saw the looks on our faces and asked if anything was wrong. We assured him that nothing was wrong; possibly just a little indigestion. Secretly, we doubted his Mercedes would ever be the same again. Fortunately, she returned about an hour later with the car intact, looking very proud of herself. She confided in us later (not to the judge) that she had never driven a Mercedes before and was unfamiliar with the controls on the dashboard. She had inadvertently activated the windshield washer and windshield wipers and could not figure out how to disengage them.

Undeterred, she drove the three miles to the car wash in the hot August sun with the wiper blades working furiously to clear off the smears made by the washing solution. Luckily, the attendant at the car wash was able to figure out how to turn them off before she drove the car through. We were all very grateful the car had not come equipped with a sun roof.

One of the tales she told on herself involved the wedding reception held after her marriage to the man who would later be her ex-husband. He was a ruggedly built deputy sheriff with many years of service. Because of his popularity, the reception was attended by most of the members of the sheriff's office. He had informed the court attendant prior to the wedding that he could father no children because of a vasectomy. She had a child by a previous marriage, so this was not a great concern to her.

During the reception, the bridegroom noticed several of his friends looking at him in a pitiable manner and he didn't have a clue as to the reason why. Later, he approached a group of well-wishers around his bride and overheard someone ask if they intended to start a family. He was dumbfounded to hear her reply, "Oh, no. That's not in the picture for us because he's impotent." He hastily drew her to one side and demanded, "Why in the world would you say such a thing, when you know it's not true?" She reminded him that he had told her he had a vasectomy. He retorted, "That makes me sterile, not impotent!" She responded cheerily, as if a light bulb had gone off in her head, "Oh, *that's* what I meant. I'm sure they all understand that. Besides, I only told about a dozen people." With such an auspicious beginning, it's probably just as well she had not reserved a hall for a golden wedding anniversary celebration.

Occasionally, if the judge was ill or on vacation, our court attendant would be assigned to work for a different judge in another department. She usually got along all right in most instances, but for some reason she felt intimidated by certain judges. One of our most distinguished jurists at the time was a judge I'll call G. Barton Phillips. She had never worked for him before and when assigned to be his court attendant for one day, her actions more or less guaranteed there would never be another such assignment.

Every bailiff or court attendant in the Superior Court in this county memorizes a little speech they make each day at the commencement of court proceedings. When the judge comes into the courtroom, the bailiff or court attendant stands, bangs the gavel and says, **"Please rise! Department three of the Superior Court of the State of California, in and for the County of Santa Clara, is now in session. The Honorable Phineas F. Featherhead, presiding. Be seated, please."** In most courtrooms the name of the judge was readily apparent on a wooden plaque in front of the bench. On this occasion either the judge was not in his usual courtroom or the court attendant had mixed up her contact lenses again, but she could not remember his name correctly.

She told me later she had rehearsed his name, over and over to herself, "G. Barton Phillips, G. Barton Phillips." When the judge came out that morning, however, he was announced as the Honorable G. Pharton Billips. This immediately produced a momentary murmur of mirth in the courtroom, as well as an icy glare from the judge. If that had been the end of it, no really lasting damage would have been done, but there was more to come. When jurors are given exhibits to examine during a trial, the first juror is given the exhibit and after it has been examined it is passed on to the next juror. When it reaches the end of the first row of jurors, it is collected by the bailiff or court attendant and then presented to juror number seven in the next row to be examined and passed on down to the end of the row. Then the exhibit is collected and returned to the clerk.

In this case the court attendant had been engrossed in a book she was reading and did not notice that the jurors simply passed the exhibit on to the next row without her assistance. When the exhibit reached the end of the final row, the last juror returned the exhibit to the court attendant and she began to pass it on to the row which had already seen it. When they declined, she became somewhat insistent until the judge inquired, "Is there a problem over there?" By then she realized her mistake and apologized for the interruption. At a later point in the trial that day, the judge asked counsel to approach the bench. Again, she had not been paying close attention and when she saw all the attorneys stand to approach the bench, she assumed the judge had called a recess and she had not heard it. Somewhat panicked, she immediately banged her gavel and said, **"Rise, please. Court is now in recess."** The jurors and the people in the audience obediently rose to their feet until the judge wearily proclaimed that there had been no recess called.

Charles Dickens advised us in *The Tale of Two Cities*, "It was the best of times, it was the worst of times." Surely, if he had witnessed the proceedings in court that day, he would have omitted the first part of that sentence. The court attendant was very relieved to return to her own department the next day. The judge in whose department she had been temporarily assigned was no doubt convinced he had just completed a frightening journey through the Twilight Zone.

⚖

Sometimes when people hire a well-known lawyer to represent them in a legal action, they are somewhat perturbed to find a younger, less experienced member of that firm has been assigned to represent their interests in court. Occasionally, the opposite arrangement may prove to be just as disconcerting. We are all familiar with the sad comparisons with earlier skills of superb athletes or entertainers who seem not to recognize the terrible toll that the inexorable passage of time has levied upon them. Usually they are financially secure, but apparently cannot survive without the heady tonic of admiration and adulation that an approving audience provides.

This can be just as true with attorneys and judges, although not as likely with judges anymore in this state. In the 1960s, legislation was passed in this state requiring the retirement of judges at age seventy or they would forfeit half of their retirement benefits. One of the compelling arguments in favor of this legislation was a judge in a neighboring county who was still on the bench at the age of eighty-nine. He slept through a good portion of most of his trials and was rapidly becoming senile.

As far as good trial lawyers are concerned, the thrill and exhilaration of adversarial competition in the arena of litigation is a very difficult thing to give up. When it becomes obvious to others that the raging fire that used to burn there is now little more than a flicker, it is painful to watch an aging lawyer who does not realize he is getting by primarily on his past reputation.

One of the personal injury trials held in the time period we are concerned with was a good example of this. The plaintiff was represented by one of the most prestigious law firms in northern California. The suit involved a woman whose death resulted when her vehicle collided with a large cement truck. The plaintiff's case was being very ably tried by a senior member of the aforementioned law firm, with sporadic appearances by the founder of the law firm. The founding partner, at that time, was in his mid-seventies. For the sake of convenience, let's call him Mr. Lasagna.

Mr. Lasagna and his firm enjoyed a well deserved reputation for winning some of the biggest and most successful law suits in the state and the nation over a period of approximately forty years. A great deal of that success was attributable to Mr. Lasagna who, in earlier days, had mesmerized juries with his flamboyant style and his instinctive drive to go straight for the jugular of the opposition. Indeed, some of the huge judgments he won for his clients were reduced by the Appellate Courts on the basis of the *prosecutorial misconduct of counsel*.

What did not seem apparent to Mr. Lasagna was the fact that today's jurors are much more sophisticated than they were forty years ago. What might have been effective with a jury then was not nearly as likely to succeed today. Nevertheless, in spite of the fact his senior lieutenant had done an excellent job presenting the plaintiff's case, Mr. Lasagna decided to pull rank and make the final arguments to the jury himself. When word got out that he was going to argue the case, a whole class of third year law students showed up to watch The Great One in action.

His greatest emphasis in the argument was placed on the fact that the lady's death had left three children without a mother. If one had not heard the whole trial, one might assume from his argument that the children were just barely out of kindergarten. While it is always tragic to lose your mother, the jurors knew from the testimony, as well as having viewed the children, that they were in their mid- to late-thirties. Finally, in an effort to really drive home the point, he emotionally recited the words to the old tearjerker, M-O-T-H-E-R, a song written circa 1915 by Howard Johnson and Theodore Morse.

In a husky voice, he began, "M is for the million things she gave me. O means only that she's growing old." Then, with his eyes glistening, he continued, "T is for the tears were shed to save me. H is for her heart of purest gold." He paused for effect, taking out his handkerchief, and then, "E is for her eyes with love light shining. R means right, and right she'll always be." Incredibly, almost in tears, he concluded, "Put them all together, they spell Mother, a word that means the world to me."

Many of the jurors were under forty and possibly had not heard the song before his passionate presentation to them. They were impressed even more, however, by his coup de grace in describing the husband of the woman, sitting there with his wife dying in his arms, waiting for the paramedics to arrive. At least that's what he intended to say. What he actually said was, "Waiting for the *paralegals* to arrive." He did not realize he had used the wrong word and went right on with his argument. The law students in the audience had a difficult time keeping a straight face and I had to forcefully tear my eyes away from a juror who was looking at me with a smile on his face.

This is an example of how even a tragic situation can result in repressed humor. The paralegal Freudian slip conjured up visions of ambulances being pursued by hoards of attorneys and yet no one could acknowledge it under the circumstances. The old warrior pulled out all the stops and gave it his best shot. The jury responded by returning a verdict for the plaintiff. Mr. Lasagna, however, had asked them for several million dollars in damages. They awarded his client several thousand dollars. When the trial was ended and the jury had been excused, Mr. Lasagna growled, "I've gotten more than that for the death of a damned Poodle." With that, he stormed out of the courtroom. Who can say what the result might have been if the attorney who tried the case had been allowed to argue it? On the other hand, if Mr. Lasagna had actually sung the song....

Once, when I was temporarily assigned to a criminal department to work for a different judge, I reported a motion to suppress evidence which might have been considered erotic narcotics. The evidence sought to be suppressed was all related to the narcotics arrest of a group of people and had been obtained by an undercover narcotics officer. The defendant's attorney alleged that the undercover officer had taken his role too literally and had a sexual relationship with one of the female informants, thus tainting the evidence. The officer denied this and stated that, while he had spent some time with the informant, he had never had sex with her.

The woman was called as a witness and was cross-examined by the deputy district attorney. He asked her, since she claimed to have had sex with the officer, if she had seen him naked. She said that she had. He then asked her if she could describe any distinguishing marks on his body, such as scars, birthmarks, or tattoos. She stated that the officer had several tattoos adorning different parts of his body. The officer was asked to remove his shirt in court and, sure enough, he had several tattoos that were very obvious. Later the officer testified they had gone to the beach together one day and that is how she knew about his tattoos.

Finally, on redirect examination, the defense attorney asked the woman if the officer was circumcised. She stated that he was. At that point a recess was taken and the district attorney and the officer went into a conference room. The court clerk was a nervous wreck. She assumed that if the officer came back and stated he was not circumcised, he would be asked to prove it. Even though such delicate matters were usually handled in the court's chambers, part of her job was to mark exhibits for identification and then, if they were admitted as evidence, she had to keep them in her custody until the trial was concluded.

Fortunately, when the officer was recalled as a witness, he stated that he was circumcised. There was an audible sigh of relief from the clerk. Despite the officer's admission, the district attorney was able to adduce so many inconsistencies in the woman's testimony that it was apparent she had simply made a lucky guess as far as the model and design of the officer. Her testimony was refuted and the motion to suppress was denied. No doubt the events of this case caused the narcotics detective to take a lot of ribbing from his fellow detectives down at the Dick Bureau.

Chapter Seventeen

"Should Our Sister Have Been Treated Like a Harlot?"

WHEN I worked for Judge X in the Municipal Court, report-ing jury trials of drunk drivers, one of his strictly enforced court rules was the disallowance of any questions by counsel of potential jurors regarding whether or not they imbibed in alcoholic beverages. Most of the local attorneys were aware of this restriction and avoided such questions, thus eliminating a potentially embarrassing situation. It was always amusing, however, when it became obvious that some attorney from out of town was working his way up to that question—very much like waiting for the other shoe to drop. In such cases, the record would read something like this. Counsel would ask, with a knowing wink:

> Mr. Gregarious: And do you, Mrs. Cartwright, occa-sionally enjoy a cold beer on a hot day or perhaps a cocktail before dinner in the privacy of your home?
>
>   Before the potential juror could respond, there was an explosion from the bench with all the force of a small thermonuclear device:
>
> The Court: **Counsel, I will not allow that question in this Court! You may ask the jurors if they have any moral, religious, or philosophical beliefs against the use of alcohol by anyone, but what they do in**

> the privacy of their homes is nobody's business. If this was a sex case, it would be like allowing you to inquire into what they do in their own bedrooms. If you try to ask it again, I will hold you in contempt!

This usually had the effect of completely demoralizing the attorney, at least temporarily, to the point where there was a reluctance to ask any further questions, lest he be further humiliated in front of the jury. In most jurisdictions the question would have been permitted, but not in Judge X's court.

In 1987 I reported one of the most lurid and bizarre sex cases I had ever encountered. It involved the prosecution of a man and his wife for the crimes of rape, sexual assault, battery, false imprisonment, oral copulation, penetration with a foreign object, and a few other charges I cannot recall at this time. The evidence disclosed that the victim was a woman in her mid-twenties who, along with her three-year-old daughter, rented a room in the home of the two defendants. The defendants also were the parents of a young child.

Over a period of months, the victim was persuaded to join the two defendants in viewing pornographic movies after the children were asleep. These movies were apparently very graphic and explicit and covered a wide range of sexual activities. As the victim grew closer and more relaxed with the couple, she revealed some of her sexual fantasies to them, which may have played a part in the violent events which I will go into later.

The selection of the jury in this case was a very lengthy procedure because each potential juror was questioned individually in the judge's chambers. This was a common practice in capital murder cases so that one juror's comments might not influence the opinions of the rest of the jury panel regarding capital punishment, as they would if made in an open courtroom. It was done in this case simply because of the subject matter and to avoid the embarrassment of jurors having to answer such questions in public.

The primary reason for this type of jury selection being so

time consuming is that when jurors are questioned in open court, the first juror is usually asked a whole barrage of questions dealing with background and experience and ability to be fair and impartial. The subsequent jurors are generally asked fewer questions, followed by the standard inquiry, *"Now, you have heard all the questions asked of Juror Number One and the responses of Juror Number One. If asked those same questions, would your responses differ in any material way from those given by Juror Number One?"* There was usually a negative response and the questioning would proceed on to the next juror.

This was not possible in chambers, of course, and each separate juror had to go through the long explanation of what the case was about, their individual histories and whether or not they felt they could be a fair and impartial juror in a case such as this. On the average, each potential juror's questioning in chambers took between twenty and thirty minutes. As each potential juror was escorted into the judge's chambers, they were introduced to the judge, the court clerk, the reporter, the deputy district attorney, the two defendants, their two attorneys, and the bailiff. The judge asked them to be seated, to try to relax, and not to be nervous. In spite of this, most of them appeared to feel like Daniel in the lion's den.

The majority of the questions they were asked dealt with whether or not they felt they could remain fair and impartial during testimony regarding the sexual activities portrayed in this case, including various exhibits of a sexual nature. The attorneys graphically described the activities and a number of women and a few men stated they would be too uncomfortable with such matters to serve adequately as a fair and impartial juror and were excused to serve on a different jury. Others stated they would have no problem and looked forward to it with interest.

One senior citizen in her mid-seventies was asked the question, "Would testimony regarding sex between one man and two women be upsetting for you, ma'am?" Her delightful response was, "Why, heavens no. I didn't know that was possible. I might learn something." She was so sprightly and forthright, she wound up serving on the jury even though her

husband was a retired deputy attorney general who had prosecuted cases for the state.

The old adage, *give them an inch and they'll take a mile*,
must have been formulated with attorneys in mind. As the
jury selection proceeded, the questions of the attorneys became more and more personal in nature. At one point, they almost persuaded the judge to allow them to inquire of the jurors whether or not they engaged in the type of sexual activity
depicted in this case. I could not help but be reminded of
Judge X in the Municipal Court, who had passed on to that
great Appellate Court in the sky some years earlier, and his ad-
monitions to attorneys in drunk driving trials. I thought surely
he must be spinning in his grave like a giant auger at this
point. Cooler heads and reason prevailed, however, and the
questions were not allowed.

As the case unfolded, the evidence revealed that the victim had
retired to her room one night after viewing films with the defendants and had gone to sleep. About two hours later she
was awakened when both husband and wife tied her hands behind her, put a gag in her mouth, and dragged her out of bed.
She struggled to no avail against their superior strength and
she was taken out into the garage. There, she found that they
had constructed a framework or rack with a bedspring attach-
ment, covered by a thin mattress. The four posts of the rack
had eye bolts attached to the ends. There was also a battery of
bright lights as well as a video camera. The inside of the garage door was covered with a quilt-like material, she learned
later, for the purpose of muffling the sound.

They roughly placed her on the rack, tying each foot to a
bedpost and then tied her hands to the upper bedposts in a
spread-eagle fashion. They told her they would remove the
gag if she promised not to scream out. She nodded her assent
and as soon as the gag was removed, she screamed as loudly
as she could. The husband immediately slapped her in the
mouth until she stopped screaming. Her tearful pleas to be released were ignored. They informed her they were going to
satisfy her fantasy. They then stripped her nightgown from her
and, while the husband operated the video camera, the wife

produced a razor and some shaving cream and proceeded to shave the pubic hair of the victim.

A variety of sex toys were then shown to the victim, including nipple clamps and a double dildo about two feet long, the latter being designed for *sharing*. First the wife and then the husband performed oral sex upon the victim and then forced her to do the same to them. Each time she attempted to cry out, she received another blow to the mouth. The ordeal continued for almost two hours during which time she was raped three times by the husband in addition to being penetrated by the dildo with the wife impaled on the other end of it.

Finally, their passions spent, the two released the victim, telling her she would be grateful when she had time to think about it. The victim returned to her room, got dressed and waited until she could hear the defendants sleeping in their own room. She then packed a few of her daughter's things, gathered up her sleeping daughter and fled from the house. She drove her car to the home of her boyfriend on the San Francisco peninsula. She told him what had happened and he immediately notified the police and took her to a local hospital. Medical examination confirmed that she had indeed been sexually assaulted and additionally had severe bruising appearing on her face, as well as her wrists and ankles. The defendants were arrested later that same morning and taken into custody.

The contention of the defense in this case was that the victim had shared with the defendants a fantasy of being kidnapped by a handsome lover and then ravaged while in bondage. Even if that was the case, comparing the imagined "handsome lover," someone like Robert Redford for instance, to the male defendant in this case was like comparing a shiny new Porsche to a General Sherman tank. The defendants claimed that prior to the night in question, the victim had been very irritable, had trouble sleeping, and had lost her appetite. They felt if they helped her fulfill her fantasy, she would be more relaxed and her health would improve.

One of the questions asked over and over again during the

jury selection process was, "*Do you believe a woman some-times says no, when she means yes? Or, sometimes says yes, when she means no?*" Almost as frequent was the inquiry, "*Do you believe a woman has the right to change her mind?*" Then, of course, there was the ever popular, "*Do you agree that even a prostitute can be raped?*" I was often amazed at how the potential jurors could refrain from voicing objections to being talked down to and to being asked such patronizing questions.

The prosecutor in this case was a nice looking bachelor about thirty-five years old. He had once been the grand prize in a charity auction to the highest bidder for a night on the town. Whenever an attractive young woman was questioned by him during the jury selection, there was a discernible lowering of his voice, almost to the level of an intimate whisper. I could not say whether this was deliberate or involuntary, but some of the ladies looked very uncomfortable and a few even blushed. I asked him at one of the recesses if he wanted me to run out and get him a large bib so he could drool without soiling his tie, but he never seemed to appreciate my humor.

One of the exhibits the defense tried to have admitted into evidence was a pornographic film alleged to have been viewed by the victim along with the defendants. For purposes of determining the possible admissibility of the film, it had to be viewed by the court out of the presence of the jury. The jury was therefore excused early one Friday afternoon and a VCR was set up for viewing the film in court. Our regular court clerk had previously scheduled that afternoon off on vacation and her substitute was a very prim and proper lady who had no idea of the subject matter of the trial until she came into court that afternoon.

The windows on the courtroom doors were covered, the doors were locked and the lights were turned low. The film was slightly more than an hour in length. As soon as the film began, I thought the court clerk was going to explode with embarrassment. Once she realized what it was, she refused to look up and covered her ears throughout the entire film. I wondered later why she could not have been excused, but this was an official court session and I suppose her presence was technically required. My only real purpose for being there was to record any comments relative to the film made by the court or counsel. At that stage of my life, there were very few things in this world that could shock me, other than an overdrawn check perhaps.

The thing that kept going through my mind was the irony of the fact that the county was paying all of us to sit there on a Friday afternoon, to watch a dirty movie which would have resulted in the prosecution of an adult theater manager if shown ten years earlier. As they say, however, it's a tough job, but somebody's got to do it. At the conclusion of the film, the judge was still undecided as to whether or not the jury should view the movie. He asked counsel to submit further points and authorities on Monday morning before reaching his decision. The prosecutor gallantly offered to review the film further on his own time over the weekend to aid the court in reaching a decision, but the court declined and ordered the film placed in the evidence locker. Ultimately, the court determined the film was not admissible and the jury was spared the collective embarrassment of viewing the film.

As noted earlier, juries are routinely instructed that they are not to let bias, personal feelings, prejudice, or sympathy influence their feelings for one side or the other. Even though the attorneys for both sides know this instruction will be given, they go out of their way to engender sympathy for the party they represent. The prosecution, of course, wanted the victim to appear as sympathetic as possible. The defendants faced a much greater challenge as far as gaining the sympathy of the jury, so their attorneys concentrated on trying to bring out the fact that their young child would be without parents if there was a conviction. There were, of course, objections by the prosecution each time this subject was brought up by defense counsel, but even though the court might order the comments stricken from the record, you can't unring a bell. Even the most conscientious juror might retain that thought in the back of his or her mind during deliberations.

Despite the allegations of the defense that the victim had encouraged the defendants to do what they did, either actually or subtly, the evidence was overwhelmingly against them. Although the videotape made during the assault was never found during a search of the home of the defendants, the presence in the courtroom of the rack, as well as all of the sexual toys, played a very convincing role for the jury. After a trial of two weeks, the jury returned a verdict of guilty on all counts. The matter was continued for preparation of a probation report prior to sentencing.

State prison sentences in California are divided into three major categories: a mitigated term, a midterm, or an aggravated term. The terms are pretty much self-explanatory, but for the uninitiated, a mitigated term might be selected for someone who had a minimal criminal record, showed remorse for their crime, or was not considered a threat to society. These things would all be considered by the court as mitigating factors. In contrast to that was the career criminal, who had a violent and extensive criminal record and displayed little hope for rehabilitation, as well as having used a deadly weapon during the commission of a violent crime. This type of history would merit an aggravated term. The midterm, obviously was somewhere between the two extremes. The law specified the number of years applicable for each of the three terms.

The defendants in this case had no criminal history, which must have greatly influenced the judge's sentencing decision. The prosecution was seeking a sentence of ten to fifteen years. The judge chose instead the mitigated term required by law. The defendants were sentenced to five years—with an apology from the judge for having to break up their family. The tearful victim attended the sentencing and left the courtroom alone with her thoughts, no doubt resolving to be more careful the next time she was invited to watch a movie with someone.

⚖

One of the judges in a local Municipal Court was a middle-aged lady who was very sociable. She enjoyed chatting with attorneys after a case was completed and would often have rather lengthy conversations with them after she stepped down from the bench, just prior to entering her chambers. During these formal talks, she would divest herself of her robe by unbuttoning it down the front while she talked and then put it temporarily on the back of a chair until the conversation was completed.

On one occasion she became so involved in the conversation that she evidently forgot she had removed the robe and started, subconsciously, to unbutton the front of her dress. By the time she realized her mistake, the dress was completely unbuttoned and she was standing there with her undergarments exposed. The young gentleman attorney, no doubt recalling Mrs. Robinson in *The Graduate*, beat a hasty retreat for the courtroom door. The embarrassed judge made an attempt to apologize, but by that time the shocked attorney was long gone. Talk about your judicial notice!

In November 1785, long before the invention of computers, the great Scottish poet Robert Burns wrote a poem called *To a Mouse*, which included the following verse:

> But, Mousie, thou art no thy lane,
> In proving foresight may be vain:
> The best laid schemes o' mice an' men
> Gang aft a-gley,
> An' lea'e us naught but grief an' pain,
> For promis'd joy.

If Robbie Burns had been alive in the 1970s, he may have modified that verse to include the *"best laid schemes o' mice an' judges."* Particularly if he had witnessed a further example of a judicial faux pas which occurred in a different branch of the Municipal Court when a class from a local middle school was visiting the courtroom as part of a civics assignment. The judge in this department had grown weary of the complaints and whining of people who had gotten parking tickets and wanted him to dismiss them. With that in mind, he had gone out and deliberately gotten himself a parking ticket. He kept it on the bench and when people complained to him about their parking tickets after that, he would show them his own parking ticket and tell them to pay theirs, just as he had paid his.

Judges usually bend over backwards to be attentive to visiting classes because it not only gives them a chance to explain the court system, but they know that they are speaking to future voters and sowing a few political seeds couldn't hurt. In this instance, the students were encouraged to ask any questions they had and the judge would be glad to answer them. After a slow start, the questions became more animated and varied. The class monitor tried to restrain one young man, who was evidently the class clown, but the judge called on him anyway. The judge had a slight hearing defect which occasionally affected his comprehension.

The young man asked the judge what would happen if he was having sex with his girlfriend in the back seat of his car and got a ticket. No one can say what the judge thought he heard the young man ask, but his immediate response was to wave his parking ticket in the air and state, *"I just got one myself the other night and I paid for it and I think everyone should do the same."* The students just howled and were convulsed with hysterical laughter. The judge was genuinely perplexed at their reaction until the court reporter told him what the question had actually been. At that point, he brusquely bade them all good evening and quickly retired to his chambers, leaving the court clerk and the bailiff to dismiss the class. It is highly unlikely that any school class ever had a more memorable visit to a courtroom.

Chapter Eighteen

Judge Not, Lest Ye Be Judged

THE RIGHT to a trial by a jury of our peers is one of the most precious rights Americans enjoy. This is a right unheard of in many of the most civilized countries of the world. This right is not always utilized for its intended purpose, however. It is often used to delay the pursuit of justice, rather than to enhance it. In both civil and criminal cases, the demand for a jury trial is often used by attorneys as a negotiating tool for the purpose of plea bargaining in criminal cases and achieving an acceptable settlement in civil cases. In the majority of cases there is a settlement of the case on the date set for the jury trial. With this in mind, most judges set a number of jury trials for the same date, with the safe assumption that most of them will settle before going to trial.

Previous reference was made to the fact that when traffic violations and other relatively minor offenses were defined as misdemeanors in this state, those charged were entitled to the same rights available to someone accused of a major crime. One of the primary reasons those offenses are now known as infractions was the considerable number of demands for a jury trial by people charged with running a stop sign, speeding, or even having a dysfunctional taillight. In some counties defendants soon learned that a demand for a jury trial was pretty much a guarantee of having their ticket dismissed, rather than the county expending the considerable funds necessary for the prosecution of a jury trial.

The judges at that time in the Municipal Court at Palo Alto vowed that would not be the case in this county and in their courts. Perhaps budgetary concerns were not quite as awesome as they are now, but each Friday was set aside in one department for what were known as *wise guy juries*. In ninety-nine percent of the cases, the defendants were representing themselves. This no doubt contributed greatly to the fact they were willing to stipulate to almost anything with the exception of their guilt. These jury trials were, I suspect, some of the most unique in the history of judicial proceedings. Often, three or four defendants would stipulate to the same jury hearing their cases simultaneously. There was also agreement to a jury of six persons, rather than the usual twelve, in many instances. I can recall one occasion when four separate jury trials were all held in one day.

The presentation of the evidence was extremely brief. The police officer would testify the defendant ran the red light. The defendant would testify the light was green or yellow. End of case. The jury instructions the judge was obliged to give the jurors in each case took at least four times as long as the case itself. The defendants were invariably found guilty by the juries. Most of the jurors were not too happy with the fact they had been called away from their jobs and their own concerns for something as seemingly trivial as a traffic ticket. At that time the cost to the county for bringing in each jury panel was approximately three hundred dollars, in addition to the salary of the deputy district attorney and a full court staff. When a defendant was found guilty of the charge of having a defective taillight, for instance, the fine would be seven dollars plus a two dollar penalty assessment. I think the most important lesson to be learned from all this is that it's a good thing the judges were not put in charge of administering the county budget. It is also fortunate those types of offenses are now considered infractions and the right to a jury trial does not apply to infractions.

In a perfect world there would always be great rapport between judges and their reporters. We obviously do not live in a perfect world, but in the real world about ninety percent of the time there is an excellent relationship between judge and reporter. In the rare instances where this is not the case the causes can be varied, but generally boil down to a lack of consideration on the part of either judge or reporter. If the fault lies with the reporter, such as consistent tardiness, improper behavior in court, or showing disrespect for the judge, the judge can usually hire another reporter to replace the one causing the problems. There is, however, an occasional exception to this judicial privilege.

When I began my employment in the courts of this county, the status of court reporters was somewhat in limbo. They were not technically classified as civil service employees, yet they enjoyed all the benefits of that classification, plus a good deal more. For example, they were granted vacation time during their first year of employment which would have required about ten years of service of a regular civil service employee. On the negative side, they were hired and fired at the discretion of the judge. In the Municipal Court, if a reporter's judge retired, the judge's replacement was not obliged to keep the same reporter. If the new judge had a favorite reporter who was looking for a job, the old reporter was history.

A court rule was established in the Superior Court to help protect the security of the reporter's job there. If a judge retired or died, the person appointed to fill that vacancy was required to keep the same reporter who had served the previous judge. The only exception to this rule was when a new department of the court was created, then the new judge could hire anyone he or she desired as their reporter. In one instance in the late '60s, a Municipal Court judge was appointed to fill the vacancy created by the death of a veteran Superior Court judge. The new judge wanted to bring along his old reporter from Municipal Court. The other Superior Court judges, citing the aforementioned court rule, said no. The new judge was forced to accept the reporter already employed in that department and the relationship between judge and reporter can best be described as very rocky.

The judge wasted no time in letting his reporter know that he was there under protest, thereby engendering a great feeling of resentment on the part of the reporter. They spoke to each other only when absolutely necessary and after little more than a year, two new departments were created in the court and the reporter went to work for one of the new judges who was very pleased with his services. The dissatisfied judge then immediately hired his former reporter from Municipal Court. There is no substance to the rumor that the judge told his colleagues at the next judges' meeting, *"nyah, nyah, nyah,"* but his demeanor was much more pleasant after that.

When a judicial appointment is made of someone who is rather cold and has little real concern for the welfare of others, it is fantasy to believe that the investiture of a black robe will suddenly change that person into a warm, caring human being. Sometimes judges show little consideration for their staff simply because they are mean-spirited to begin with. This is, by far, the exception rather than the rule, but it does happen occasionally. Judges operate under a handicap from which we mere mortals are exempt and which may ultimately make their jobs more difficult. When the rest of us act in a rude or imperious fashion or get out of line in some other way, there is always someone there to remind us of the high cost of dental repair work if we don't shape up. Because of their position and the power they wield, judges are, for the most part, denied these gentle corrections.

Some judges say things to attorneys which, under any other circumstances, would be considered very insulting. The attorneys are expected to grin and bear it because to do otherwise might not only be detrimental to the interests of their client, but also result in a finding of contempt of court. No matter how contemptuous an opinion of the judge the attorney may harbor in his or her mind, verbalizing it may result in some very undesirable consequences. (Of course, if a good attorney is convinced that his client's interests are being prejudiced by an obviously biased judge, the attorney has a duty to strongly advocate the rights of his client even at the risk of a few days in jail.) Judges of this type usually find themselves surrounded by a cortege of courtiers and sycophants who fervently believe the perpetual osculation of judicial derrieres may prove to be beneficial to them at some point in the future.

I knew of one reporter who, over a period of time, developed an intense dislike for his judge. They started off on a very amicable basis, but as time went by the judge's demands on the free time of the reporter became more and more frequent. The wife of the judge traveled a lot and on several occasions, at the end of a long day in court, the judge would ask the reporter to pick up his wife at the airport because he had other pressing business. This meant a round trip of about sixty miles in rush hour traffic which would result in the reporter getting home about three hours late. This was in addition to many instances of working late in the evening, long after the other courts had adjourned.

You might ask why, under those circumstances, the reporter did not resign and seek employment with another judge. Basically, the reasons were that the reporter had an excellent relationship with all of his co-workers, the calendar was very productive of transcript income, and his home was not that distant from the courthouse where he was employed. Besides, he kept hoping that things would improve. There was no improvement, however, and things continued to get worse. The judge had no idea of the cauldron of seething fury boiling just a few feet away from the bench.

Inevitably, the reporter began telling his troubles to the friendly bartender of a French restaurant about five miles from the courthouse. He would stop there on his way home and have a few drinks with some attorneys he knew and unburden himself of the latest atrocities perpetrated against him by the judge. The judge happened to be of Irish descent, so let's call him Judge Shaughnessy. Just as Norm had his special greeting when he entered *Cheers* on the television show, it became the reporter's habit to rhetorically ask the bartender, immediately upon entering the bar of the French restaurant, "You know what that son of a bitch, Shaughnessy, did today?" Soon he didn't even have to ask the question because the bartender would beat him to the punch as soon as he saw him come in. He would shout out, in his French accent, "And what deed that son of a beetch, Shaughnessy, do today, *mon ami*?" This went on for some time until one day the judge got wind of the fact that his reporter was in the habit of socializing with some of the attorneys on his way home. On one of the evenings when the judge's wife was out of town, the judge told the reporter he would like to join them for a little diversion. The reporter quickly discouraged the judge, assuring him it would be very boring for him and it would not be proper. The judge persisted, however, even offering to pay for the drinks.

Unable to dissuade him and suffering great anxiety, the reporter jumped into his car and sped off for the restaurant because he knew he had to get there before the judge did. He drove down a major thoroughfare, exceeding the speed limit, and the judge was right behind him. He ran a couple of red lights and the judge followed him relentlessly. It was much like a car chase scene from an old Steve McQueen movie. Finally, the reporter arrived at the restaurant, leaped from his car and raced inside with the judge right on his tail. As soon as he opened the door, the bartender shouted out his customary greeting, "And what deed that son of a beetch...," but he was interrupted by the reporter frantically screaming out, **"This is Judge Shaughnessy! He's going to join us for a drink tonight."** Rarely, if ever, has disaster been so narrowly averted.

⚖

Adaptability is an asset of great value to court reporters in performing their jobs. The ability to understand and comprehend the various accents and idioms of our diverse population is a skill that is developed only through experience. Strangely enough, my biggest problem in that regard was dealing with what passed for English in testimony by witnesses whose native language was the same as my own. In my earlier years as a reporter, I was lulled into believing there was a certain rhythm to the manner in which a sentence was constructed. For example, if someone were relating a previous conversation with a friend, they might be expected to say, "I told my friend what his wife said. He stated he still wasn't interested."

The court reporter, always struggling to keep up, develops a tendency to anticipate what the next word will be in a commonly used phrase, such as, "I said," "He told me," or "She asked me," etc., etc. If your assumption proves to be wrong, you can instantly correct it. Then along came the 1970s and everything changed. I think of the '70s as the decade of ugliness, not only as to fashions in clothing, shoes, and outrageous hair styles, but also as to the bastardization of the English language. I was working in Juvenile Court when I first encountered, "He goes, why? And I go, because." I stopped the witness and asked him to repeat his statement. He repeated it and I wrote it down, assuming the poor young man had been deprived of any schooling in the language skills. I soon learned his was not an isolated case. It became apparent to me that all American teenagers had sworn a mighty oath, not only to use such phrases as, "He goes" and "I go" in place of the jaded "He said" and "I said," but also such atrocities as, "We don't gots enough money for the concert." There was no doubt in my mind that this was a deliberate plot on the part of the electronic recording industry to drive reporters insane and thereby take over our jobs.

That, needless to say, put an end to my habit of anticipating what the next word would be in a previously common phrase. A short while after I partially recovered from that culture shock, the Watergate hearings were televised and introduced the nation to the ubiquitous usage of *"At that point in time."* While there is nothing grammatically wrong with that phrase, its usage soon became *de rigueur* for an attorney or a witness who was trying to appear more erudite than perhaps was justified. I guess the thing that bothered me most about that phrase was the fact that I had a stenographic brief for "at that time," but none for *"at that point in time."* Also popular during that time period (I mean at that point in time) was the valley girl vernacular selected by many young ladies as a means of communication. Somehow, *"like, totally awesome,"* did not grate on my nerves to the same extent as, "He goes" and "I go." Besides, I secretly admired their originality in the use of vocal inflection. When making such a declaratory statement as, "He looked totally awesome," they would accent the word "awesome" to make it sound like a question. Emphasizing the last word of the sentence to make it more like a question was actually more definitive of the valley girl sound than the words themselves.

While not strictly confined to the '70s, homage should also be paid to the generous and almost infinite usage of the term, "you know," which enriched our language to such a magnificent extent. Some people seemed incapable of giving you the time of day without also sharing at least six "you know's." It is my understanding that the Guinness Book of Records at one point kept track of the most times "you know" was used in one sentence, but they had to abandon the idea due to the high cost of constant revision. It seems that every time a professional athlete was interviewed on television, a new record was set and it just became too expensive. Actually, many people of this era never violated any laws, yet they still had their development arrested.

I once had a nightmare in which everyone involved in court proceedings talked in a manner which incorporated nearly all these speech variations and buzz words. Naturally, I kept a typewriter beside my bed so that I could prepare the transcript that follows:

Ms. Phitt: Like, Judge, the dude goes he read it in, you know, the paper so that's, like, hearsay and I, you know, object.

The Court: The dude gots a right to, you know, indicate the basis of his, you know, opinion because the dude's, like, an expert. So your objection is, like, overruled.

Ms. Phitt: Like, wow, man. That's totally awesome.

Mr. Smegma: May I continue my, you know, questions, like, Your Honor?

The Court: Right on.

Q (by Mr. Smegma): At that point in time, Dr. Dork, can you, like, tell us what the dude told you?

A: Well, like, the dude goes, you know, like, "Get out of my face." I go, "Your face scare me so bad, like, I wouldn't get close to your face." I thought it was, like, important to establish a good doctor/patient relationship at that point in time. You know.

Ms. Phitt: That's, like, totally rad!

The Court: Like, chill out, Counsel.

Ms. Phitt: Sorry, you know, Judge.

Q (by Mr. Smegma): At that point in time, did the dude, like, tell you why he got, you know, busted?
    (Whereupon, at this point in time, a loud, like,

explosion was heard in the, you know, jury box.)

The Court: What was that, man?

The Bailiff: Juror number six just shot himself in the, you know, head. You know?

Ms. Phitt: Oh, gross me out with a spoon!

The Court: Was he the accountant?

The Bailiff: No, he was, like, the English teacher.

The Court: Bummer.

My vocabulary was also bountifully blessed during this time by the ever changing terminology involved in drug offenses. Some of the terms made a little sense, such as a nickle bag meaning five dollars worth of marijuana, but the majority of the terms went right over my head like so much funny smoke. At this time I can recall such colorful and creative descriptions as the ever popular pot, Mary Janes, joints, roaches, bombers, doobies, angel dust, K.J., horse, speed, smack, acid, crank, crack and the indelicate *shit*. Just about the time I thought I had it all down pat, I would have occasion to work on a different calendar for a few months and by the time I returned to either Juvenile Court or a criminal calendar, so many new additions had been added to the vernacular I had to start all over.

It has always been interesting to me how certain words and phrases seem to catch on in our society. They arrive on the scene in a blaze of glory and then usually disappear, like a star that has gone nova. Phrases all the way from *Oh, you kid*, in the 1920s to Bart Simpson's *Eat my shorts* in the 1990s. Time has a way of changing the meaning of different sayings as well. When I was a teenager (no, not in the Jurassic period, but in the early '40s...and that's the 1940s), *making out* meant going all the way—scoring! These days, making out simply means what we called necking or heavy petting.

Also at that time, to be reprimanded by an employer's serious tongue lashing was commonly called being *eaten out*. I got in a lot of trouble with a young female deputy sheriff in the 1980s by using that term. She was our temporary bailiff and she had been late getting to court on one or two occasions. When I asked her if her sergeant had eaten her out for being late, she almost slapped my face. She explained to me later that the term today has a specific sexual connotation, which I had certainly not intended.

As this is being written, the current buzz words are *empowerment* and *enabling*. It seems every time I turn around, someone's empowerment is being impacted or endangered by the enabling technology of someone else. When I first began to get acquainted with a computer (still a very casual acquaintanceship), it took me a little time to understand the terminology. Wouldn't you know that just about the time I began to accept the fact that P.C. stands for personal computer, they've gone and changed that on me already. P.C. is now, of course, politically correct. Why, it's enough to emasculate my empowerment as an enabled P.C. operator and leave me just plain P.O.'d (*post officed?*).

Chapter Nineteen

Many Are Called,
But Few Are Chosen

IT IS always fascinating to observe the various approaches and methods utilized by attorneys in selecting a jury. A few attorneys adopt a very cavalier attitude towards jury selection and may accept the first twelve people called into the jury box, leaving the fate of their clients more or less up to chance. They seem to feel that their superlative skills cannot help but be obvious to any twelve people off the street. Experience proves this to be very unwise, however, because picking the right jury can be one of the most important functions a trial lawyer can perform.

In the early 1960s some attorneys seemed to pass judgment on the qualifications of jurors based upon the bumper stickers they admitted to having on their cars. It was not uncommon at that time for a defense attorney in a criminal case to inquire of a potential juror whether or not their car sported the bumper sticker, *support your local police*. Not to be outdone, the prosecution might inquire if anyone's bumper was adorned with the popular phrase, *when guns are outlawed, only outlaws will have guns*. (With reference to the latter phrase, I suggested my own version of that sticker which simply stated, *when in-laws are outlawed, only outlaws will have in-laws*. My major talent being procrastination, however, I never got around to having it circulated on a national basis.) Another sticker, favored by police officers on their private vehicles during this time when police were referred to as *pigs*, proclaimed, *if you hate cops, the next time you're in trouble, call a hippie!* One obviously religious juror confessed that the only bumper sticker he had announced that, *Jesus is coming—and boy, is he pissed!*

Jurors are also often asked which television shows they watch, what books they read, and which movies they attend. They are asked, in criminal cases, if they or any members of their family have ever been charged with or been a victim of a similar offense. In civil cases the same questions are asked as to previous accidents, injuries, or surgeries which might influence their judgment in the present case. I never ceased to be amazed at the remarkable things a skillful lawyer could compel a juror to say as if it were absolute gospel. The following *voir dire* questions of a potential juror may illustrate what I mean:

Q (by Mr. Svengali): Mrs. Dupe, the fact that my client has a swastika tattooed on his forehead, wears a dead kitten for a necklace, and smells like an outhouse will not have any bearing on you giving him a fair trial, is that correct?

A: That is correct.

Q: And if the People should prove that he has suffered seven prior convictions for this same offense, that would not tend to prejudice you against him in any way?

A: No, Sir.

Q: You will give his testimony the same credibility as you would give the police officer and the elderly victim in this case, will you not?

A: Absolutely.

Q: If, after hearing the evidence in this case, you find yourself in disagreement with all the other members of the jury in the jury room and you feel my client is not guilty, notwithstanding the fact you have been in deliberation for ten days and your only daughter is having her wedding the next morning, you will not change your vote just to get out of there?

A: Absolutely not.

Q: The fact that my client's mother intends to testify against him will not cause you to make any assumptions about his guilt or innocence?

A: Certainly not.

Q: If you were my client, would you be satisfied with twelve jurors with your same frame of mind?

A: Oh, yes, Sir.

Mr. Svengali: Pass the juror for cause, your honor.

Whether as a result of pride or intimidation, some jurors take the ability to be fair and impartial as a personal challenge. They seem intent on proving they can be just as unbiased as the next juror. One trial we had in the Municipal Court involved a woman charged with stealing merchandise from a local department store. One of the potential jurors called in that case informed the court she had been a security officer for many years at a nearby Sears store. While admitting she had dealt extensively with cases of petty theft in that capacity, she firmly maintained she could be fair and impartial in deciding the defendant's guilt or innocence. The defense attorney, to everyone's amazement, left the woman on the jury.

Out of the presence of the jury, the defendant admitted on the record several prior convictions for petty theft. Because of that admission, the prosecution was precluded from mentioning that fact to the jury. During the defendant's testimony regarding her arrest, however, she stated she had never been in such a situation before. That false statement opened the door and allowed the prosecution to bring her prior convictions to the attention of the jury.

In most instances, this would have been a fatal mistake for the defendant. The case went to the jury and after long deliberation the foreman of the jury announced that the jury was hung eleven to one and the court declared a mistrial. When the jurors were questioned later, it was learned that the lone holdout for a not guilty verdict was the security officer from Sears. Evidently her desire to prove her impartiality proved greater than her ability to recognize what was obvious to the other eleven members of the jury.

⚖

The academic community surrounding the Palo Alto area in the '60s and '70s contributed greatly to a higher than average intellectual level among people called for jury service in the local courts. It was not at all unusual to discover several college professors, scientists, or nuclear physicists on the same jury panel. Because of liberal university attitudes and the general informality of the times, the mode of dress adopted by these people left a lot to be desired. It became a generally accepted premise that the scruffier the appearance of the potential juror, the more likely it was that a Ph.D. was the least of his accomplishments.

During this time period one young deputy district attorney, who was new to the area, made a regrettable error in phrasing while selecting a jury. After asking all the other jurors individually about their various occupations, he turned his attention to juror number twelve, who, in truth, looked as though he had slept under a bridge for the last few weeks. He asked the juror, with thinly veiled contempt, "and, Mr. Frowzy, what do you do for a living—*if anything?*" The juror immediately objected to the court that he was insulted by the D.A.'s inference and an apology was instantly forthcoming. The juror turned out to be a professor of calculus at one of the local universities. The deputy district attorney had to use one of his peremptory challenges to excuse the juror because he knew he had made an enemy for life. I'm sure when his boss found out, the deputy received a few choice words about judging books by their covers.

Although attorneys usually deny it, certain occupations of potential jurors will almost always cause them to be excused by one side or the other during the jury selection process. Engineers have a very high mortality rate as far as jury service. Some attorneys feel that engineers, because of the precise and exacting requirements of their work, would demand the same high degree of proof before accepting the evidence presented. This, of course, would put a higher burden of proof on the prosecution than is required by law.

Another vocation that is frowned upon by the prosecution in criminal cases is that of social worker. Most prosecutors feel that a person trained in social work will spend more time worrying about how society failed the defendant to cause him to lead the life he does, than whether or not a crime was committed and he should be punished. Legal secretaries, investigators and insurance claims adjusters are also likely to be challenged in civil actions because the attorneys feel they possess too much inside information and might not buy the evidence presented to them.

Needless to say, practicing attorneys are almost always excused from the jury. I vividly recall one case, however, where a potential juror was not only married to an attorney, but she herself was also a member of the county Grand Jury. The prosecutor decided to take a chance and left her on the jury. When the verdict was returned, not only was the defendant acquitted, but the deputy district attorney was verbally chastised by that same lady for being rude to the defendant during his testimony.

I was surprised many, many times by very competent attorneys who seemed to lack the important instinct needed to spot a potential juror who was going to be the source of trouble if allowed to remain on the jury. Perhaps court clerks and reporters have an advantage because they see so many hundreds of jury panels, compared to a relative few by the attorneys, but many times a juror would be allowed to be sworn in whose behavior almost guaranteed future problems. It was usually easy to spot them in the audience, even before they were called to the jury box. Their mannerisms, body language, and general attitude were almost as obvious as waving a red flag.

Occasionally they would have to be stopped by the bailiff from listening to their transistor radios rather than listening to the proceedings in court. Of course, the attorneys sat with their backs to them so they could not observe their demeanor until they entered the jury box. Their responses to the inquiries of the attorneys were usually somewhat flippant and should have given the attorneys a clue, but unless they said something really outrageous, they were not challenged. Nine out of ten times, these were the jurors who kept everyone else waiting for them at the conclusion of recesses, were late getting back from lunch and whose stance during deliberations resulted in a hung jury.

I have encountered many attorneys over the years who have learned to *play* a jury just as one would a musical instrument. Many lawyers make a habit of using the court reporter as a tool for enhancing their side of the litigation before a jury. If a witness gives an answer that is favorable to their side, the attorney will feign a hearing difficulty and ask the reporter to read it back, thus giving it added emphasis in the minds of the jurors—much like a pianist who uses the sustaining pedal to emphasize a certain chord. Another trick is to loudly ask the reporter to *mark* that portion of his notes so it might be referred to later. It seldom is, but it makes the jurors think it must be very important or else it would not have been requested.

An additional ploy used by some attorneys during their final arguments (which infuriates most reporters) is to exhort the jury to have the testimony read back to them during their deliberations. While the jury has the right to have testimony reread to help them settle any conflicts in the testimony, they are usually sufficiently intelligent to decide on their own whether or not it is necessary without the urging of counsel. Most jurors take such copious notes anyhow that their collective recollections are almost as complete as the written record.

What is not taken into consideration regarding having the record read back is the fact that it takes almost as long to read it back as it does to give the testimony in the first place. If a witness testified for three days, it would take at least two days or longer to read it back—even by the fastest talking reporter. Many times an attorney will refer to it as having the *transcript* read back, which gives the impression to the jury that it is all neatly typed up and they can take it into the jury room. That is, of course, not the case and it uses up precious time the reporter could be spending in his office getting out other transcripts. Personally, the attorneys who galled me the most were the ones who would tell the jury, while smiling in my direction, *"If you have any questions, Mr. Reily will be happy to read back the entire testimony for you."* I have never really learned to appreciate other people gratuitously volunteering my services and I was often tempted to stand up and respond, "Oh, yes. And if any of you have a legal problem, Mr. Grunge will gladly represent you free of charge." Actually, all I could do was to fantasize about how nice it would be to shave the attorney's throat with a straight razor and maybe have it slip—just a little bit.

The great majority of people who serve on juries are very conscientious and take their duties quite seriously. They may be required to listen to very offensive testimony or, in some cases, crushingly boring testimony. They try diligently to follow the instructions of the court, even though some of the instructions may sound quite confusing and contradictory. The jury instructions have been formulated and compiled over a period of many years by judges, lawyers, and the legislature, yet a jury of twelve lay people is expected to absorb them in about a half hour.

There are, unfortunately, occasions when some jurors do not abide by the rules and their misconduct can result in serious consequences. Most of these occasions are not discovered until after the trial, the verdict has been rendered, and the jurors speak to the attorneys informally. Jurors are specifically instructed not to consider any evidence except that presented during the trial. Yet there have been instances where a juror has brought in a magazine dealing with the subject matter of the trial and has read it to the other jurors. I was involved in a trial concerning arson and during deliberations one of the jurors went to the library at night and made a detailed report on the subject of arson investigation and presented it to the other jurors. A verdict of guilty was returned after a long trial, but when this jury misconduct was discovered, the defendant's conviction was set aside by the trial court and he had to be retried. This, of course, meant that the tremendous expense to the taxpayers of the first trial just went down the drain and was added to the cost of the second trial.

At other times jurors have complained, after the trial, about bullying tactics on the part of other jurors and near physical violence. One man, who had a heart condition, admitted that he changed his vote because he was afraid the stress of holding out further might bring on another heart attack. Sometimes jurors will state, under oath, they have no prejudice against the police, minorities, or anyone else and then get inside the jury room and relate tales of persecution by such groups in complete contradiction to what they stated in open court.

When a verdict is rendered by a jury, the attorneys in the case have the right to ask that the jury be polled. This is done by the court clerk asking each juror individually whether or not that is his or her verdict. In civil cases there must be audible conformation that at least nine out of twelve jurors voted for the verdict. In criminal cases, of course, the verdict must be unanimous. Many times, after a lengthy period of deliberation, the polling process can become very emotional, especially when the jurors have to look the person in the eye their finding is against. Some jurors break down and cannot bring themselves to admit that that is their verdict. In such cases, the jury is sent back into the jury room for further deliberation until a verdict can be reached or it is determined that the jury is hung and there is a mistrial.

In my experience, rarely is a juror punished in any way for misconduct, other than perhaps a stern lecture by the court. I have seen instances where people who refused to answer the summons for jury duty were found in contempt of court and fined. As far as conduct that resulted in a verdict being set aside, however, the conduct would have to be extremely egregious to result in punitive action by the court. I believe this is true because there is an unwritten law whereby the court does not want to be put into an adversarial relationship with juries. The distinct provinces of the court and the jury work best when there is cooperation between the two. It is difficult enough trying to get people willing to make the personal sacrifice necessary to serve diligently on a jury without the additional worry that they might go to jail if they don't follow all the court's orders. Fortunately, only a very small percentage of juries present such problems.

One of the most basic tenets for an attorney's criminal defense before a jury is to create in the minds of that jury a reasonable doubt that the defendant is guilty. Sometimes if there is only marginal evidence of guilt, the defense attorney's job is relatively easy. However, if the evidence against the defendant is overwhelming, the task becomes much more of a challenge. Under such circumstances it is quite common for some defense attorneys to attempt to put everyone on trial *except* the defendant. I have seen rape cases where an effort was made to portray the victim, who looked as innocent as Julie Andrews, as little more than a hooker who had just begged to be brutalized and have her eyes blackened and her teeth knocked out.

In drunk driving cases, where the blood alcohol reading is extremely high, there is usually an attempt made by the defense to claim a mistake on the part of the district attorney's crime lab. The reasoning being that, while the defendant may have had a few drinks, he certainly did not drink enough to reach *that* level so the analyst must have mixed up the sample with one belonging to someone else. Even the prosecutor is not exempt from insinuations by the defense that the case would have been dismissed by a more experienced prosecutor. However, the police, by far, are the greatest target of allegations and accusations by the defense when the defendant doesn't have a leg to stand on. For many years the credo has been said to be, *"when you don't have a case, try the police officer."* Charges against the police may range anywhere from mistaken identity to racism to police brutality or that the officer was prejudiced against the defendant because he had a bad hair day. Any one of these allegations just might trigger a memory in the mind of a juror of the time he was given a ticket he didn't deserve by a very mean cop and, therefore, maybe what the defense is claiming is true. And you know what? Once in a while it works. It only takes one juror to cause a hung jury and when that happens, it is a partial victory for the defense. At the very least it gives the defendant more room to negotiate a plea to a lesser charge so the People may avoid the expense of another trial. Of course, if the jury is hung eleven to one for acquittal, the defendant may successfully move for a dismissal of the charges—assuming the victim was not the judge's grandmother.

In the trial of criminal cases, the most difficult challenge for many jurors seems to be the reasonable doubt instruction. Although many defense lawyers will stand before the jury and tell them their clients can be convicted only if the jury finds them guilty *beyond all shadow of a doubt*, that is not what the instruction says. In most cases when this happens, the prosecutor will either object or the judge will remind the jurors that what the attorneys say is not evidence; it is only their interpretation of the evidence. The instruction itself reads as follows:

A defendant in a criminal action is presumed to be innocent until the contrary is proved, and in case of a reasonable doubt whether his guilt is satisfactorily shown, he is entitled to an acquittal, but the effect of this presumption is only to place upon the state the burden of proving him guilty beyond a reasonable doubt. Reasonable doubt is defined as follows: it is not a mere possible doubt, because everything relating to human affairs, and depending on moral evidence, is open to some possible or imaginary doubt. It is that state of the case, which, after the entire comparison and consideration of all the evidence, leaves the minds of jurors in that condition that they cannot say they feel an abiding conviction, to a moral certainty, of the truth of the charge.

This instruction has probably helped more guilty defendants walk out of the courtroom to freedom than any of the skills displayed by the attorneys in their trials. Conversely, it very well may have resulted in the acquittal of many people charged with a crime who were truly innocent. The problem many jurors have with this instruction is defining in their own minds just what is reasonable. Some jurors feel that if a defendant swears under oath that he is innocent of the alleged crime, that is cause for reasonable doubt. After all, they reason, he was under oath. Other jurors determine that if the defendant is truly guilty of having committed an armed assault, for instance, he would not hesitate to perjure himself.

The more astute jurors will simply accept that instruction along with all the other instructions and then attempt to reach a just and proper verdict. The majority of jurors are sufficiently intelligent to decide, if the case for the prosecution is very weak, to acquit the defendant—even though they may think he is probably guilty—because the case was simply not adequately proven according to the instructions given to them by the court. It is almost a given, however, that when a jury in a criminal trial asks the court to repeat some of the instructions to aid them during their deliberations, the reasonable doubt instruction is number one on their list.

⚖

I have previously commented about how despicable I consider the crime of child molestation, which hardly makes me unique. It is a charge, however, which falls into a special category. Those charged with this crime are, of course, to be considered innocent until proven guilty, as is the case with any other crime alleged to have been committed in this country. The defendant does not have to prove his innocence. The People have to prove his guilt. Yet, when a defendant is found not guilty of this charge, there is always a nagging doubt in the minds of people—family, friends, business associates—that the charge may have been true. The stigma of such a charge is very difficult to escape even after an acquittal.

With this in mind, there has been a devastating tendency over the last decade to allege such conduct in many bitterly contested custody battles. Belief in the old bromide, *all's fair in love and war* is never more evident than in a fierce divorce action where custody of the children is at stake. Sometimes the hatred and bitterness is so great that one parent does not even want the other to be entitled to visitation with the child. If the party making the allegation truly believes it is true, then those feelings are understandable. Too many times, however, revenge is the sole basis for making such a claim.

When the seed of such an accusation is planted, there is usually a bountiful harvest of suspicion and skepticism as to the character of the accused. Regardless of how irrational the claim may seem to be, the court cannot ignore it. Immediate steps must be taken to ensure the safety and welfare of the child and to begin a thorough investigation of the party accused, with the aid of the Children's Protective Services, while recommending professional counseling for all the parties involved.

One such custody battle in our department took seventeen days to try, which was a result of a failed custody stipulation that had been agreed to in a different department of the court a year earlier and which had been reached only after months of negotiations. The child in question was slightly more than three years old. The father of the child was a physician and the mother was a registered nurse. The father had remarried and had a child by his new wife. His new wife was younger than his former wife. The former wife alleged that while spending time with the father, the child was improperly touched and thereby traumatized. She also alleged that indecent photographs had been taken of the child, as well as alleging the father's ingestion of cocaine in front of the child.

Medical evidence in the case indicated that the child suffered from a recurring vaginitis condition. It was evidently the father's attempts to treat this condition which resulted in the mother's allegation of molestation. There was an admission by the mother that, while using a tape recorder, she and her sister had interrogated the child for six and one half hours into the wee small hours of the morning. After that length of time it would not be unreasonable to assume the child's fatigue would have persuaded her to agree to anything the mother might have suggested. During the testimony of the main therapist who testified in behalf of the mother, it was revealed that during the interviews with the child, the child refused to even speak to the therapist if she saw a tape recorder in the room.

This same therapist had been appointed by the court to make a custody evaluation regarding the child and then, on her own volition, decided to extend her investigation further into the allegation of possible molestation. She interviewed both sets of grandparents, the mother and father of the child separately, and then conducted a number of further interviews with the child alone. She read transcripts made from the tapes the mother had made of the child and it became obvious to the father that the therapist considered him guilty of molesting his own daughter. During his interview with the therapist, he became so angry that he threw a cup of coffee in her face, thereby guaranteeing the removal of any vestige of impartiality she may have retained.

Prior to these interviews, the mother had alerted the police department of the community in which the father resided about her suspicions regarding cocaine usage in front of the child. A search warrant was executed of the father's residence and no trace of any drugs was discovered. The father did confess to having taken some photographs of his daughter while she was in the bathtub—an act which, if deemed criminal, would indict most parents of young children.

The rights of the child in this case were protected by a court-appointed attorney who performed her assignment very capably, despite being in the awkward position of being caught in the middle between the two adversaries. The testimony of the therapist on direct examination by the mother's attorney was devastatingly incriminating against the father. On cross-examination by the father's attorney, however, as well as the child's attorney, it left something to be desired. A large number of drawings which had been made by the child were introduced in evidence. There were drawings of houses, balloons, and people, along with a variety of other subjects. The therapist alleged that almost every drawing by the child contained some phallic symbols. A balloon on a string, for example, was representative of a testicle and the string to which it was attached was identified as pubic hair by the therapist.

If a drawing portrayed a person, the inclusion of a navel was an indication that the child was obsessed by sexuality because she could only know about navels if she had seen her father naked. If there were pictures of houses, the portrayal of a domed roof was irrefutable proof of molestation, based on the therapist's extensive history of doing evaluations of children, because a domed roof could only be identified with a penis. She later recanted this latter claim, when confronted with the works of experts who had done evaluations of children from the Middle East. One of the drawings was supposed to represent a picture of the child's bedroom. The picture showed a series of dots on the wall of the bedroom, which the therapist interpreted as being ejaculate stains. A photograph was later produced of the child's bedroom which revealed the walls were covered by a floral wallpaper design featuring little dots of flowers.

As the testimony by the therapist continued, I could not help but be reminded of Humphrey Bogart's excellent portrayal of Captain Queeg in Columbia Picture's adaptation of the *Caine Mutiny* by Herman Wouk. At any moment I fully expected the therapist to begin rolling around a pair of steel ball bearings in her hand, just as the skipper of the U.S.S. Caine had done whenever he was under pressure. Subsequent to the testimony of the therapist, there was testimony by a substantial number of other therapists, psychologists, and psychiatrists who testified that the child enjoyed an excellent relationship with her father and they could find no evidence of any molestation. It was the finding of the court that there had been insufficient evidence presented to prove the allegation of molestation, drug usage, or indecent photography.

Because this was a civil action (*although the parties were very uncivil to each other*) the level of proof required was a preponderance of the evidence. This is usually demonstrated to juries by envisioning the scales of justice which start out equal on both sides. If there is the slightest tipping of one side of the scale, then the trier of fact must find in favor of the side which preponderates. In a criminal case the level of proof is beyond a reasonable doubt. In that instance, the scale would have to be completely tipped in favor of the prosecution. A civil case, therefore, requires less proof than a criminal case.

The fact that the father of the child was never charged in the Criminal Court leads to the logical assumption that the hard evidence was just not there. Prior to the breaking down of the stipulation which resulted in this hearing, the shared custody arrangement had been that the child would spend half the week with her mother in Southern California and then fly up to Northern California for the rest of the week. I could not help observing that such an arrangement must have created a great deal of stress for a three-and-a-half-year-old child. All parents have their priorities, however, and must handle them as they see fit. The only thing more certain than the fact that the child was a victim in this case, one way or another, is the fact that the therapist who testified for the mother is no longer used by the court for purposes of evaluating possible molestation victims.

⚖

For many years after I began my court reporting career, whenever the court clerk would administer the oath to a prospective witness, I would not write it down verbatim. I would simply note on the record: (*witness sworn*). I would do the same thing when the oath was administered to a jury, except the notation would read: (*jury sworn by clerk*). I had one trial, however, which caused me to change this practice forever. I was working in a different department than was customary and a jury had been selected and sworn in by the clerk. There was an immediate request by defense counsel for a recess because he wanted to put something on the record out of the presence of the jury.

As soon as the jury was excused, the defendant's attorney stated that the clerk had sworn the jury to make a finding for the plaintiff in the case. He then asked me to read back the oath and I had to confess that I had not taken it down. The clerk, however, stated that he had indeed administered such an oath and apologized because he had not had a jury trial in many years. When the jury returned to the courtroom, the judge explained the error and had the clerk administer the proper oath, including the phrasing that they would "try the case fairly and impartially and a just decision render, to the best of their ability." From that moment on, I always made it a point to write down everything the clerk had to say, with the possible exception of an occasional sneeze or an involuntary expression of flatulence.

Chapter Twenty

Driving Out Demons

UNTIL THE late 1960s, people in the State of California who were committed to state mental hospitals and deemed to be mentally ill might well have thought they were locked up and the key thrown away. Responding to the public outcry over this practice of simply *warehousing* these patients for an indefinite period of time, the California Legislature enacted a law which became effective July 1, 1969, called the Lanterman-Petris-Short Act, named for the authors of the bill. This law, now included in the California Welfare and Institutions Code as section 5001, states its purposes, in part, in the following general provisions:

> *To end the inappropriate, indefinite and involuntary commitment of mentally disordered persons, developmentally disabled persons, and persons impaired by chronic alcoholism, and to eliminate legal disabilities; to guarantee and protect public safety; to safeguard individual rights through judicial review; and to protect mentally disordered persons and developmentally disordered persons from criminal acts.*

Under the provisions of this law, if a determination is made by competent medical authority that a person is a danger to others, himself or herself, or gravely disabled as a result of mental disorder, that person may be detained for no longer than 180 days without a judicial review. On a preliminary basis, section 5150 of this law authorizes the detention, treatment, and evaluation of an individual for a period not to exceed seventy-two hours, providing a Superior Court judge determines, based on medical evidence, that the previously stated criteria have been met. This law also provides for court-appointed counsel or the public defender to protect the rights of the person whose detention is sought by the People.

In these hearings, the People are usually represented by the county counsel who adduces evidence by nurses, psychiatrists and therapists who have examined the individual and who give their reasons why they feel the subject should be detained. These are not criminal hearings and therefore, the person the People want detained is not a defendant, but rather a respondent to the petition of the People. These hearings are held at least twice a week in the Superior Court and they are referred to as LPS hearings—shorthand for Lanterman-Petris-Short, the authors of the legislation.

I have reported many of these hearings and while few things are more tragic than mental disorders, these situations often have their lighter side. It is obviously not my intent to ridicule people suffering an infirmity as that would be morally indefensible. I also firmly believe in the old saying that people who live in glass houses shouldn't throw stones. Besides, most of the humor is a result of the actions of other people in the hearings, rather than the respondents themselves. It is a fact, however, that some of the hearings are less doleful than others.

One such hearing that stands out in my mind involved a respondent testifying about voices that spoke to him from outer space. He told the judge the voices often emanated from flying saucers and, to emphasize his point, turned suddenly to the window and stated, *"There goes one right now!"* The judge reflexively craned his neck to peer out of the window, before realizing what he was doing. When reality set in, his face turned red and he made a rather futile attempt to regain his dignity and look cool again. Fortunately, this was not a jury trial or he would have had twelve more reasons to be embarrassed.

Sometimes people who have mental problems display such convincing evidence of lucidity that it requires astute perception by the judge to determine the fact that there is a real basis for the detention request. It is of primary importance in these hearings that the respondents try to convince the judge that they are able to provide for their own food, housing, clothing, and personal hygiene as well as guarantee they will take their medication as prescribed. In one such case in 1984, a lady respondent's answers to the judge's questions all seemed to be quite adequate and she seemed well on her way to obtaining a favorable ruling by the court.

She then stated to the court that her fiancé, with whom she planned to live if released, was a pilot and she greatly enjoyed flying with him in his plane. When the judge asked her to state his name, she proudly announced that he was Jimmy Doolittle. There was no reaction whatsoever by the attorneys to this revelation by the witness. With the exception of the respondent who was testifying, the judge, the clerk, and the reporter were the only ones at the hearing old enough to recognize the name of Jimmy Doolittle. Both the deputy county counsel and the deputy public defender were just barely in their thirties and did not recognize the name of the air force general who led the first bombing raid on Japan in World War II. After further inquiry verified that was indeed the same person referred to by the respondent, the judge had no difficulty in making his decision. Her fate might have been much different had she appeared before a younger judge.

During my early years in the courts of Montana, I had only a few occasions to report hearings involving rulings on the sanity of a person, but they were quite memorable in their own right. In one instance a gentleman was alleged to be so violent the authorities did not want to risk bringing him into the courtroom, which was located on the third floor of the courthouse. It was decided, therefore, that the hearing would be conducted outside so the gentleman could remain secure in the back seat of a car. Accompanied by the judge and the clerk, I took my machine, along with a chair, and set up shop as best I could just outside the car door.

At that time the temperature was around twenty-eight degrees and the wind was blowing with near gale force. The paper my notes were being written on was blowing all over the place and I considered it a minor miracle I was able to salvage my notes. My fingers were almost frozen by the time we finished and I had serious doubts about whose sanity was in question—the respondent, seated comfortably inside a nice warm car, or the freeze-dried reporter, scrambling after his notes and trying to write everything down before the ink froze in his machine.

On another occasion, a gentleman who was considered non-violent appeared in the judge's chambers for a sanity hearing and, like so many others, seemed to fade in and out of reality. During the latter part of his hearing, he seemed to be completely rational and in touch with what was going on. After the judge, who was a bit rotund, asked him if he understood all of the legal rights he had just been advised of, he stated he did, but he had one question. The judge asked him what it was and the gentleman inquired, *"Did the county pay for that fat belly of yours or did you pay for it yourself?"* There was no audible response from the judge, but his face looked as if there had been a sudden forty degree increase in the room temperature of his chambers. The attendants in charge of the respondent displayed remarkable self-control in maintaining a straight face. One can only surmise the level of their outburst, once they had safely exited the court's chambers.

Section 5302 of the aforementioned LPS law in California grants the right of a jury trial to persons who have been previously certified to mental hospitals and feel they should now be released. It further grants them the right to be represented at that trial by the public defender. Even though it is not a criminal case, the jury's verdict is required to be unanimous. One jury had a rather unforgettable experience during the presentation of the case of a young man who had been detained at a state mental hospital for a number of years.

The People called the usual parade of witnesses consisting of psychiatrists, psychologists, and hospital personnel who testified to the respondent's behavior, which they had observed at the hospital over a span of years. They painted a pretty dismal portrait, citing numerous instances of failure to cooperate, refusal to take his medication, refusal to bathe, and assaultive behavior towards other patients as well as the staff personnel. They also testified to several attempted rapes of other patients, as well as a general disdain for responsibility of any type.

When it became time for the respondent to try to convince the jury that he should be released, he testified that none of the allegations made by the witnesses for the People were true. He stated that he was very cooperative and considerate with everybody and that, more than anything else, he was a very responsible person. Near the end of his testimony, his attorney asked him if there was something he wished to show to the jury and he said there was. He reached into his pocket and withdrew a long, unrolled condom. He slowly swung it back and forth before the jury and stated, *"This proves what a responsible person I am because I use this every time I have sex."*

The deputy county counsel almost swallowed her pencil. To their credit, not a single member of the jury even cracked a smile. I am sorry to say the same cannot be said for the clerk and the reporter. After considering all the evidence, the decision of the jury was to return the respondent to the hospital for further treatment. The clerk was particularly gratified that she had not been required to receive any exhibits in evidence in this case.

Often the people who are brought before the court in these LPS hearings must be heavily sedated prior to their court hearing to ensure that they will not become violent or disrupt the court in some other fashion. Hopefully, the attorneys representing them are free of sedation by the time of the hearing. In one such case, the respondent was in a very somnolent state. His speech was extremely slow and he seemed to have little awareness of the proceedings. As the hearing progressed and the various doctors testified as to his condition, he seemed to take more interest in their testimony to the extent of mumbling something each time they spoke. His muttering eventually became more distinct and it was soon apparent that each statement of the doctor evoked the response from the respondent, "F-u-u-c-c-k y-o-u-u-u, D-o-c." The words were laboriously drawn out, but unmistakable.

Judges are, of necessity, very tolerant with the respondents in these hearings, but finally the judge decided to admonish the respondent that he must remain silent. This seemed to be effective for a few minutes, but then the doctor said something else the respondent disagreed with and once again voiced the painfully slow, "F-u-u-c-c-k y-o-u-u-u, D-o-c." At that point the judge sternly advised the respondent that he was ordered to remain silent. Without batting an eye, the respondent answered, "F-u-u-c-c-k y-o-u-u-u, J-u-u-d-g-e."

The judge's face grew red with frustration and embarrassment because, under the circumstances, there was little he could do about the respondent's behavior. Fortunately, the hearing ended shortly thereafter and the respondent was ordered held for further treatment. There were a number of attorneys in the audience, however, whose faces revealed the likelihood that they would have gladly changed places with the respondent for that brief moment in order to be able to express the same sentiment with impunity.

In this part of the western world it seems that there is open season all year long in the sport of attorney-bashing. While some of this is no doubt justified, a lot of it is not. Many attorneys provide a great deal of service to the courts, as well as doing pro bono (free) work for indigent clients, without any compensation whatsoever. Attorneys in this state frequently volunteer their services as a judge pro tempore, more popularly known as a pro tem judge. These pro tem judges are granted, on a temporary basis, the same legal authority to make binding rulings and judgments as a regular appointed or elected judge.

These assignments usually are for only one day because most attorneys cannot afford to leave their private practice any longer than that. There are some exceptions, however, where a pro tem judge may serve throughout a whole trial of several days, but these are generally older and more successful attorneys who need not be concerned about the loss of income to their practice. All parties to the litigation must agree to have their case heard by a pro tem judge. If either side declines, then the case is put over until a regular judge can hear it. This usually results in the case being continued for a matter of weeks or even months, so there is a great time saving advantage in presenting your case to a pro tem judge.

In my experience the greatest service a pro tem judge performs for the court is in domestic cases and in hearing settlement conferences. These calendars are usually quite backed up and without the services of pro tem judges would be almost unmanageable. Great effort is made to ensure that the pro tem judge has extensive experience and expertise in the subject matter of the trial he or she is asked to preside over. For example, an attorney who specialized in probate work would not be assigned a domestic case to try. This has not always been the case, however.

In the late 1970s, I was given the assignment of working for a pro tem judge one afternoon and found that the presiding judge had referred two LPS hearings to be heard before the pro tem judge. The first case to be presented involved a lady who, the evidence revealed, had been in and out of mental hospitals for more than twenty years. She was one of the most pitiful respondents I had observed in these hearings. She was hallucinating right in court and stated she saw people walking through the walls, coming to get her. When she testified, she asked for a drink of water. The bailiff brought her a cup of water and as soon as she tasted it, she screamed out her throat was burning because the bailiff had given her acid to drink.

There was abundant medical evidence presented to attempt to establish her diagnosis as a paranoid schizophrenic with little, if any, hope for recovery. There was also ample evidence that the respondent had no income, no means of support, and no place to live. I assumed, based on all the evidence and the symptoms exhibited by the respondent in court, the pro tem judge's decision was a foregone conclusion. Instead, the judge decided to release the respondent from her seventy-two hour detention and further treatment. I was so shocked that I asked the judge to repeat his decision, fearing I had misheard it. He repeated the same ruling, at which time the county counsel made a motion to challenge the judge from hearing the second case which had been assigned to him. The motion was denied on the basis that once there had been agreement that the two cases could be heard before a pro tem judge, it was too late to challenge the judge at this juncture.

The respondent in the second case was a gentleman who appeared to be in at least one hundred percent better condition than the lady in the previous case. There was minimal evidence presented as to the serious nature of his condition, his living conditions seemed adequate and he had the support of family members. After consideration of the evidence, the judge decided that the seventy-two hour detention was a necessity in the second case and the gentleman was held for further observation and treatment. This took place late on a Friday afternoon. I was so astonished by the performance of the pro tem judge that I called the deputy county counsel on Monday morning and offered to read back my notes of the hearing to the presiding judge. He thanked me, but said it wasn't necessary because the lady in question had evidently regained sufficient lucidity to voluntarily commit herself for further treatment and care. Up until the time of my retirement in 1990, I never heard of another assignment of an LPS case to a pro tem judge in this county.

One lady, who was a ward of the court under a conservatorship, almost became a fixture around the courthouse for a number of years. She was not deemed to be a danger to herself or others, but she was not capable of handling her own finances, such as making her house payments or managing her own bank account. This lady, who I will call Mrs. Morton, was always dressed impeccably and carried a briefcase with her most of the time and looked, for all intents and purposes, like a very successful attorney. She was an attractive middle-aged lady who carried herself with an air of great confidence and dignity.

She enjoyed attending court hearings as a spectator and, for the most part, created no problems. On occasion, however, she would shout out something inappropriate or react in a bizarre fashion. She had to be removed from the courtroom in one instance for blowing kisses to all the members of the jury.

In another case, she stood with all the other spectators when the judge entered the courtroom, but when everyone else sat down she complained loudly that her clothes were soiled from the oily hair of the man in front of her, who happened to be a very bald and embarrassed attorney.

This type of behavior might have been expected of someone who went about with glazed eyes, tangled hair, and was generally unkempt in their appearance. This lady looked very professional, however, and that added to the shock of many people who engaged her in conversation, only to do a double take and move away a few moments later. One day I was waiting in the lobby of the courthouse for an elevator and I was bumped very hard from behind. I immediately presumed it was some friend of mine clowning around. I turned around, raising my fist in a mock stance of attack, only to discover it was Mrs. Morton.

She screamed loudly that I was trying to attack her and demanded that I be arrested by the deputy sheriff in the lobby because I was a communist and I had also murdered the emperor of Mexico. Fortunately, the deputy knew both of us and the matter ended there. For reasons unknown to me, she always recognized me when she would see me out of court. Perhaps it was because of my large mustache which distinguished me from the court clerk (hers was smaller), but every time I found myself in the vicinity of Mrs. Morton she had some embarrassing comment to make to the people around her. Once I strolled through the courthouse lobby and she shouted out, *"There goes that communist who draws pictures of naked girls on the courthouse walls!"* I swear I never did any murals of naked girls. At least not on the courthouse walls.

I don't know why she thought I was a communist, unless it was because I had red hair. One evening I had reason to visit a local medical facility and no sooner had I entered the lobby than I encountered Mrs. Morton. Even though I was dressed in jeans and a sweat shirt, she recognized me and ran to the information booth in the lobby, shouting that I was a communist and should be arrested. Evidently the people staffing the booth were familiar with her and pretty much ignored her dire warnings. She eventually stopped frequenting the courthouse and I have no knowledge of whatever happened to the poor soul. I can only conjecture that she would have made an excellent lieutenant for Joe McCarthy, the late Senator from Wisconsin, had she been around in the '50s.

Some attorneys who volunteer their time as pro tem judges walk a thin line between a feeling of true altruism and the heady enjoyment of a sense of power and prestige, however temporary it may be. I had the misfortune once of being assigned as the reporter for a pro tem judge I will call Judge Dull, who enjoyed his role as a judge so much that he volunteered to hear jury trials, some of which lasted for several weeks. He could do this because he had been a member of a prestigious law firm which made him independently wealthy and he was free of the usual worries about lost income.

I must admit that he handled the jury cases very capably and the presiding judge was very grateful for his service in relieving the backlog of jury trials. His attitude towards the court staff assigned to him, however, was complete indifference. He thought nothing of going on for hours without a recess and, while most courts adjourned their jury trials between 4:30 and 5:00 P.M. to give the jurors a jump on the rush hour traffic, he would often continue his trials until 6:00 P.M.

During one trial I informed him that I absolutely had to leave at 5:00 P.M. that evening to drive my family to the airport because they were flying to Disneyland for a vacation. At 4:55 that afternoon, one of the trial attorneys wanted to call a new witness to the stand. The judge informed him that even though it would be preferable to proceed and it would help in expediting the conclusion of the trial, not to mention being more convenient for the jury, the court reporter had made other plans and court would be forced to recess at 5:00 P.M. Nothing like being made the goat for daring to request adjournment at the same time all the other courts adjourned.

When the trial of that case was concluded, it went to the jury for deliberation in the late afternoon. The jury took a break for dinner and then resumed their deliberations. As the hours passed, there was no indication of a verdict. Most judges will permit the jury to deliberate for a reasonable period of time, but then send them home for a good night's rest so they may return with a fresh outlook in the morning. This is not only for the jury's benefit, but also for the benefit of the court staff. Sometimes even if the jury desires to continue its deliberation, if the hour is too late the judge will send them home.

I had to be available in the event the jury wanted testimony read back. The pro tem judge and the trial attorneys decided to avail themselves of the hospitality of a nearby cocktail lounge, with instructions to the clerk to call them if the jury had a question or reached a verdict. Finally, at 12:45 A.M., the jury indicated they had reached a verdict. The pro tem judge and the attorneys were summoned from the local gin mill where they had been drinking *coffee* and they hurried back to court. The judge remarked to me facetiously that he had been considering sending the jury out to breakfast. By that time I was steaming and I told him I thought that was about as funny as a broken leg and that I didn't get a dime's worth of overtime for staying so late. He later reported my *disrespectful attitude* to my supervisor, but under the circumstances no action was even contemplated.

By the time the verdict was rendered and the jury polled and excused, it was close to 2:00 A.M. The icing on the cake for me was the revelation that the gentleman working as the court clerk had just had his driver's license suspended because of an alcohol problem and he had no way home since the buses did not run that late. After driving him home, I reached my home at around 2:45 A.M. With my family in Disneyland, I could only vent my frustration by whining to my dog. He just yawned sympathetically and went back to sleep. All things considered, it was not one of my better days—or nights.

This same pro tem judge was so fond of being a judge that he often wore his black robe while walking in the corridor or taking the elevator downstairs for coffee. Many people in the courthouse assumed he was a regular judge and addressed him as Judge Dull. Eventually he became so enamored with the idea he decided to challenge one of the incumbent judges who was running for re-election. He began a vigorous campaign, making serious allegations against the incumbent judge. As previously noted, money was no object in his campaign and he invested heavily in billboards and newspaper advertising. The game of politics being what it is, however, once the incumbent judge suggested the public might be interested in the challenger's previous conviction for wife beating, the would-be judge decided to withdraw from the race and ended his quasi-judicial career.

As an example of the other side of the coin, I was contacted once by a lady whose divorce action I reported before a pro tem judge and she wanted a transcript of that hearing because she thought the order prepared by her attorney was in error. I was so deluged with requests for transcripts that if the hearing was no more than about five minutes, I would often ask people if they would be satisfied with me reading my notes to them over the telephone, for which there would be no charge. (*I can hear the muttering of other reporters now!*) This lady agreed to that procedure. Her contention was that her husband had been ordered to assume the debts of the parties and the order prepared by her attorney stated that she was to assume the debts. A reading of my notes verified that she was correct in her recollection of the pro tem judge's order.

She further informed me that her attorney agreed that the order he prepared was in error, but that it would cost her another five hundred dollars to go back to court to have the order corrected. He wanted her to pay to rectify the mistake he had made in her case. I told her I would call her back and I contacted the attorney who had served as the pro tem judge in the case. I explained the situation to him and read back the entire hearing to refresh his recollection. He told me to call the lady back and have her bring him the order and he would correct it on its face free of charge.

I informed the lady of the pro tem judge's willingness to assist her and she was very gratified. I also suggested she might wish to contact the County Bar Association and report her former attorney's attempted extortion, but I doubt if she ever followed through with it. The same attorney still has a full page ad in the yellow pages of the telephone directory, advertising his skill and expertise in domestic cases. I hope it doesn't sound as if I am participating in attorney-bashing because I have no license, poetic or otherwise, to do so. After all, if it weren't for attorneys and judges, I would have had no career and might still be contemplating the beginning of page one of this book. (*Upon reflection, I probably should have given it more thought.*)

⚖

It must be gratifying to have one's accomplishments recognized on an international level. A few years ago, one of our local judges was assigned to a calendar dealing with criminal defendants who had violated their probation and were facing sentencing to prison. One of the defendants who appeared before him had made no attempt at all to abide by the terms of his probation. He had failed to even contact his probation officer after having been granted probation. He had been subsequently apprehended for other violations and the recommendation of the Probation Department was that he be sentenced to prison. The defendant, of course, wanted his probation reinstated. The judge declined and sentenced him to a term in the state prison. After the sentencing, the defendant, who was in custody and wearing jail clothing, asked if he might make a statement. The judge agreed and the defendant spun around, dropped his pants and mooned the judge while yelling, *"Go to hell!"* The defendant and his pants were immediately removed from the courtroom and the judge apologized to the spectators in the audience. A few days later the defendant pled guilty to a charge of indecent exposure, which added another six months to his prison sentence.

Several weeks later, a local attorney advised the judge that while he had been vacationing in Africa he purchased a copy of the *London Times* and was very impressed to find that the mooning of the judge in San Jose had been duly noted in that distinguished daily. Once again, international acclaim must be very rewarding and must make all the hard work that is necessary to achieve it seem worthwhile.

Chapter Twenty-one

The Law Is Good
If a Man Use It Lawfully

I SERVED as an enlisted man in the U.S. Navy from 1948 to 1952. I would be in a much higher income tax bracket now if I had a dollar for every time some old salt with twenty years or more of experience told me that in the *old navy*, whenever the navy sponsored a social event open to both officers and enlisted men, the announcement would invite officers and their *ladies* and enlisted men and their *women*. I never actually saw such an announcement myself, so it is possible this story was merely one of the many legends passed on to gullible young sailors. Quite apart from the naval regulations prohibiting fraternization between officers and enlisted personnel, however, there was definitely a covert effort on the navy's part to encourage an active caste system.

There is a caste system also, to a much lesser degree of course, among judges, attorneys, and in some cases even among court reporters. Many corporate attorneys, ensconced in their high-rise luxury suites, look down contemptuously upon the district attorneys and public defenders fighting in the trenches each day in court, simply because the corporate lawyers are paid a great deal more than their brethren (*and sistern?*) who look to the public for compensation. The fact that many of the corporate attorneys do not possess a fraction of the skills of the public attorneys, developed through daily experience in court, does not seem to be a part of their equation.

The alleged justification for such an attitude seems to be, *"I must be better or they wouldn't pay me more."* As is the case with most caste systems, the bottom line for establishing a delineation always seems to be the amount of income of the respective parties.

In the early 1960s, when women first began to swell the ranks of attorneys, they were confronted by a very thriving *old boy* network which consisted not only of male attorneys, but also many judges on the bench at that time. There was much rolling of the eyes and subtle winks between the male-dominated bench and bar whenever some fledgling female attorney was attempting to make her point in court. Some of the more experienced women lawyers did little to dispel such prejudice by creating a persona of eccentricity which only added to the myth that women lawyers should not be taken seriously. I can recall one such attorney who was very successful and who made herself famous in Los Angeles and San Francisco simply by the outrageous hats she wore when appearing in court. Regardless of her considerable legal talents, she was much more famous for her hats than for her victories in court. (I could never understand why, if a man was forced to remove his hat or cap when appearing in court, a woman could appear before the court wearing a hat that would have made Carmen Miranda jealous and it was perfectly acceptable.)

On the other hand, when some male attorneys developed a *trade mark* that set them apart from others, it was not considered a reflection on all the rest of the male members of the bar. The members of one law firm in San Jose, consisting of a father and his two sons, made themselves somewhat unique by always wearing a bolo or string tie when appearing in court. Another elderly attorney had a fixation on Abraham Lincoln to the extent that he grew his beard in the same shape as Lincoln's and also wore a long, stovepipe hat, and clothing suitable for that time period. He gave out Lincoln-head pennies along with his business cards and he even had a mole on his face similar to that of Honest Abe. He was not as tall as Lincoln, but there was enough similarity to cause a lot of double takes by people who casually sat next to him in court.

As time goes by (*what a great title for a song!*), things tend to even out. As more and more women entered the legal profession—and more women were appointed to the bench—a grudging recognition of their talents helped them gain the reluctant respect of their male counterparts. At least in most instances. There are still a few remaining diehards even today who not only would consider trying a case against a female adversary completely repugnant, but would do everything in their power to avoid appearing before a female judge.

One such attorney who comes to mind was a fiery Italian (oh, I forgot about being P.C. *Italian-American!*) who was always getting in shouting matches and even fistfights with his opponents in and out of court. For these purposes, I will call him Mr. Zucchini. I liked to refer to him as the Billy Martin of the Santa Clara County Bar because despite his proclivity for somewhat violent behavior, he was very good at what he did. His sarcasm in court and his profanity out of court were legendary.

In 1970 my son and I participated in a YMCA program called *Indian Guides*. My son was nine years old at the time. During one of the weekly meetings, the father of another young boy, upon learning that I worked in the court system, told me that he and his wife had met a local attorney at a social function and were very embarrassed by his crude language. He could not remember the name of the attorney who had made such an impression. When I inquired if it might possibly have been Mr. Zucchini, he immediately recognized the name and was very impressed that I had guessed right. All things considered, it wasn't much of a guess because the odds were all in my favor.

Inevitably, because Mr. Zucchini had no control over who his opposing litigants chose to represent them, he had to try some cases against female attorneys. Distasteful as it was to him, he determined that if they wanted to do *men's work*, they would get no special consideration from him simply because they were women. Although he made a point of always being very courteous to the court, he walked a thin line between proper conduct and contemptuous behavior when it came to dealing with opposing counsel. When speaking to the judge during a pre-trial motion, he would make reference to his opposition's *alleged attorney* or to their *so-called* counsel. He was much too smart to do such things in front of a jury because he knew that might alienate them completely.

After one such motion, his female opponent was furious and they continued to berate each other on the elevator until they reached the lobby. They continued their heated discussion there until Mr. Zucchini called her a vulgar four-letter word commonly associated with the southern portion of a woman's anatomy. At that point she hauled off and slugged him in the face as hard as she could. She then spun around and left the courthouse. Mr. Zucchini was stunned and, for the first time since he was six months old, speechless. Although he had experienced more than his share of such altercations with male attorneys, this was the first time he had been sucker-punched by a woman. There must have been more than just a physical impact involved because in addition to Mr. Zucchini gaining more respect for his female adversary in that case, his office is now almost equally divided between men and women attorneys. So I guess you could say, first he saw stars and then he saw the light.

Lest you become convinced that he was an evil ogre, I should point out that he could be very charming and was always very kind and courteous to the personnel of the courthouse. He was very generous in supporting many charitable organizations being promoted by public employees and he was a court reporter's dream. He paid for his transcripts *on the spot!* Despite the fact his colorful behavior may have been somewhat unorthodox, he was an excellent trial attorney who gave one hundred percent of his efforts towards achieving the best interests of his clients. I always felt that if I ever got into trouble, I would rather have him represent me than some mild-mannered attorney who was barely aggressive enough to state his name for the record.

Referring yet again to Judge X in the Municipal Court, he was very bitter that he had never been elevated to the position of Superior Court judge prior to his retirement. Although there is an annual salary difference of around ten thousand dollars between Muni and Superior Court judges, that is rarely the reason for aspiring to the higher position. Recognition of one's intellectual ability and performance as a judge can only be fulfilled by promotion to a higher court with greater responsibility and prestige. At least that is the belief of some Municipal Court judges and, to some extent, many Superior Court judges who long for appointment to the Appellate Court. As far as remuneration is concerned, many attorneys actually take a cut in pay when appointed to the bench, compared to the former income from their private practice.

In the case of Judge X, he never realized he was his own worst enemy. When governors appoint attorneys to the bench or elevate judges to a higher court, it is almost always the result of political favors done in the past. Judge X was a man of enormous intellect, but had great difficulty controlling his temper. Additionally, he was almost obsessed with not wanting to appear obligated to anyone. It didn't seem to matter who was in power at the time in Sacramento, but whenever an attorney appeared in his court who was known to have great clout in either the Democratic or Republican party, the judge seemed compelled to find some reason to roar at him and embarrass him before the whole courtroom. This no doubt endeared the judge to these attorneys immeasurably, but he never made a connection between that and his remaining on the Municipal Court bench for so many years.

Courts of the same jurisdiction sometimes have different names in various states. When I began my career in the District Court in Montana, that court had the same jurisdiction as the Superior Court in California. An appeal taken from the Superior Court in California first goes to the Appellate Court and if a further hearing is demanded it then goes to the state Supreme Court, the highest court in California. In the state of New York the Supreme Court has the same jurisdiction as the District Court in Montana or the Superior Court in California. If a litigant wishes to appeal a decision of the New York Supreme Court, the appeal must first be pursued through the Appellate Division of the Supreme Court and then finally to the Court of Appeals of the state of New York.

Think how confusing that must be for the pilot of a galactic flying saucer who is pulled over for driving with an expired license. It sounds very much like someone a long time ago amused himself by inventing a very appealing game for the courts, using such adjectives as superior, supreme, and perfectly punctilious. Why not have, in the state of Massachusetts, for instance, the Quintessential Court of Quincy? Or in Michigan, the Superlative Court of Lake Superior? Or even the Court of Gloria in Excelsior at Excelsior Springs, Missouri? However, I suppose you have to draw the line somewhere—at least, that's what Mason said to Dixon.

Common sense dictates that for something to be superior or supreme, something else must be somewhat less than that. With that in mind, I will tell you that I went to the funeral of a highly regarded Superior Court judge many years ago which was also attended by many attorneys and most of the judges in the county. A rosary was held the night before the funeral at the mission church at Santa Clara University and there were many hundreds of people at that service. The next morning the funeral was held at a small funeral home a block from the downtown Superior courthouse so that the other judges and attorneys and court personnel could attend.

After the conclusion of a brief service, the funeral director stood up in front of the coffin and stated, *"All of you Superior Court judges may now come forward, form one line and pay your last respects to your fallen compadre. After that, you Inferior Court judges may come up and say farewell."* That went over with the Municipal Court judges, as an old bailiff used to say, like a turd in a punch bowl. It also embarrassed the Superior Court judges. In a strictly grammatical sense the funeral director may have been correct, but it was a grossly insensitive example of a lack of diplomacy. Under the circumstances, nobody made any comment, but I would hate to have been that funeral director if he had to appear before any of the Municipal Court judges for even the slightest infraction. Coincidentally, that funeral home went bankrupt less than a year after that occasion.

Sometimes attorneys really do go above and beyond the call of duty in attempting to perform their duties. One day in the early '70s a deputy district attorney was walking in front of the courthouse in San Jose reading a court file. All of a sudden, he heard a disturbance ahead and looked up to see a man running towards him at full speed, wearing the clothing of a jail inmate. The man was pursued by several deputy sheriffs who were shouting at him to stop or they would fire.

As the man reached the area of the deputy district attorney, the D.A. brought him down with a flying tackle that would have made a linebacker for the San Francisco '49ers green with envy—or at least '49er scarlet and gold. Within seconds the deputy sheriffs arrived at the scene, handcuffed the man and took him back into custody. The would-be escapee weighed approximately 220 pounds. The D.A. weighed in at 145 pounds, soaking wet. As a reward for his heroics, the D.A. was chewed out by the judge for being late to court.

Another example of a prosecutor being willing to risk life and limb in the pursuit of justice occurred during the trial of a defendant in a murder trial. The victim had been stabbed to death in the back seat of an automobile. The defendant alleged that it was a case of self-defense. He claimed he had been sitting in the driver's seat of the car when the victim, who was in the back seat, reached over and attempted to stab him with a long knife. The defendant allegedly attempted to wrest the knife away from the victim and they both wound up on the floorboard of the rear portion of the car. He stated that while he was on top of the victim, the victim was slashing at him with the knife and his only recourse was to grab the arm of his assailant, inadvertently forcing the knife into the victim.

On cross-examination the prosecutor asked the defendant to demonstrate for the jury just how the incident occurred. Four chairs were set up to represent the front and back seats of the vehicle. The defendant in this case was a very large man with a menacing look about him. The D.A. was a man of average size, but in very good physical shape because of a passion for playing tennis. A kitchen spatula was utilized to represent the knife for the demonstration.

The reenactment was performed step by step, with the D.A. playing the role of the victim in the case. During the final part of the demonstration, the D.A. was on the floor with the spatula in his hand and the defendant astride him. The D.A., in his role as the victim, was attempting to move the spatula in a stabbing motion to correspond with the defendant's version of the attack. The defendant had the wrist of the D.A. locked in his grip. Despite his great arm strength from years of playing tennis, the D.A. could not begin to budge the defendant's arm. The defendant told the D.A., "Try to stab me now."

As far as the D.A. was concerned, he was trying as hard as he could. Because of his great effort, his face was very red. He had beads of perspiration on his forehead and his hand, straining against the defendant's arm, was completely white and shaking with the strain. At that point the defendant smiled and said to him, "No, *really* try to stab me now." The D.A. could not have tried any harder if he had been a clone of Arnold Schwarzenegger. The demonstration was concluded at that point and the jury had been provided with a splendid example of the strength and power of the defendant. It is difficult to imagine why the defendant's attorney allowed him to be used in such a fashion, but he made no objection. A guilty verdict was reached in the case after just a few hours of deliberation.

Once during a criminal law and motion calendar, a defendant charged with murder was attempting to make a motion to compel the state to furnish him with a new pair of glasses so he could work on his defense more effectively. He had chosen to represent himself, rather than having court-appointed counsel. The D.A. was opposing the motion. When the court inquired as to the reason for the D.A.'s opposition, the explanation was offered as follows:

> Prosecutor: The People are seeking the death penalty in this case, Your Honor, and we believe a jury should decide whether he gets the death penalty or life imprisonment before the Court rules on this motion.
>
> The Court: What has that got to do with whether or not he gets a new pair of glasses?
>
> Prosecutor: It would be relevant, Your Honor, as to whether we buy him a pair or lend him a pair.

⚖

In another case in which a defendant was charged with murder, he was represented by the members of a two-man law firm which had sorely tried the patience of the court on several occasions by their tactics. When they made their first appearance before the judge in this case, proceedings were held as follows:

> The Court: I will call the case of the People versus Genghis Khan.
>
> Mr. Farpsnoodle, III: Yes, Your Honor. Busleford Q. Farpsnoodle, III, appearing with my co-counsel, Cornelius P. Farpsnoodle, Jr., for Mr. Khan. We are ready to proceed.
>
> The Court: Are you two brothers?
>
> Mr. Farpsnoodle, III: No, Your Honor. We are unrelated. When we first met, we so admired each other's name we decided to enter into a partnership.
>
> The Court: Is this lady with you part of your firm?
>
> Mr. Farpsnoodle, III: Yes, Your Honor. This is our paralegal, Ms. Sue Asponte. She volunteered to come down here with us this morning to make sure we did things right.

In almost every subsequent appearance before the court, the attorneys were late or in some cases did not show up at all. At one point the court threatened to issue a bench warrant for their arrest if they did not show up for their next scheduled appearance. Finally, on the day set for the trial of the defendant, who was in custody, the attorneys showed up on time, but they had failed to bring any suitable clothes for the defendant to wear during his trial. The judge refused to allow the defendant to proceed to trial dressed in his jail clothing.

The judge's patience had long been stretched to the limit with these attorneys and he found them both in contempt of court and fined them five hundred dollars. He informed them that a jury panel was waiting downstairs to be called up and that he would give them one hour to find clothes for the defendant. He stated very emphatically that the fine would be increased by five hundred dollars per hour for each hour of further delay. Mr. Farpsnoodle, Jr., asked if they might confer with the defendant in the empty jury room and the Court agreed.

When the judge entered his chambers, he commented to his clerk that the defendant should have pled not guilty by reason of insanity and the jury would have believed him, based on who he hired to represent him. This was at a time when lapel microphones were first being introduced into the court system and he had forgotten that his mike was still turned on. The clerk quickly reminded him of that fact and then stepped back into the courtroom to ask the bailiff if the judge's comment had come over the loudspeaker. The bailiff stated that it had, but that the defendant and his attorneys were inside the jury room by then and probably did not hear it.

When the proceedings in court resumed after the recess, the defendant appeared before the court wearing a rather ill-fitting suit and tie, which looked vaguely familiar to the judge, along with dusty brown shoes. Mr. Farpsnoodle, III, was attired in a trench coat and his socks. The trench coat was buttoned to the top because he had nothing on beneath it but his underwear. Except for the lack of a glass eye and a chewed up cigar, he was a dead ringer for Lt. Columbo. Rather than running up a tab with the court at five hundred dollars an hour, he had given the defendant his own clothing and his shoes to wear during the trial. Later, despite all this effort on the part of his counsel, the defendant decided to change his plea to guilty. Only the defendant could say for sure whether that decision was prompted by his lack of sartorial splendor or the ultimate realization that with these lawyers, he might as well have wired ahead for a reservation at San Quentin.

During my early years as a Municipal Court reporter, there were somewhat strained relations between Superior Court reporters and Municipal Court reporters, again involving income, but for a different reason. In those years the Superior Court reporters were the ones who did the negotiating with the county for salary increases, benefits, etc. But when the increases were granted, they were extended to both Municipal and Superior Court reporters as well. This irked the Superior

Court reporters, who felt the reporters from the Municipal Court were getting a free ride.

Since that time, reporters from both courts have been represented as a single unit by various associations and unions which serve as bargaining agents. There are still a few reporters in the Superior Court who try to convince themselves they are truly *superior* to the Municipal Court reporters because of the longer trials and more technical terminology encountered in the Superior Court. Having worked for a number of years in both courts, I can attest to the fact that it all balances out and there is no basis for one group of reporters feeling superior to another group when both groups are performing basically the same type of work. Ideally, the construction of courthouses would embrace a whole complex of different courts. The Municipal Courts would be on one side of the complex and on the other side would be the superiority complex.

⚖

In 1961, prior to the opening of the North County Courthouse at Palo Alto, as has been previously noted, the Municipal Court was located above the police station in a very antiquated building. The courtroom was a barn-like structure, very uncomfortable and heated inadequately during the winter months. The court clerks, required to sit there for hours at a time, wore heavy sweaters to help ward off the cold. One day, during an unusually cold spell, a clerk decided to bring in her electric heater to protect her from the chill. There were only two electrical outlets in the whole courtroom so she also brought a long extension cord which extended all the way from in back of the court's bench to her desk in front of the bench.

The Naval Air Station at Moffett Field was located only a few miles from the Municipal Court and it was not uncommon for naval personnel to be included on the court's calendar for traffic violations, etc. At that time Judge X had a standing rule that the punishment for anyone found guilty of driving one hundred miles per hour was an automatic five days in jail. On the same day the clerk brought in her electric heater, a nervous young sailor appeared before the judge and pled guilty to speeding at one hundred miles per hour. He was terrified because he had observed the sentencing of other defendants found guilty of the same offense. He pleaded with the court to reconsider and show him some leniency because his squadron was leaving for Japan in two days and if he was unable to join them because of his incarceration, he would be considered A.W.O.L. and his naval career would be in jeopardy.

His plea must have touched a spark in the judge because, after reading him the riot act, he fined him one hundred dollars and even gave him time to pay it off. Then, as he was ending his remarks to the sailor, he roared, **"You're getting a break that very few people get and if I ever see you in my Court again, you'd better give your soul to God, because..."** At that point there was a loud crackling noise, a flash of light and then smoke swirled up from behind the judge's chair. The clerk's extension cord had shorted out and started a small electrical fire behind the judge. The sailor, of course, knew nothing about the extension cord being there and his eyes nearly popped out of his head. He was convinced he had been sentenced by either Mephistopheles or, at the very least, the Wizard of Oz. The fire was quickly extinguished and the young sailor was never seen in the area again.

Chapter Twenty-two

Lamentations

THE YEAR of 1987 had to rank as one of the busiest and most stressful years of my entire career. The judge I worked for at that time had nothing but criminal trials all year long and historically, ninety-eight percent of criminal convictions are appealed. Many times even defendants who are sentenced to prison as a result of a plea bargain will be convinced by their fellow prison inmates, or *jailhouse lawyers*, to appeal their sentences as well. Convicted criminals have everything to gain and nothing to lose. The state will pay for their appeal, for a lawyer to handle their appeal, and will pay the court reporter to prepare their transcript on appeal.

The Appellate Court strictly enforces its rules governing the preparation and completion of Reporter's Transcripts on Appeal. The time allotted by the Appellate Court for completion of the transcript is twenty days from the date of the filing of the appeal. In most cases the reporters are not notified of the appeal until four or five days have elapsed, cutting their time even more severely. Upon a showing of good cause and due diligence by the reporter, two separate thirty-day extensions *may* be granted if extenuating circumstances can be proven—such as a heart transplant or a slight case of death.

In some jurisdictions there are *reporter pools*, presided over by a chief reporter, who makes sure that no one reporter is overwhelmed by an unmanageable number of appeals. That is not the case in this county where, traditionally, judges have preferred to have a reporter of their own selection with them on a daily basis. While this arrangement is conducive to attaining the goal of a close-knit staff and hopefully a good rapport between the judge and reporter, it can place a substantial burden upon the reporter when that department has an endless parade of criminal trials.

Even though a reporter may be backed up with several appeals to prepare, he or she is continuing to generate additional appeals because of the requirement of working on new criminal cases every day. Remember, the transcripts can only be prepared on the reporter's *free* time. When reporters become severely overloaded with appeal transcripts, some judges will allow them to temporarily swap with another reporter in a department that has much less transcript volume until they are able to catch up. Other judges insist that they have the same reporter every day because they feel more comfortable with their own reporter, especially if they need their recollection refreshed by frequent read-backs of the record.

If there is no conviction, there is no appeal. The prosecution cannot appeal an acquittal. The People may appeal a judge's ruling which leads to a dismissal of the charges, but that is about the extent of their appellate rights. By now it is probably no secret that I have always been sort of a law and order guy. I must confess, however, that on more than one occasion I was hoping that the jury would bring in a not guilty verdict simply because I already had an impossible schedule of appeal transcripts to complete. Despite what you may have heard through the media, the vast majority of criminal trials result in convictions rather than acquittals. I am not trying to paint a portrait of poor, pitiful reporters (*yes, I remember what Harry Truman said*), but prior to the advent of the use of computers by reporters, it was quite common for them to work on their transcripts late into the night, many hours after court was adjourned. There was one period of over four years when the only vacation I had was an occasional long weekend. My main vacation time was spent in my office getting out transcripts.

The procedure by which the Appellate Court enforces its time limits on the completion of transcripts begins with the issuance to the reporters of an order to show cause why the reporter's license should not be suspended as punishment for not completing the transcript on time. If a license suspension is imposed, the reporter can no longer work in the court and his or her employment is usually terminated along with all benefits such as health coverage, etc. This is an extreme measure which generally is resorted to only after it has been shown that the reporter has not made a real effort to complete the transcript.

In some cases reporters have been fined several thousand dollars until the transcript is completed and I know of one case in another Bay Area county where the reporter was actually jailed for ten hours each day while he worked on the transcript in his cell until it was completed. I mention this only to illustrate that, just as there are imperfect lawyers and judges, incredible as it may seem, there may occasionally be one in ten thousand reporters who doesn't have his head screwed on properly. Remember, it only takes one bad apple to make a whole barrel of rotten Americans!

Ironically, even though a criminal calendar can bring as much misery as income into the life of a reporter, it is undeniably more interesting than a civil calendar. Watching the grass grow is only about one tenth as boring as listening to the trial of a breach of contract action. I believe that requiring a jury to sit through a civil trial for breach of contract should come under the heading of cruel and inhuman punishment. On the other hand, many criminal trials provide the excitement that gives people the perception that they are on the inside track of something big that the general public may catch only a glimpse of through newspapers and television.

During the year of 1987 I reported not only the strange rape case covered in an earlier chapter, but many other criminal trials which would have lent themselves to TV movie adaptations if that had been such a popular trend at the time. One of the trials involved a professional car thief who had been stealing and selling cars for a living for almost a decade before being apprehended. During that trial the evidence educed from experts in auto theft investigations made potential expert car thieves out of all the jurors. Everything from discovering where hidden vehicle identification numbers are located to the practice of buying or stealing old license plates off wrecked cars in a junkyard to be later attached to a stolen vehicle. At that time when a car was junked, there was no longer a current record kept with the department of motor vehicles and there was less chance of the vehicle being stopped.

One of our trials involved a defendant charged with assault with a deadly weapon. The weapon alleged to have been used in a lethal manner was an automobile. It seems that a drug deal had gone sour between the defendant and his victim so the defendant decided to include the victim as an additive to the asphalt of a supermarket parking lot. According to witnesses, the defendant made three or four high-speed passes at the victim, missing him only by inches each time. Only the timely arrival of the police prevented the victim from becoming a permanent part of the landscaping.

As the investigation progressed, it developed that the victim also had a number of heavy duty warrants out for his arrest and he was subsequently arrested and convicted of felonies and sentenced to the state prison at Soledad, California, one of the toughest prisons in the state. During the trial of the defendant who had tried to run him down, the victim was returned to court from Soledad prison to testify for the prosecution. Evidently, the passage of a few months had been very detrimental to the memory of the victim. He claimed that he had no memory of the incident and could only barely recognize the defendant. The prosecutor, realizing he would get little help from the victim, strategically revised his questioning of the victim as follows:

Q: (By the prosecution:) Would you mind telling the members of the jury where you presently reside?
A: Soledad State Prison
Q: How much more time will you be required to serve?
A: Five and a half years, with good behavior.
Q: Could you tell the jury what other inmates of the prison consider the lowest form of life in the prison population?
A: That's easy. A stool pigeon or snitch.

Q: What happens to snitches in prison?
A: They die.
The Prosecution: No further questions.

This proved to be a very telling demonstration for the jury. The defendant was subsequently convicted and the victim was returned to Soledad to serve out the remainder of his sentence, without having been labeled a snitch.

One of our major trials of that year had sort of an international flavor to it. Two defendants were charged with attempted murder. Both defendants were German-Americans, one a man in his early twenties and the other a woman about sixty years old. The intended victim in the case was the former husband of the woman defendant. The prosecution alleged that the female defendant had conspired with and paid the male defendant to considerably shorten the longevity of her ex-husband.

The evidence at the trial established that the woman defendant and her former husband had both immigrated to this country from Germany many years earlier. After a long and stormy marriage, they had divorced a few years prior to the incidents involved in the trial. The evidence showed that in the years following the divorce, there had been a number of incidents of malicious mischief suspected to have been perpetrated by the husband, but never proven. The wife's home had been set on fire at one time and sugar had been put in the gas tank of her automobile. She owned and operated a German restaurant and many times telephone reservations would be made for a large group of people with special orders and then nobody would show up. This was also suspected to be the work of the ex-husband, but again there was no proof.

Finally, she had enough and allegedly contacted the young male defendant, who was also a German immigrant, and he agreed to put an end to her former husband's devilish harassment, promising to make him holier than a piece of Swiss cheese. His planned instrument of conversion was a special pistol he had been practicing with in a make-shift firing range behind his home. A fee was agreed upon and the young man began a stake-out of the ground floor apartment of the husband in Santa Clara. After several days of surveillance, he was satisfied that he knew when the husband was alone. He approached the front door of the apartment one morning and rang the doorbell. When the husband opened the door, he found himself looking at a long barrelled pistol with a silencer attached, pointed straight at his chest.

The husband was then about sixty-five years old and had a well-developed stomach as a result of bellying up to the bar of many a German beer garden. He immediately grabbed the would-be assassin's arm, attempting to dislodge the gun. They wrestled in the alcove outside the apartment and fell to the ground. The husband was not able to gain control of the gun, but he did manage to break the arm of the young man, who then fled the scene. A neighbor gave police a description, both of the young man seen running from the scene clutching his arm, as well as his car and license plate number. With this information, the young man was traced to his residence and arrested within two days. The victim had never seen the young man before in his life so he immediately suspected his attacker had been hired by his former wife. He quickly informed the police of his suspicions and their investigation resulted in the young man admitting that he had indeed been recruited by the former wife for the purpose of putting an end to the problems caused by the husband. He claimed, however, that it was their intention only to frighten the victim, not to render him *kaput*.

The prosecution produced expert evidence in the trial from agents of the U.S. Department of Alcohol, Tobacco, and Firearms to help educate the jury concerning the use and construction of silencers for guns. I found this testimony to be rather fascinating, especially the opinion that despite the sophisticated development of silencers today, a carved-out common potato can be just about as useful for that purpose. (*Remember that the next time you want to shoot a cockroach in your bedroom without waking the kids!*) During the defense portion of the trial, the younger brother of the male defendant was called to testify as a character witness for his accused brother. The witness was not a naturalized American citizen, but was here on a temporary visa. (Or MasterCard.) When he completed his testimony and left the courtroom, he was arrested by agents of Interpol on warrants issued by both Germany and France. I was so intrigued by the cosmopolitan nature of the trial that I had lunch that day at the International House of Pancakes.

The jury found the evidence sufficiently convincing to find both defendants guilty of attempted murder. Although the male defendant had been in custody throughout the trial, the woman defendant had been out on bail for the entire period and the district attorney requested that her bail be revoked and that she be remanded into custody pending sentencing. He attempted to convince the court that, now that she had been convicted, she represented a flight risk—especially since she had relatives in East Germany. This was two years prior to the fall of the Berlin wall and there was, of course, no extradition agreement with Communist East Germany.

Her attorney countered that she had made every appearance required of her since her arrest and she had many ties to the local community and he implored the court to allow her to remain free on bail until the time of sentencing. Because of her age and her health, the judge decided to allow her to remain free on bail, but ordered the bail increased substantially. Because of the bail increase, it was necessary that she go through a re-booking procedure.

About thirty minutes after court recessed, she and her attorney, along with the district attorney and several booking officers, returned to the courtroom to reopen the case. It seems that during the booking procedure her purse was searched and inside were found three valid passports: a Chinese passport, one for West Germany, and one for East Germany. Her purse also contained twenty thousand dollars in cash and several thousand dollars in traveler's checks. Confronted with this additional information, the court revoked her bail and remanded her into custody while awaiting sentencing.

At that time the mandatory sentence for attempted murder was twenty-five years to life in the state prison and that is the sentence each defendant received. Ironically, the prescribed sentence was the same for murder as attempted murder. It must have been frustrating for the defendants to realize that with a little more effort they might at least have accomplished their purpose, with no increase in their sentences. About four years after the trial, the former husband died of natural causes. A year later, the woman defendant died in prison. If she had just been a little more patient, she may have died a free woman.

These trials were obviously more interesting and thought-provoking than watching television. The positive aspect was that there were no commercials. The negative side was that they just made my pile of appeal transcripts grow higher and higher. Through an unexpected source in the late summer of 1987, I did manage to obtain some limited relief from the parade of new trials, among other things. Although I had never had the desire to play the role of *Hamlet,* one phrase kept repeating itself over and over in my mind: *"To pee or not to pee, that is the question."* I was required to undergo prostate surgery to alleviate this difficult dilemma. The three weeks I spent recuperating at home helped me to at least make a good dent in my transcript situation. My transcriber should have been awarded a medal for being able to understand my dictation during this period because I was having a new roof put on my home at the time and the tape picked up, not only the constant hammering on the roof, but the incessant barking of my dog.

In January of 1988, the judge I worked for elected to return to the Palo Alto Court facility and his staff, of course, went with him. I had hopes that the somewhat serene atmosphere of Palo Alto would enable me to spend more time working on my ever increasing volume of appeal transcripts. Because of all the criminal trials held in our department in 1987, the appeals continued to trickle in (*that word has a familiar ring to it!*) and each time I felt I might actually see some daylight, there was another deluge of appeals. The judge was very adept at settling cases, but in March of 1988 we had a criminal trial scheduled to begin which was estimated to last a minimum of five weeks. I knew there was no way that I could allow myself to be involved in a trial of that length, which would only worsen my appeal situation.

I was finally able to convince the judge that it was an absolute necessity for me to temporarily swap with another reporter until I got myself out of the hole. He agreed and I made arrangements with a reporter in the Domestic Court in San Jose to change places with me. She had recently invested in an expensive reporter's computer system and was eager for transcripts to help defray the cost. Boy, did she pick the right department! The fact that I was *volunteering* to work in a Domestic Department is an indication of the extent of my desperation.

Under the circumstances, I could hardly have made a better selection for a department that would provide me the time required to complete my transcripts. The judge in that department was the presiding judge of the Domestic Court and, as such, assigned out most trial matters to other departments. This would take about forty-five minutes to an hour in the morning and then he would hear settlement conferences for the remainder of the morning. The procedure would then be repeated in the afternoon. I was required to be present to record any settlements or stipulations, but in the interim was free to work on my transcripts.

This additional time was invaluable to me and I was really beginning to make some headway, when disaster struck. Five criminal appeals were filed all within the same week. This meant, for all intents and purposes, that time was running simultaneously on all five matters. Three of the five cases were trials which had lasted more than three weeks. The Appellate Court made no exceptions for situations like this and, try as I might, I had no idea how to solve the problem. It was much like trying to bail out a rowboat with a sand pail, while three firemen filled it with their hoses. I put out an S.O.S. to my fellow reporters and to the Court Executive's Office.

By this time I had established a fairly good record for reliability, so the Court Executive allowed me a full two weeks to stay in my office working on transcripts without going to court. Additionally, two very kind women reporters came to my rescue by agreeing to do two of the shorter appeal transcripts for me. They were each from departments which generated very little demand for transcripts and were not nearly as burdened with transcript orders as I was. While court reporters all use basically the same stenographic system, there are always unique briefs and phrases adopted by individual reporters which have meaning only to them. It was necessary, therefore, for me to go through each fold of my stenographic notes and make notations by pen whenever I thought there might be a question on the part of the other reporters. Even with this precaution, they still had to check with me on several occasions before the transcripts were completed.

With the assistance of those two reporters, the patience of the Court Executive's Office, and utilizing all the extensions of time available through the Appellate Court, I was finally able to deliver and file the appeal transcripts on time. You cannot imagine the weight that was lifted off my shoulders and I will always be grateful for the help I received in that time of need. I still had a large backlog of transcripts to complete which were not appeals. Attorneys often order partial transcripts of hearings to be used at a future hearing of the same case for purposes of impeachment.

One of the quandaries facing a reporter in the situation I had just escaped was handling the transcript requests which were not appeals. On the one hand, it is unfair to expect an attorney to wait for his partial transcript until you finish all your appeals because that might take months. On the other hand, if you keep interrupting your work on appeals to get out short transcripts, you will never finish your appeals. Legally, appeal transcripts take precedence over any other transcript and criminal appeals take precedence over civil appeals—but not by much. Only a very skillfully performed balancing act, honed through years of experience, can save a reporter from being tarred and feathered by angry and impatient attorneys in such a situation.

By this time my regular judge had completed his tour of duty in the Palo Alto facility and returned to San Jose. The swap of reporters between the two departments had been agreed to on a temporary basis and I had a decision to make. During the battle to successfully meet all my appeal transcript obligations, the considerable angst generated thereby caused my blood pressure to jump off the charts. My doctor warned me that if I did not manage to lessen the stress in my life, I could expect a massive stroke or a coronary attack in the not too distant future.

My former judge continued to have a criminal trial calendar and, under the circumstances, I did not think it was wise to return to that department and risk putting myself right back into the same deep chasm from which I had recently been exhumed. My doctor's remarks may have contributed to some preoccupation with thoughts of holes in the ground. I discussed the matter with both judges, as well as the other reporter, and they all agreed to make the transfer of reporters permanent. I left that department with some sadness. I had worked with the same court clerk for ten years and we had become close friends during that time. I was very fortunate, however, in joining a department which was just as friendly and efficient and made me feel quite welcome.

⚖️

The Domestic Department of the Superior Court at that time was concentrated in what was known as *the old courthouse.* This was a three story building which had its first use as a courthouse in 1868. It started out as a one story building with a huge dome on top. Then, in 1879, a second story was added. The building survived the 1906 earthquake which leveled San Francisco, but in 1931 a devastating fire gutted the interior of the building. The building was then refurbished and a third story was added. The ceilings were so high that when you walked up the stairs to the third floor, you were actually walking up the equivalent of four stories. Inside, the building featured beautiful oak-paneled walls and oak furniture. The floors and staircases were built of Italian marble. If you just had to get a divorce, you couldn't ask to do it in a more impressive building.

Located directly across the street from the old courthouse was St. James Park. This park was designed by a gentleman named Frederick Olmstead, who later landscaped New York City's famed Central Park. St. James Park was graced with stately old trees which had been there for many decades. It provided a shady retreat from the heat of summer as well as the heat of courtroom battle. It also provided a haven for many people who had lost their battle with Muscatel. Near the turn of the century, prior to the establishment of a county jury commissioner, judges would sometimes send their bailiffs across the street to press into service anyone found in the park to serve as jurors when their official panels had been exhausted. Based upon the sobriety of most of the park regulars, there were no doubt some very interesting verdicts rendered in those days.

On May 13, 1901, President William McKinley delivered an address at St. James Park in San Jose. Just four months later, on September 14, 1901, he died as the result of an assassin's bullet suffered a week earlier in Buffalo, New York. The citizens of San Jose at the time were so impressed by his speech and the fact that he had visited San Jose so close in time to his assassination, they erected a bronze statue in his honor which was dedicated on February 21, 1903. It was a very imposing statue, high upon a pedestal and resides there to this day. One of the more poignant sights I witnessed in the park involved a gentleman who was obviously in the grip of the grape and felt a need to commune with his God. I don't know whether his vision was too blurred to read the inscription on the statue or he believed it to be a likeness of St. James, but he knelt in front of the statue, crossed himself and prayed for about five minutes. I never knew whether he was a nearsighted Catholic or just a very devout Republican, but I hope his prayers were answered and I wish him well wherever he may be.

I had worked in the old courthouse many times over the years on a temporary basis and on numerous occasions older attorneys, who were long time residents of San Jose, would point out one of the tallest trees in the park to me and state proudly, *"That's the tree where they hung those two kidnappers in 1933."* They were referring, of course, to the last known lynching in San Jose which occurred when a mob broke into the jail and brought out two prisoners charged with the kidnap and murder of the popular son of a local department store owner.

I always assumed the attorneys were correct because they had been around the area a lot longer than I had. It wasn't until I read Harry Farrell's excellent account of the events leading up to and beyond the lynching in his book *Swift Justice* (St. Martin's Press) that I learned there had actually been two trees utilized for the execution. I learned further that, because of the community shame resulting from the event, the two trees had been taken down and cut into firewood to be given to the poor. Since I know for a fact that an attorney would never intentionally say anything that was untrue, I can only assume that the attorneys who told me that may have just been hanging out with the wrong crowd.

⚖

The deputy sheriff who worked as a bailiff in our department of the Domestic Court was a Latino weight lifter who rarely had any problem maintaining order in the courtroom. Many times, even when people merely cleared their throats too loudly, he would give them a look that indicated he would be quite willing to perform a tracheotomy if it would help them breathe better. He could make some of the hottest salsa I ever tasted and I suspect that may have had something to do with his steamy disposition. Deputy Cojones really should have been a docent in an art museum because of his great concern for the safety of things of beauty.

To his great dismay, he discovered that nearly every time an attractive young woman was involved in a Domestic Court dispute, her former husband represented a great physical threat to her safety and it was necessary for the deputy to accompany her to the parking lot and the security of her vehicle. Some of these women must have been required to park a considerable distance from the courthouse, based upon the amount of time it took the deputy to return. Hey, you don't suppose that...nah. That would be ridiculous. But, more about Deputy Cojones later.

Chapter Twenty-three

Apocalypse

WHEN I reentered the world of the Domestic Court in April of 1988, I was amazed at the extent of specialization which had taken place since my last visit. My first real experience with Domestic Court had been in 1972 when one judge handled all but the most lengthy cases. Now, three judges were assigned to handle the domestic case load with occasional assistance from other departments of the court when the calendar was really overloaded. Additionally, a new position of *attorney-mediator* was created by the court for the purpose of aiding in settlement conferences and acting as a permanent judge pro-tem. Later, a *domestic commissioner* was appointed by the court. The commissioner had her own designated courtroom and handled most regular domestic matters, unless there was some objection by the parties, in which case the matter would be referred to a regular Superior Court judge for determination. There were also fully staffed departments offering family court services, mediation of visitation disputes, and representatives from Juvenile Probation to investigate any claims of child abuse.

I could not help but note the contrast between the Domestic Court judge sixteen years earlier, laboring feverishly to write down all the numbers cited in the income and expense equations of the parties—sometimes with the help of an early calculator—and the sophisticated software designed just for that purpose to be used in today's modern computers. No doubt the court's proximity to Silicon Valley gave it a leg up on the rest of the courts in the nation in that respect.

As noted earlier, until the time I retired, I remained totally ignorant on the subject of computers. (*E. Pluribus Unum?*) When I finally took the plunge and bought a computer, one of the first things I was told by my instructor was how to turn it off. Rather than simply pushing the off button, there was a procedure for *parking* the computer so as not to risk losing or damaging any of the programs operating at the time. When I first began my Domestic assignment in April of 1988, my primary concern was completing my large backlog of appeal transcripts. To that end, I would often spend weekends working in my office at the courthouse. At those times I was usually alone in the building and, being the conscientious taxpayer that I am, I would make it a point to turn off any lights that had been left on by others. I would also notice, with some irritation, that the computer had been left on, using up electricity unnecessarily, so I would punch the off button. Every Saturday I would discover the computer had been left on Friday night.

Somewhere in the periphery of my awareness, it would register in my subconscious that there was a lot of grumbling on Monday mornings about the computer being down and having to be re-booted with new programs. I never gave it a second thought because I was concerned with transcripts, not computers. It wasn't until my computer instructor informed me of the parking procedure two years later (plus the fact that most users leave their computers on all the time) that I finally made the connection between my frugal attempts to save power and the down time of the Domestic computer. I think such dedication to stupidity in the face of the obvious must be a sign of strong character. Certainly, if ignorance is bliss, I may very well have discovered a universal cure for clinical depression.

Most people in Domestic Court cases elect to have attorneys represent them, but there are some who choose to represent themselves. This decision is usually based upon their inability to afford attorney fees, but in some cases it is because they consider their case simple enough to handle on their own with a little help from a paralegal along the way. People who represent themselves in legal matters are known as *pro pers*, from the Latin *In Propria Persona*, defined literally as *in one's own proper person*. If a marriage is of short duration, there are no children resulting from the marriage and little property involved, there is usually no reason why the termination of the marriage cannot be achieved without the aid of counsel. There are many form books available today on do-it-yourself divorces and the necessary forms are generally available at legal newspaper offices located near the courthouse. There is one form in use in California wherein, if everything is stipulated to, neither of the parties even has to appear in court.

The standard litany of required testimony for obtaining a dissolution (no more divorce in California) is available in most form books and if not, a visit to a Domestic courtroom a few days prior to the time your case is called would certainly be very educational. Assuming all the facts stated in the petition are stipulated to by both parties to the action, the following testimony would assure a legal end to your marriage.

> Ms. Gabor: I am the petitioner in this action. All of the facts stated in the petition are true and correct to the best of my knowledge. I have been a resident of the state of California for six months and the county of Santa Clara for three months immediately prior to the filing of this petition. During the course of our marriage, irreconcilable differences have arisen, which have led to an irremediable breakdown of the marriage relationship. We both agree that further counseling would be of no avail. There are no children resulting from the marriage and we have divided our property equally. Both sides are waiving spousal support. I therefore request the court grant us a dissolution of our marriage.

The portion of the testimony relating to residency and irreconcilable differences leading to an irremediable breakdown of the marriage is known as the *jurisdictional testimony*. This testimony establishes, for the record, the court's jurisdiction to grant the dissolution and is required in all dissolution actions, whether contested or not. I must reiterate, however, the importance of having a good attorney represent you if there is child support involved, a long marriage, medical coverage, the issue of spousal support, division of community property, and the evaluation of a business, among other things. You will note that I said a *good attorney*. Many people, faced with the shock and despair caused by the breakup of their marriage, reach out for the first attorney they can find—sometimes a second cousin they haven't seen in years—and suffer great consequences for that decision years later.

Domestic law has become a highly specialized field. Just because you may know of an attorney who successfully sprung Uncle Dexter on that drunk driving charge, that doesn't mean he would even have a clue as to how to proceed in a complicated Domestic action. By the same token, even the best Domestic lawyer could be out of his league in a criminal trial. Remember, a surgeon who specializes in heart transplants or brain surgery might leave a lot to be desired if called upon to treat a dislocated shoulder.

Just as specialists in any field may command a higher fee for their services, the same is true for expert Domestic attorneys. I often found it amusing when people would tell the judge they were almost penniless and would be out on the street if they were ordered to pay any spousal support, yet they were represented by one of the most expensive lawyers in town. Many people subscribe to the adage, *you get what you pay for*. Unfortunately, being charged high attorney fees does not always guarantee quality representation. I knew some attorneys whose fees were outrageous and they could barely remember where they parked their car. Their reasoning seemed to be whatever the traffic would bear. The court usually took this into account when modifying the attorney fees requested.

I am convinced that a few people choose to represent themselves in court simply because they know they can get by with a lot of things an attorney would not be allowed to do. They can, for example, attempt to argue with a witness rather than ask questions; they can make hearsay statements which are impossible to verify; they can neglect to properly serve opposing counsel copies of motions they have filed and they try to milk the court's sympathy by the forlorn plea that they are not attorneys and should not be held to the same standard of conduct.

Most judges are extremely patient when dealing with pro per litigants, but it is not their job to tell them how to present their case. It is also not the job of court clerks or people working behind the counter of the clerk's office. Court employees are not lawyers and are forbidden to give anyone legal advice. Yet, few people can be more demanding than a pro per litigant who wants his or her matter to be put on calendar and expects a clerk to drop everything and do their work for them immediately. Certainly, the majority of pro pers are not like this, but if you get the impression that some are a real pain in the butt, your perception is not far off the mark.

One case worthy of mention in this time period involved a lady who chose to represent herself throughout a very extended and confrontational Domestic action. She would file motions to be heard on certain dates in court and then not show up on that date, causing her former husband to incur additional attorney fees to his lawyer. At other times, she would show up when her matter was not on the calendar and demand that the Court hear her matter, even though it was not scheduled for hearing and the other side had not been notified.

She could be very abusive to the clerk when she was not allowed to speak to the judge in his chambers. During the times when the matter was heard in court, she would conduct herself in an extremely melodramatic fashion, proclaiming how unjustly she had been treated by men in general and the courts specifically. She would alternate between sobbing and screaming and would calm herself only when the judge threatened to put her in jail for her subtle insinuations that the judge had been paid off to rule against her.

At one point the judge even issued a restraining order against her to keep her away from his car. He had to have Deputy Cojones accompany him to his car at the end of the day to ensure that he was not accosted by this lady. He did not want to have to send her to jail because that would simply enhance her role as a martyr. Eventually, a settlement was agreed upon and the courtroom no longer resembled a bombed-out neighborhood in Beirut. You know what this lady did in between court appearances? She was a full-time public school teacher. When I found this out, I was very grateful that my children were all grown by that time.

The case brought to mind a somewhat similar situation I had reported for a different judge a few years earlier. This was also a bitterly contested Domestic case involving nonpayment of child support. In this instance it was the former husband who was in pro per. He had remarried and his new wife already had three children from her first marriage. He maintained that the upkeep of his new family left him nothing to contribute towards the support of his children by his former wife. There were protracted hearings conducted in this case over a period of at least a year. During these hearings, the behavior of the husband would range from pleading, to threatening, to nearly psychotic. His speech was rambling and at times almost unintelligible. His occupation? A senior pilot for a major airline. Coffee, tea or Prozac?

One of the sadder cases I reported in 1988 involved a love affair between two women. They decided they wanted a child so one of the women became pregnant through the means of artificial insemination and gave birth to a healthy baby girl. The woman who played the role of the man in the relationship decided to go all the way and had a sex change operation, along with prescribed applications of testosterone and other hormones. With the passage of time, the two grew apart and no longer wished to be lovers. The child, of course, knew only one person as her father and was deeply attached to him.

The mother of the child eventually met and married a gentleman from Georgia who took both the mother and the child back to Georgia to be part of his family there. The putative *father* of the child sued to attempt to gain rights of visitation with the child and that is how the matter ended up in our court. When I first saw the transsexual gentleman in court, it was difficult to believe he had ever been a woman. He had a full length beard, a deep voice and several colorful tattoos. Subsequent evidence revealed that he swore like a sailor and had developed a serious drinking problem, having been con-victed twice of drunk driving. Obviously, he had decided to adopt only the noblest attributes of the male persuasion. The only thing he could not change was his bone structure. He was a very slight man, approximately five feet, four inches tall and weighing no more than one hundred five pounds.

The husband of the mother, however, was a six-footer and well over two hundred pounds. His demeanor identified him as almost a burlesque of the stereotypical southern red-neck image, especially when he uttered such comments as, *"That baby don't need to spend no time around no danged queer."* There had been several attempts at visitation made prior to the matter coming to court and each time the child's *father* had been severely beaten by the new husband. At the time the matter came to court, the child was four years old and could not understand why she was not permitted to visit her father, whom she dearly loved. The court finally ordered that some visitation be permitted and both parties were admonished not to risk traumatizing the child further by revealing the past gender history of the father. The father was also warned that if there was any reported drinking around the child, he would lose all rights of visitation immediately. The family went back to Georgia and I have no knowledge of the ultimate results of that arrangement. Assuming the child one day becomes a healthy adult, she will certainly be in for a shock if she ever decides to trace her family history.

At the end of 1988, the judge announced that he had agreed to preside over the civil law and motion calendar for the first six months of 1989. I believe I previously may have hinted at the extent of my fondness for that calendar. I would have much preferred to have slivers of bamboo driven under my fin-gernails. It was pointed out, however, that that might possibly hinder the operation of my Stenograph machine so I resigned myself to my fate. It was customary to conduct the law and motion calendar in the *new courthouse* (even though it had been there since 1964) so it was necessary to move into the other courthouse building.

Over the previous decade, the appointment of new judges

had exceeded the number of courtrooms available and it was necessary to share quarters in some instances. The law and motion calendar was to be held in the same courtroom that the main presiding judge used to call his calendar in the mornings. It was decided, therefore, to hold the law and motion calendar in the afternoon, which caused considerable confusion on the part of many Bay Area attorneys because such calendars were called in the morning in the courts of every other Bay Area county. After some initial procedural problems, however, the attorneys managed to adapt to the new hours and rarely missed a scheduled appearance—much to my disappointment.

Sharing the space of someone else often leaves something to be desired. In this case, it left a lot to be desired. The judge had to make do with makeshift chambers in the jury room of the presiding judge's courtroom. The court clerk was given a desk in the corner of the courtroom between the witness stand and the window. There was a dividing screen placed in front of her desk and that was her office. The bailiff just sort of hung out in the courtroom all day because the regular bailiff's office was occupied by the presiding judge's bailiff.

I guess I was the luckiest of all because at least I had some privacy in which to prepare my transcripts. I was granted temporary possession of an attorney's conference room—something like a cross between a large broom closet and a concrete tomb. There were no windows in the small room, but it was certainly preferable to a corner of the courtroom. One of the most annoying aspects of that location was the fact that attorneys kept trying to open the locked door all day long, assuming it was still an attorney's conference room. I had affixed a sign to the door identifying it as a reporter's office, but, as the tailor in the convent said, old habits are hard to alter. They finally got the message, but then conducted their conferences right outside my door which made dictating my transcripts that much more difficult.

If my doctor ever tells me I only have six months to live, I am going to go back to work and volunteer to report the law and motion calendar. It won't cure me, but it will be the longest six months of my life. This calendar made the law and motion calendar in Palo Alto seem like child's play. For openers, it had at least five times as many cases on it and some cases involved as many as ten attorneys. In the majority of cases, the attorneys ordered transcripts of the proceedings and each attorney considered his or her case much more important than that of anyone else.

While these transcripts were usually not appeals and did not generate pressure from the Appellate Court, the attorneys wanted them as soon as possible. They could not understand why there should be any delay when the transcript was not expected to exceed twenty-five or thirty pages. What they failed to take into consideration was the fact that thirty or forty attorneys before them had also ordered transcripts and I felt obligated to take them in the proper order. It was also necessary to obtain each case file to check the proper spelling of various citations and other documents from which quotations had been made. Court reporters usually do their own billing and bookkeeping and the sheer number of transcripts resulted in the consumption of large blocks of time expended for that purpose alone.

The daily calendar can only be described by a series of four-letter words: *dull, dull, dull.* (Depending upon the credibility of the attorneys involved, it might also be appropriate to substitute *bull, bull, bull.*) Aside from the occasional case in which one attorney finessed his opponent by a superior performance in presenting a motion, there was none of the usual amusing byplay between counsel that was an integral part of most trials. (I suppose, based upon the result of the trial, you might call it foreplay.)

Generally, attorneys are a combination of thespian, humanitarian and con artist—not necessarily in that order. For example, I can recall one criminal hearing I reported a few years ago in which the defendant's attorney kept pacing back and forth behind the chair of the district attorney while the D.A.'s witness was testifying. Finally the D.A. objected and asked the court to order defense counsel to stay in his seat. The defense attorney quickly apologized and explained that he had a very bad back and sitting down only aggravated it. The judge accepted that explanation. As soon as defense counsel began his cross-examination of the People's witness, it became obvious that he had knowledge of the case which could only have been gained by looking over the D.A.'s shoulder at his case file. This may very well have been the same lawyer who was said to be so slick he could get a charge of sodomy reduced to following too close.

On July 1st our law and motion assignment was mercifully terminated. I felt impelled to recite Martin Luther King, Jr.'s speech about *"free at last, free at last...,"* but I couldn't remember all the words. I did the next best thing and celebrated Independence Day three days early. I felt certain that nothing could happen in the remainder of 1989 as traumatic as the first six months had been. Ironically, a short while after leaving that assignment, a new position was created of a Law and Motion Discovery Commissioner who was charged with hearing a lot of the lengthier matters on the calendar which had taken up so much of our time. Nothing like locking the barn door when it's too late.

We moved back into the old courthouse, but this time on the top floor. At this time I was given an office which was about as opposite from the broom closet I had recently inhabited as an architectural genius could imagine. It was almost as large as the judge's chambers and was really the nicest office I have ever had in my career. It was sunny and cheerful and I looked forward to a long and pleasant occupancy. Our new assignment was a civil assignment which covered jury trials, court trials, and extended matters which were too long to be heard on a short calendar. It was a real treat to get back into interesting trials rather than the incessant legal motions of our former calendar. (See, I'm not *always* complaining.) The judge I worked for had a lot of talent for settling cases. Many times, even after a trial had commenced, a settlement would be reached within a few days of the beginning of the trial.

In late September we began a trial which had been originally designated as a jury trial, but then both sides waived a jury on the day the trial commenced. That jury panel never knew how lucky it was, in more ways than one. There were two attorneys on each side of the litigation and it soon became apparent that there was no love lost between the two teams. As the questioning of the plaintiff's witnesses began, there were objections to almost every question the plaintiff's counsel asked. Then, on cross-examination, the questions by the defendant's attorneys were objected to just as frequently. It was obviously developing into a game of tit for tat and I doubt if I ever spent so much time in reading back the previous question. That trial, as a matter of fact, was the inspiration for the title of this book.

The attorneys in the case ordered a daily transcript of the testimony of certain specified witnesses so that meant I got to share with another reporter much of the spitefulness between the attorneys for each side. There was some suggestion that there was a deliberate attempt by counsel to run up the costs of trial, the presumption being that the winner would have those costs paid by the losing party. I don't know if that was true or not, but I did notice that neither team of attorneys even bothered to look at the daily transcripts we had knocked ourselves out to deliver to them. I might add that a civil daily transcript is more expensive than a criminal daily transcript because the source of payment is private counsel, rather than public funds.

The trial finally began winding down around the middle of October. I can recall how relieved and exhausted I was when both sides finally rested their case and closing argument was scheduled for the following morning. It is always more difficult to report a case that is filled with bickering and acrimony. I decided, therefore, instead of working in my office as I usually did, I would go home early and kick back and relax. The third game of the first ever Bay Area World Series was scheduled to be televised between the San Francisco Giants and the Oakland Athletics from Candlestick Park in San Francisco. The Oakland A's had taken the first two games at the Oakland Coliseum and the Candlestick fans were eager for revenge. I locked my office door, walked to the elevator and pressed the button. As I got onto the slow moving elevator, I glanced at my watch and noted it was 5:03 P.M., Tuesday, October 17th.

I knew from experience that the elevator proceeded at a snail's pace. It normally took almost a full minute to get from the third floor to the first floor, assuming nobody got on at the second floor. About two seconds after it inched its way past the second floor, I was almost knocked down by a violent shaking motion of the elevator—I could hear the car actually being slammed against the rails in the shaft—and I realized immediately we were in the midst of a very large earthquake. I knew I was between the first and second floor so I wouldn't have too far to fall if a cable snapped.

The car finally reached the first floor, the door opened and I got out fast! The instant I stepped out of the elevator, the power went off in the building. If the power had gone off even a second earlier, I would have been trapped inside that elevator for at least sixteen hours. I suffer from claustrophobia and would have been a raving lunatic by the time I was rescued. (There are those who are convinced I may have suffered a similar trauma sometime in my early childhood.) If a jury had not been waived in the trial we had just finished, the elevator may well have been filled with twelve jurors and an alternate at that time because it would have taken them longer to get on the elevator at the third floor. Along with my knees, the building was shaking as I stood inside the marble entryway to the elevator.

Suspended from the ceiling of the main lobby of the building were four decorous chandeliers. The design of each chandelier consisted of four large glass balls, about fourteen inches in diameter, attached to brass frames which hung from chains approximately six feet long. These chandeliers were all swinging in unison in a perfect 180-degree arc and the sight was so awe inspiring I was temporarily fascinated by them. I could only marvel at the master choreography involved in such a spectacle. Fortunately, my instinct for self-preservation kicked in about then and I realized if the extent of the arc of the chandeliers was increased by even an inch, I could be showered with shattered glass and end up looking like a large minute steak. I would have given my front seat in hell to have a video camera at that time, but I didn't so I made my way to the back door of the building, dodging falling debris along the way. Luckily, the back door was not jammed so I escaped the building unharmed, suffering only the damage to my nerves and my shorts.

When I got outside, there was not so much a sense of panic as there was of shock. The parking lot was full of people who had just been about to leave for home. Everyone seemed concerned about the physical well-being of each other. Some pointed to the tall buildings across the street, which dwarfed the courthouse, and swore they had actually seen the buildings moving from side to side. None of us knew at that point that we had survived an earthquake that measured 7.2 on the Richter scale. To my knowledge, I was the only one who had still been in the old courthouse at the time of the quake. It was not until a few days later that I learned that I had been permanently evicted from the lovely office I had occupied for the last few months.

None of the traffic signals downtown were operating and I was pleasantly surprised to find that most drivers were cooperating with each other and treating each intersection as a four-way stop sign. At one intersection near my home, the signals were still working. As I sat in my car waiting for the light to change, there was a sharp aftershock that shook the whole car. People in automobiles during an earthquake usually do not feel the jolt because of the suspension system of the car. This one would nearly have aroused a sleeping bailiff. The driver in the car next to me shouted, *"Did you feel that?"* I told him that I certainly had. My first concern was the welfare of my family and I was very relieved to find they were uninjured when I got home, although they were quite shaken—no pun intended. (*Moi?*)

Aside from a chimney which had to be replaced, the damage to my home was minimal. A number of lamps and a few potted plants were overturned, but there was nothing that could not be cleaned up fairly easily. Most of us are familiar with tales about straws penetrating barn walls during tornadoes in the Midwest. The forces at work during an earthquake are just about as mysterious. When I entered my kitchen, I found a heavy glass blender on the floor where it had fallen from the top shelf of the cabinet. On the shelf immediately beneath it were four fragile champagne glasses which had not moved at all. Go figure. As the events of the next few days revealed, most of the folks in San Jose came out of this catastrophe smelling like a rose, compared to the rest of the Bay Area. The epicenter of the earthquake was in the Loma Prieta section of the Santa Cruz hills and that area, as you might expect, suffered terrible damage. Some homes in the hills literally disappeared. Also extremely hard hit were the people of Santa Cruz, Watsonville, and the town of Los Gatos. We are familiar by now with the massive damage to the Marina district of San Francisco, due mostly to its construction years ago on an unstable landfill. The disastrous collapse of the Cypress Freeway in Oakland, as well as the section of the San Francisco-Oakland Bay Bridge which fell, are images not soon forgotten.

A few days after the quake, KRON-TV, the NBC affiliate in San Francisco, advised us that authorities had cheered us with the news that the day before the quake, there was a fifty percent likelihood of the Bay Area being hit with an earthquake of the magnitude of 7.2. They stated further that the day after the quake, there was still a fifty percent chance of a 7.2 magnitude quake occurring in the Bay Area. Have a nice day!

Chapter Twenty-four

Exodus

THE MORNING after the earthquake when I returned to work, I was informed that county engineers had determined that the damage to the old courthouse was so great that it was too hazardous to permit public entry. I informed officials at the entrance to the courthouse that I had to get to my office to obtain my Stenograph machine or I could not perform my job. After some argument back and forth, I was finally allowed to be escorted up the back stairs by a deputy sheriff with a flashlight. The power to the building had not yet been restored. Upon reaching my office on the third floor, I was allowed to retrieve my Stenograph machine, tripod, and a couple of pads of paper and nothing else. Because of the many severe aftershocks which were still occurring, the deputy was not overjoyed with such an assignment.

I commented earlier on the lack of adequate space to accommodate all of the judges and their staffs. As a result of this catastrophe, six judges and a commissioner, along with their staffs, had to be squeezed into whatever available space might be found. Shortly after the quake, the county leased private office space and moved the Domestic Department into an office building a block away from the courthouse. Our department, however, was not associated with the Domestic Department and we were pretty much like orphans. We never knew from one day to the next where we might be holding court the day after that. For about two weeks, we held court in the jury rooms of various departments where no jury was present or used the courtrooms of vacationing judges in the criminal an-

nex building located two blocks from the downtown courthouse.

Sometime during the first week following the earthquake,
arrangements were made for those people who had worked in
the old courthouse to go to their offices and retrieve the things
they needed most. During that time period, dire warnings
were issued by the county that a sharp aftershock might cause
the whole building to come tumbling down. Because of the
fact that I was working in various jury rooms and courtrooms
two blocks away during that week, I was never notified of this
window of opportunity to regain entry to my office. When I finally got the word, it was too late and nobody was allowed
inside the building.

I was quite disturbed about this because I was very anx-
ious to get into my office to obtain, not only things I needed
for my work, but many personal items as well. All of my income tax information was there along with my transcript bill-
ings and personal family information which I felt had no need
to be pawed over by some evacuation crew. The exterior of
the building was roped off and deputy sheriffs patrolled the
area during working hours. I was doubly disturbed when I observed exceptions being made for members of the Court Executive's office. Wearing hard hats, they were granted access to
the building to obtain personal items for the judges who
wished to have them. But, when I sought permission to enter
the building at that time, I was denied entry.

Actually, to say I was disturbed is as much an understate-
ment as saying the ocean is slightly damp. I thought it was
very unfair and I commented to a deputy I knew that I had a
key to the back door of the building and I planned to come
down the following weekend, when the area was not patrolled, and enter the building and get what I needed from my
office. I very nearly suffered a meltdown when he told me the
locks had been changed. Not having immediate access to a fire
extinguisher, he cooled me down somewhat by confiding to me
that the locks could be opened with a credit card. Prior to that
time, I had only seen such things done in private eye movies or
on television. But, I decided, if that's what it took, so be it.

I revealed my plan to two close friends and each of them

tried to dissuade me. Realizing they could not convince me to change my mind, they begged me to at least arrange for someone to stand by outside in the event of a damaging aftershock. That person could then notify the authorities that some fool had gone into the building and might need help. This made sense to me so I decided to call up my old pal, Charley the bailiff, who had long since retired from the court system. When I related my plan to Charley, he was somewhat less than enthused. He was always fond of lecturing me on my shortcomings, usually employing several biblical quotations. In this instance, he quoted from Max Shulman's *"Barefoot Boy with Cheek,"* and stated, *"John, the Lord never told nobody to be stupid!"* I finally talked him into it, using such persuasive terms as *a free six-pack* and he met me at my home the following Saturday morning.

Armed with several large plastic trash bags and a number of credit cards, I drove my car to the courthouse parking lot, which was nearly deserted on a Saturday morning. I had barely turned off the engine when I spotted the presiding judge pulling into his parking space, presumably to do some work in his chambers. Even though he was fifty yards away from me, I was afraid he might recognize me and wonder what I was doing there at that time. I therefore hunched down behind the steering wheel as best I could, while Sir Walter Scott's famous quotation from *Marmion* ran through my mind—*"Oh, what a tangled web we weave, when first we practice to deceive."* He probably had no idea I was even there, but I waited until he had entered the building before sitting up straight again.

Just as I was preparing to move my car closer to the old courthouse, I noticed a resident of St. James Park who had decided to have an early lunch on the courthouse steps which I had to use to get to the back door. I had no choice but to wait for him to finish his entrée. Finally, the bottle empty, he ambled off towards the park across the street. Without further delay, I moved my car adjacent to the back door of the courthouse and prepared for my incursion. I knew from experience that I would be visible to the presiding judge from his chambers, should he decide to look out at that time, but I kept my fingers crossed and proceeded to the door.

I was very discouraged when the first two credit cards I used failed to work on the lock, but I finally gained entry with the third card—possibly due to a higher line of credit with that bank. Quickly gathering up my trash bags, I started up the back stairs, which were well illuminated because the power had been left on as usual. My heart was racing, not only because of all the stairs I was climbing, but because of the fear which had been drilled into us all since the earthquake and the very likely possibility that the whole building might come tumbling down should a severe aftershock occur. I noticed many little cracks in the cement stairs that I had never noticed before. Each time I placed my foot on another step, I wondered if that might be all that was needed for the whole flight of stairs to collapse. The old building was famous for many creaks and noises even before the quake and my adrenaline level at the time simply magnified every sound to perilous proportions.

When I reached my office on the third floor, I had to pause and let my heart settle down a bit. It was not merely the exertion of climbing the stairs, but the fear and uncertainty resulting from each step I took. I used my key to open my office door and found everything virtually untouched by the effects of the quake. I began loading things into my trash bags, as well as several empty cardboard boxes, and made my way back down the stairs. Obviously, there was no way in hell I was going to risk using the elevator again. All together, I made four trips up and down the stairs before gathering together my personal effects and leaving the building. To my knowledge, my little adventure was not observed by anyone. I rushed back to my car, assuming Charley would be a nervous wreck by this time, possibly even more concerned for my safety than I was. When I finally succeeded in waking him up, he helped me load the bags into my trunk. When the whole project was completed, I was as high as a kite. I felt as if I had consumed four or five glasses of wine. A career change was not a consideration at that time of my life, but if it had been, judging by the way I felt, I believe a job as a cat burglar might have been given a high priority.

Many weeks later, when a special task force was assigned

to fully eviscerate the old courthouse building, my electric typewriter was presented to me in a very damaged condition. I had to bear the cost of the repair because I could hardly tell anyone that it had worked fine at the time of my unauthorized office visit. In my mind this even further justified the action I had taken. I can only hope that by this time the statute of limitations on trespassing has run its course.

⚖

The judges of the Superior Court held weekly meetings in a large conference room on the fifth floor of the downtown courthouse. To help alleviate the cramped situation resulting from the earthquake, the judges agreed to allow their conference room to be modified so that it could be used as another courtroom. The only real modification required was the construction of a judge's bench in one corner of the room and the removal of the long table around which the judges sat during their conferences. A regular counsel table and chairs were then brought in with folding chairs available for juries. When juries heard cases in this makeshift courtroom, they were required to deliberate in whatever jury room was available in an adjacent courtroom.

Probably because our department had been shunted about more than any other since the quake, we were given the use of this courtroom which had formerly been used by the judges for their conferences. Once again, my office consisted of a large closet-type room which was originally an attorney's conference room. It was a treat, however, not to have to wonder where we would be working the next day. In mid-December, during one of the court trials held in that courtroom, the plaintiff was represented by a lady attorney. During the trial proceedings one day there was a loud backfire from the street down below. In a flash, that lady was under the counsel table faster than an Olympic sprinter. She had assumed we were having another earthquake and was taking no chances with her safety. When she realized her mistake, she felt rather foolish—muttering something about looking for a contact lens. That is one small example of how traumatized one can become as a result of experiencing a large earthquake.

As it turned out, our department made use of that court-

room for a little less than two months because the judge selected the department in Palo Alto for his next assignment in
January of 1990. Once again, I put on my commuter's hat and
headed for the train station. Since I knew I was going to retire
in September of 1990, it seemed somehow appropriate that I
wind up my career with the county where it had begun in October 1961. I have previously described the calendars handled
in that department—probate matters, Law and Motion hearings, and some Domestic actions; this time there was also the
added attraction of a criminal sentencing calendar every Monday afternoon.

The sentencing calendar consisted of cases which had been
settled downstairs in the Municipal Court either through plea
bargaining or the entry of a guilty plea. The final disposition
had to be decided by a Superior Court judge who was charged
with making the ultimate judgment on what the proper sentence would be after discussing the matters with the prosecution, the defense, and the Probation Department. These calendars were difficult to report because there were often thirty-
five to fifty cases to be handled in one afternoon. Additionally,
groups of prisoners were being brought in and out of the
courtroom on a rotating basis and the attorneys were talking
to their in-custody clients who were seated in the jury box.
Consequently, I made myself very unpopular by suggesting,
none too gently from time to time, that the attorneys whisper
to their clients, rather than screaming at them. These were
usually the same attorneys who, six months to a year later,
would complain that something had been omitted from the
sentencing transcript, conveniently forgetting the near chaos in
the courtroom at the time of sentencing.

In California, the victims of a crime have a right to be
present and address the court at the time of sentencing of the
defendant who is convicted of committing the crime against
them. The statements of these victims were usually very emotional and poignantly illustrated the terrifying incidents which
they had been forced to endure. My heart went out to them
and I was grateful that neither my family nor I had ever been
involved in such a situation. Then, on Saturday evening, January 27, 1990, I decided to go to a local supermarket near my

home in San Jose to pick up something for dinner. I was looking forward to watching the Superbowl the following day and enjoying a nice meal that night. As I pulled into the parking lot, it was very crowded and I had to circle around the lot several times before finding a space. Out of the corner of my eye, I noticed two young gentlemen standing at the front of the store looking at me intently each time I drove by. At that time my car was only about a year old and still looked quite nice.

As I pulled into the vacant space located some distance from the store, I noticed the two men walking toward my car. I thought, with some exasperation, they were probably a couple of panhandlers who would try to hit me up for a couple of bucks. They walked up between my car and the one next to it and seemed to be arguing with each other. I got out of my car, pushed the automatic locking mechanism and shut the door. As soon a I turned around, one of the men stuck a revolver in the left side of my stomach and said, *"Open up your car and get in the back seat!"* I knew if I did that, I was a dead man, so I grabbed the barrel of the gun and forced it away from my stomach, while inviting the young man to participate in an intimate relationship with himself. I believe my precise words were, *"Oh, fuck you, man. No way!"* We struggled a bit as I tried to get the gun away from him, but I was using my left hand against his right and it was no contest. The fact that he was almost thirty years my junior may have had some bearing on the matter as well. I did succeed in slicing open my finger on the gun sight and he may have been somewhat startled by the sight of all that blood. I finally turned and walked away towards the store, looking back once to see if he was going to shoot. At that time I could hear the other man saying words to the effect of, *"Don't worry—he has to come back to get his car."*

I continued walking into the store where I told one of the checkers what had happened and asked if I could use their telephone to call the police. He took me into the office so I could make the call—as well as stop bleeding on his floor—and after I dialed 911 he was kind enough to wash and bandage my hand for me. The police were there in about five minutes, but by that time of course my assailants were long gone.

As I stood outside describing them to the police sergeant, I began shaking uncontrollably all over my body. It was not that cold outside, so it must have been a delayed shock reaction. He suggested we go back into the office, where I gave him a more complete description of the two men. Later, he accompanied me to my car and it had not been damaged in any way. My former appetite had disappeared completely and I drove home and had a large glass of brandy to steady my nerves.

The enormity of the situation really did not dawn on me until I looked more closely at the card the officer had given me which read "attempted robbery and kidnapping." Anyone who knows me will attest to the fact that I have always been a dedicated and devout coward. If someone had predicted that I would react in such a way, I would have considered it ludicrous. I guess we never know, until it happens, just how we will react in any given situation. The two culprits were never apprehended, but as later events have evolved I realized I must have been a party to one of the first attempted carjackings, before it became such a popular sport.

One of the interesting sidelights to this occurrence was the fact that whenever I related this incident to anyone, the first questions most of them asked were, *"Were they Black? Were they Mexican?"* They seemed almost disappointed when I told them the two men were Caucasian. During the remainder of the time I spent in Palo Alto, each time we had a criminal calendar I closely scrutinized every defendant brought into court, but I never saw the pair I had encountered that night. I was very lucky and I would not recommend my actions to anyone in a similar situation. I just hope it never happens again because I've already used up my allotment of luck for three lifetimes.

With the exception of the criminal calendars, the days went by very slowly. Thanks to the ability of the judge to settle the majority of the civil cases that came before our department, I had sufficient time to complete the necessary transcripts of criminal sentencings as well as catch up with appeal transcripts pending from other courts. Eventually, I even reached the point of being able to enjoy some of Palo Alto's fine restaurants and take long walks through the lovely old residential areas at the noon break. I used to gaze enviously at the fine old mansions which served as breeding grounds for so many future Stanford students. I never reached the point where I became bored, but I was tired and found myself looking forward to September.

Most of the citizens of Palo Alto take great pride in their city and enjoy an income level which provides a very comfortable standard of living. They also go to great lengths to ensure that their streets remain safe. Some of the local wags in neighboring Mountain View refer to Palo Alto as *Mountain View with an attitude*. During my service in the Palo Alto Municipal Court in the 1960s, Palo Alto juries had a well-deserved reputation for returning a very high percentage of guilty verdicts in drunk driving cases. Many defense attorneys in such cases complained to me that their clients probably would not have been convicted had the case been tried in San Jose. Indeed, if the blood alcohol reading was on the low side, in other jurisdictions there would have been no trial and the defendant would have pled guilty to reckless driving.

I can recall many guilty verdicts in Palo Alto where the blood alcohol reading was below .10, the legal limit at the time, and even some where there was no sample taken at all. In one case, a very enterprising defendant agreed to give a urine sample, during which time he complained of being very thirsty and was given a cup of water to drink. He poured it into the sample container instead and the resultant blood alcohol reading was infinitesimal. Despite his heroic efforts, a blood alcohol expert testified for the district attorney that to get any reading at all with that amount of added water, the alcohol level would have had to be almost as high as the defendant was alleged to have been at the time of his arrest. The jury bought it and the defendant was convicted. Personally, I thought he should have been given a break after having the presence of mind to do what he did, but it was not my place to make the call.

In another interesting drunk driving trial, the defendant and his attorney had almost succeeded in convincing the jury that the defendant's actions on the night of his arrest were the result of diabetes rather than the consumption of alcohol. Medical testimony was presented regarding the similarity of symptoms of intoxication and the symptoms of a severe diabetic attack. It was also established that the defendant was a diabetic. Unfortunately, the trial was not completed in one day, but had to be put over to the following day. Incredibly, at the end of the first day of trial, the defendant went out and managed to get himself arrested again for drunk driving. His attorney bailed him out of jail at four o'clock in the morning and the trial resumed at 9:30 A.M. The jury knew nothing of the defendant's arrest the previous night, but when they were confronted by a defendant with bleary, red eyes, still somewhat disheveled and smelling like a brewery, it took them little time to return a verdict of guilty on the original charge.

For a relatively brief period of time, beginning in 1979, some judges conducted criminal jury trials in the Palo Alto branch of the Superior Court. During that time, it was to this jurisdiction that a bizarre murder case was transferred from another county as a result of the granting of a Motion for Change of Venue. Coincidentally, this trial was held at about the same time as the trial in San Francisco in which Dan White was charged with the murders of San Francisco Mayor George Moscone and Supervisor Harvey Milk.

I have mentioned earlier how difficult it is for a prosecutor in a criminal case to prevent jurors from empathizing with a defendant in a case involving something like drunk driving. In many instances it can be just as difficult for a defense attorney to convince a jury in a serious felony case to consider only the facts and not the defendant himself. In some cases, of course, the defendant's appearance and history may work to his advantage. The defendant in the murder trial which was held in Palo Alto was affectionately known as the *vampire killer* because of his predilection for drinking the blood of his victims. It was generally agreed by everyone associated with the trial— off the record, even by the prosecution—that the defendant was insane. He certainly did not possess any winsome characteristics with which the jury could identify. Dan White, on the other hand, had been a United States Marine, then a San Francisco police officer and finally a respected member of the San Francisco Board of Supervisors.

Both defendants entered pleas of not guilty by reason of insanity or diminished capacity. The test, under the law at that time, was basically whether the defendant knew the difference between right and wrong at the time of the commission of the crime and whether or not he had the capacity to plan or premeditate his actions. There was little doubt that the defendant in the Palo Alto trial was wildly schizophrenic. In Dan White's case, the consumption of too many *twinkies* had supposedly raised his blood sugar level to such a degree that he had some difficulty in choosing the proper course of action and should, therefore, not be held accountable. One might almost be tempted to draw a parallel to the diabetic drunk driver I spoke of earlier.

The jurors in the Dan White trial were torn between the fact that the defendant had obviously committed the crimes and should be punished, but that he was one of the good guys. *He was one of us!* They could not bring themselves to arrive at a verdict of guilty of first degree murder. Therefore, when the so-called twinkie defense was presented to them, they clutched at it desperately and returned a verdict of guilty of manslaughter, which meant a much shorter prison term. In the Palo Alto case, the defendant was adjudged to be sane and was found guilty of first degree murder. After all, one doesn't want people of that ilk walking about in a free society, even though he didn't live in Palo Alto. Ironically, not too long after these trials and the jury's findings, both defendants committed suicide, which led some folks to opine that maybe there was some justice after all.

In 1850, Elizabeth Barrett Browning wrote in *Sonnets from the Portuguese*: *"How do I love thee? Let me count the ways."* In 1990, one of the world's oldest court reporters wrote, *"When do I retire? Let me count the days."* My career was drawing to a close and after thirty-one years of listening to other people talk, I was finally going to be able to make a few comments myself: *"Sayonara, adios, auf Wiedersehen,"* and of course the moving and sentimental, *"I'm outta here!"* I had accumulated quite a bit of unused vacation time, so I decided to retire one month earlier than planned. That way I could cut down by at least a month the amount of transcript demands I would have to face after my retirement. (As it turned out, I spent the first full year of my retirement doing nothing *but* transcripts.)

In the early part of August the judge I worked for went on vacation so I was assigned to fill in for other reporters as the need arose. My target date for retirement was August 24, 1990. On that morning I was assigned to work in Juvenile Court to replace a reporter who was ill. I had begun my Superior Court service at Juvenile Court in December 1969, so I thought it was quite fitting that my last day on the job should be in that same court. Also, it was quite apparent to everyone that I had entered my second childhood with a passion so that made it even more appropriate. Some of my friends took me to lunch that day and a month later I was the guest of honor at a lovely retirement party given in the home of my best friend.

I had previously moved all my personal things out of the Palo Alto office, so at the end of the day I simply gathered up my notes and my Stenograph machine and said good-bye. It was a warm and sunny Friday afternoon (as opposed to a dark and stormy night) and I could hear everyone telling each other to *"have a nice weekend."* I thought to myself that this was going to be the longest weekend of my life. I left with a mixture of joy and sadness. With the possible exception of being a rock star, I could not imagine having a more interesting and rewarding career. It was over now, but—as they said about the fellow who stumbled and fell from a ten story window—it was quite a trip.

ᛞᛞ

I promised you earlier that you would hear more about Deputy Cojones, the sheriff's deputy who worked as our bailiff in Domestic Court and who was with us until the end of 1989. He resided in Gilroy, a town about twenty-five miles south of San Jose. When the judge opted for the Palo Alto assignment in January of 1990, Deputy Cojones did not want to add an additional round trip of thirty-four miles to his daily commute, so he arranged to go to work for a different judge in San Jose and we were assigned a new bailiff for the Palo Alto court.

On the morning of August 12, 1992, Mr. Hamilton Burger, an unemployed engineer in San Jose, arose and dressed himself in a suit and tie in preparation for making a court appearance downtown in the Domestic Court. Glancing in the mirror, he paused and decided that something was not quite right with the image that greeted him. Almost immediately, he realized what was missing so he took off his coat and strapped on a shoulder holster which contained a loaded, semi-automatic pistol. He felt much more comfortable with this minor adjustment to his ensemble and, after donning his coat once again, he began his journey downtown. His ultimate goal, after reaching his destination, was to shoot the judge and social worker who had deprived him of custody of his children.

Approximately an hour earlier in the city of Gilroy, Deputy Cojones and his wife were preparing themselves for the daily challenge of freeway traffic, which was a burden they had to overcome before reaching their workplace in San Jose. Mrs. Cojones worked as a court clerk at the downtown courthouse and Deputy Cojones worked as the bailiff for a Juvenile Court commissioner about two blocks from the main courthouse. The August sun was already reminding everyone who was boss, even this early in the morning. The pungent aroma of the garlic fields was heavy in the air. Gilroy is very proud of its nationally known Garlic Festival, which is held every July and had been celebrated two weeks earlier. During the peak of the season you won't find a vampire around for a thousand miles. Things had been rather slow in Deputy Cojones' court the last week and he was thinking how nice it would be if something happened to break the monotony. He didn't really expect that anything would, but he could dream. Actually, he was looking forward to coming home that evening and planting some new jalapeño plants that a friend had given him. He wasn't impressed much by the Garlic Festival. He thought instead there should be a jalapeño festival featuring something a man could really sink his teeth into. Now, *that* would be a fiesta!

Shortly before 9:00 A.M., Mr. Burger approached the entrance to the Superior Court annex where some of the Domestic matters were heard. Since completion of the construction of a new criminal courthouse about a mile away, this annex was now utilized for certain Domestic cases, some Juvenile Court matters and some departments of the Municipal Court. Members of the public entering this building were still required to pass through a metal detector to ensure that no weapons were brought into court. When Mr. Burger entered the building, he had no intention of passing through the metal detector. When he attempted to walk around it, he was immediately challenged by the deputy sheriff on duty and told that he must pass through it if he was going into the building. At that point, Mr. Burger withdrew his weapon from its holster and said, *"Oh, is this what you're looking for?"* The surprised deputy told him to put the gun down, while attempting to draw his own weapon. The other parties waiting in line raced for the safety of the outer door.

When Deputy Cojones and his wife reached the downtown courthouse that morning, they left their car in its usual spot in the employees' parking lot. Mrs. Cojones went into the courthouse and Deputy Cojones walked the two blocks to the courthouse annex. Following his standard routine, he turned on the lights in his department, plugged in the coffeemaker and turned on the radio, while glancing at the newspaper. At 8:45 A.M., he decided to go out to the front of the building to have one last cigarette before court convened. As he was chatting with someone in front of the building, a very alarmed woman came running out of the front door. His curiosity aroused, he moved toward the entrance and peered inside. What he saw was a man holding a pistol aimed in the general direction of the metal detector. Deputy Cojones drew his weapon and momentarily hesitated—the man inside had the same kind of gun many policemen use and he was dressed much like other police detectives who come to court, even including the shoulder holster. He didn't know at that point whether he was a good guy or a bad guy. He soon found out.

The instant Mr. Burger saw Deputy Cojones assume the standard police firing position, that is, with his knees slightly bent and both arms outstretched aiming his gun, he fired. His marksmanship was very good. Later, Deputy Cojones would recall seeing the flash and hearing the report of Mr. Burger's weapon. The bullet took off the little finger and part of the ring finger of Deputy Cojones' left hand, then traveled along his right hand, leaving a gaping wound in the knuckles and the palm of his right hand. At that point it hit a bone which caused it to ricochet away. Deputy Cojones was spun around by the impact, but never dropped his weapon. He could hear more shots from inside the building, but Mr. Burger had left the entrance lobby and was now out of sight. People began running from the building in panic and one young woman tried to enter the building, but was pulled down by Deputy Cojones who placed her behind the front fender of a parked car as a shield. He also warned others away from the building, including a woman with two small children, as they were nearing the facility.

Inside, Mr. Burger shot and wounded two other deputies as he tried to reach the courtroom, but their return fire forced him to use an exit door leading to the street where Deputy Cojones was waiting. As soon as Mr. Burger reached the street, Deputy Cojones told him to drop his gun. Instead, Mr. Burger raised his gun towards Deputy Cojones and the deputy fired four rounds at Mr. Burger. Almost simultaneously, another deputy followed Mr. Burger out of the door and fired three rounds at Mr. Burger. Mr. Burger then ran down the full length of the building, crossed the street, and ran through a parking lot with the two deputies in pursuit. Finally, Deputy Cojones brought him down to the ground and made him drop his gun by punching him with what was left of his right hand. Fueled by a mixture of anger and pure adrenaline at this point, Deputy Cojones screamed at Mr. Burger, *"Why did you shoot me?"* To which Mr. Burger replied, *"You guys stole my kids."*

Several other deputies arrived at this point and Mr. Burger was handcuffed and taken into custody. Later at the hospital, it was determined that Mr. Burger had been shot four times, but no vital organs had been affected. Apparently, the bullets also had no effect on his ability to run like a deer. He was taken by ambulance to a nearby medical center and after a short period of recovery he was placed in the county jail awaiting trial on five counts of attempted murder, along with several other felonies.

Inside the downtown courthouse, Mrs. Cojones was just preparing to enter the courtroom when she received word that her husband had been shot. She was given no information at that point as to whether he was still alive or how severely wounded he may have been. She raced from the building toward the crowd that had gathered and reached the scene just as Deputy Cojones was being lifted into the ambulance. He spotted her in the crowd and gave her a wink and a smile, which seemed to say, *"Ho hum. Just another boring day."* His smile reassured her, even though his hands looked more like two pieces of salisbury steak than the hands that had caressed her just the night before. Deputy Cojones spent the better part of a year recuperating from his injuries. He had to undergo plastic surgery to his hands on several occasions before recovering sufficiently to hold down a desk job at the Sheriff's Department. Compared to his previous post, he felt this job was rather restrictive. Even he had to acknowledge, however, it was a lot less confining than the pine box he had come so close to occupying on that earlier day in August.

When Mr. Burger's case finally came to trial, he displayed the same keen judgment he had shown on the day he turned the Superior Court annex into a shooting gallery. He refused to cooperate with or even talk to the attorney who had been appointed to defend him. He was subsequently found guilty of numerous felonies, including the five counts of attempted murder. The probation officer assigned to prepare a presentencing report for the judge met with the same lack of cooperation. He simply would not talk to her. On the day of sentencing, the probation officer's report stated, *"At this point it can only be assumed the defendant is an extremely dangerous individual who, if ever released from custody, might again resort to violence when feeling threatened."* Mr. Burger was sentenced to five consecutive life terms in state prison.

Well, Dear Reader, thanks for hanging in there. With the recalling of these events, I have just barely chipped at the proverbial tip of the iceberg as far as tales emanating from your friendly, neighborhood courthouse. I hope I haven't bored you to tears, but if I have, maybe it will help wash out some of the pollution left over from the election campaign in 1994. I will leave you now with the words uttered by the immortal Tiny Tim—*God bless us—everyone!* (...Or was that *Tiptoe Through the Tulips?*)

Epilogue

ONE OF the sad things about writing a book of recollections concerning people we have known and worked with for over thirty years is the fact that so many have left us by the time the book is completed. A very high percentage of the judges, prosecutors, public defenders, and bailiffs—along with a few court reporters—who were the inspiration for many of the anecdotes mentioned in this book have gone to their final reward just in the last five years.

My old buddy, Charley the bailiff, died in his sleep on the Ides of March 1991. It has previously been abundantly illustrated that Charley was a very unique individual in many ways. He had many other gifts, however, which I have not mentioned. He was an excellent automobile mechanic, which made it very handy for friends whose cars were in need of a tune-up. He was also very proficient at buying old cars, repairing them, and then selling them at a profit. He had a real estate license and even a certificate to be a substitute teacher in an elementary school. But, what made Charley more unique than almost anyone else was a birth defect which gave him a talent few could equal. He was born with a small opening on the right side of what he called his *lizard*, which required covering with his finger when relieving himself, to prevent the gentleman standing to his right at the rest room urinal from receiving a warm, but misguided, surprise.

He told me of several incidents in which an unscheduled sneeze caused him to wreak great distress upon his immediate neighbor, while Charley automatically covered his nose with his right hand. At first the gentleman would note, with some irritation, the fine spray in the air and assume he had been sneezed upon. Then the reality of something warm running down the side of his leg would finally jolt him into a full understanding of the situation. Fortunately, Charley was a pretty big man so his apology was usually sufficient to diffuse any potential violence on the part of the gentleman who had suffered such an unwarranted and humidifying experience. Charley rests with the angels now and hopefully there is no hay fever season in his present location.

Subsequent to the 1989 earthquake and the closing of the old courthouse because of quake damage, there was much deliberation and discussion among county officials as to whether the old building should be razed and a modern courthouse erected in its place, or the old building should be saved and made more secure to ensure the safety of the public. The county owned the land under the courthouse and the construction of a new building would solve the problem of never having enough courtrooms for the number of judges appointed. It was decided, however, that because of the historical significance of the old courthouse, it should be retrofitted against future earthquakes, renovated, and preserved for future generations to enjoy as an example of early western architecture. To that end, the foundation of the building was reinforced, the outside of the building was sandblasted and repainted, and the interior was given a face-lift as well. This proved to be a very time-consuming procedure, but if time heals all wounds, the building should now be fit as a fiddle because the old courthouse re-opened for business in May of 1994 and it is now one of the most splendid and polished examples of old-fashioned courthouse design in Northern California. Just don't get on the elevator without a flashlight and some emergency rations.

Speaking of courthouses, I can't end this book without some comment on the televised coverage of the trial of O.J. Simpson in Los Angeles. It must surely be apparent to almost everyone by this time that the decision to allow TV cameras in the court

room was one of the costliest and most ill-conceived judgments ever made in the pursuit of justice. The participants in a
trial, whether they be judge, jury, prosecutor, defendant, court
reporter, clerk, or witness, are under a tremendous amount of
pressure already, just being in trial. Add to that the stress of
realizing that every word you say is being flashed across TV
screens all over America and you have multiplied the element
of terror for most people several times over—including yours
truly. It is just not possible to be unaffected by such constant
and unrelenting scrutiny. Even though it is a public trial and
the public has a right to know, the immediate broadcast of every slip of the tongue or mistake in grammar by the participants is comparable to an invasion of privacy. On the other
hand, some attorneys would consider television coverage a
great opportunity to take advantage of free advertising and
milk every chance they have to show off their latent thespian
abilities to a national audience. And let us not forget that
judges are former attorneys as well. The temptation to create
an instant national fan club is not conducive to either the presentation or reception of the facts in a concise and direct manner.

In my opinion, based upon my experience, this trial could
have been completed in less than six months if it had been
tried in Santa Clara County—without television. The media
hype for the case has been unbelievable. The so called *trial of
the century* does not even begin to compare with the excitement generated by the Manson trial, the trial of the Chicago
Seven, the trial of Julius and Ethel Rosenberg, the Lindbergh
trial or even the trial of the cop killer mentioned in chapter
nine of this book. Obviously, if it were not for the great celeb-
rity of the defendant, the trial would have garnered perhaps
two or three paragraphs in the *Los Angeles Times*.

In the majority of states, most judges still will not admit
anyone in the courtroom with a camera. When I began my reporting career, no cameras of any type were allowed in court
and no tape recorders were permitted to be used. Sketch art-
ists were allowed to depict certain witnesses or defendants and
that was it. The attempted murder trial I wrote about in
Chapter Seven was covered by a local newspaper and the arti-

cle was headlined by a partial sketch of me at my machine. I say partial sketch because my moustache was continued on page twenty-seven. My only experience with television in the courtroom occurred in the early 1980s and that was only because the defendant was NBC. The trial itself was not televised, but portions of the closing arguments were. I had no problem with that, but if the trial had been covered as well, I probably would have had great difficulty even reading my name back because of stage fright. I certainly take my hat off to the court reporters in the Simpson trial for remaining so cool under fire.

Finally, I must pay tribute to the courage and spirit of my long-suffering wife. Sadly, in 1982, we decided to end our marriage of twenty-six years. After raising four children, we had grown apart more each year, I believe because each of us had such a competitive nature and it seemed that we could not be in the same room for more than five minutes without an argument. She was employed at the district attorney's office and retired in 1988 as a supervisor of the secretarial pool in the felony section. We remained very close after our separation and still celebrated holidays, birthdays and family functions together. Because our children were grown, there were no visitation problems or child support problems which most divorced couples fight about.

In 1989 she decided to give up smoking and began taking long walks and then jogging to keep her weight under control. She continued this practice for more than a year and then one day she expressed the thought that she might like to run a marathon. I scoffed at the idea that anyone her age should even consider such a thing and, of course, that's all she needed. She began serious training then, running sometimes more than sixty miles a week. Because one of our daughters lived in New York at the time, she aimed for the New York City Marathon. I was very surprised when she met the requirements for qualifying for the marathon. Then, just six months prior to the marathon, she fell and fractured her ankle. I naturally presumed that would end her aspirations towards racing until at least the next year.

Once again, I had underestimated her determination. Through various methods of therapy, including running in water (*not to be confused with judicial walking on water*), she was back on her feet in time to still attempt the race without a postponement. As she flew off to New York, I thought, balancing her age against her great resolve, that she might even complete half the marathon before being forced to call it quits. On the morning of the marathon, while slicing a high energy power bar to eat along the way, she cut her finger severely enough to require several stitches at a local emergency room. Later that day, Sunday, November 14, 1993, she completed the entire 26.2 mile race at the age of sixty-seven. I was amazed, along with her friends and family, at her incredible feat. (*Feet?*)

She returned to California for Thanksgiving and while she and the rest of the family dined on turkey, I had a large portion of crow. She enjoyed immensely the awed congratulations and wonder from her friends and admirers, while continuing her running practices with the thought of planning for another marathon in 1994. Fate, however, had other ideas. On February 10, 1994, she suffered a massive stroke on the right side of her brain which rendered her entire left side paralyzed. The doctors called it a CVA or cerebrovascular accident. It is also frequently referred to as a brain attack, as opposed to a heart attack. We were completely devastated and shocked, along with the doctors, that such a tragedy could happen to someone who had been in such superb physical shape.

She survived through, what we came to understand, was the usual routine for stroke survivors. She remained hospitalized for one week, then was placed in a skilled nursing facility for a month, while she regained sufficient mobility to be accepted at a rehabilitation center in Vallejo, California, seventy-five miles north of San Jose. She remained in the Vallejo facility for three weeks, undergoing very concentrated and intense physical therapy along with occupational and speech therapy. When it was determined that nothing further could be done for her there, I brought her back to my home in San Jose because her home in Santa Clara was an upstairs condo and there was no way she could negotiate the stairs with her left side paralyzed. She was also in need of constant care and the fact that I was now retired made it more logical for me to care for her than anyone else.

We have learned that there is a great variance in the severity of strokes among individuals. Some people have a minor stroke and a few months later they are just as capable as they were prior to their stroke. Others are affected for years and never fully regain all their faculties. My wife's stroke was more serious than most. It resulted not only in the paralysis, but also a marked change in her personality. This has proven to be too difficult for some of her old friends to handle. The vibrant and independent person they knew has disappeared and someone else has taken over her body. Even though the new person is a warm, caring, and highly motivated individual, many old friends feel uncomfortable and simply stop coming around. In *The Road Ahead: A Stroke Recovery Guide*, published by the National Stroke Association, the observation is made that, *"Only after mourning the loss of the person they knew can families (or friends) learn who that person has become and begin to develop a comfortable relationship."*

The same tenacity of spirit and courage that helped her complete the marathon is still very evident in her daily efforts to speed up her recovery. She can now walk a short distance with a quad cane and do many things that were impossible for her shortly after her stroke. She has a great sense of humor and has no time to waste on self-pity. She can tell you very precisely what happened on a date twenty years ago; just don't ask her what happened yesterday.

It is not my intent in writing about this incident to end this book on a sad note, but rather a joyous one. During the year and some months I have been caring for her, we have found each other once more and decided to begin our marriage anew. We will no longer face the prospect of spending our declining years alone and I will double the remote chance of someone laughing at my jokes. People have often told me that I never know when to shut up. They were wrong.

JOHN R. REILY
SAN JOSE, CALIFORNIA